C000179231

The United Kin

The United Kingdom

The Unification and Disintegration of Britain since AD 43

By

John D. Grainger

Pen & Sword
MILITARY

AN IMPRINT OF PEN & SWORD BOOKS LTD.
YORKSHIRE – PHILADELPHIA

First published in Great Britain in 2019 by
Pen & Sword Military
An imprint of
Pen & Sword Books Ltd
Yorkshire – Philadelphia

Copyright © John D. Grainger 2019

ISBN 978 1 52674 819 5

The right of John D. Grainger to be identified as Author of this work has been
asserted by him in accordance with the Copyright, Designs and Patents Act 1988.

A CIP catalogue record for this book is
available from the British Library.

All rights reserved. No part of this book may be reproduced or transmitted in any
form or by any means, electronic or mechanical including photocopying, recording
or by any information storage and retrieval system, without permission from the
Publisher in writing.

Printed and bound in the UK by TJ International Ltd, Padstow, Cornwall

Pen & Sword Books Limited incorporates the imprints of Atlas, Archaeology,
Aviation, Discovery, Family History, Fiction, History, Maritime, Military, Military
Classics, Politics, Select, Transport, True Crime, Air World, Frontline Publishing,
Leo Cooper, Remember When, Seaforth Publishing, The Praetorian Press,
Wharncliffe Local History, Wharncliffe Transport, Wharncliffe True Crime and
White Owl.

For a complete list of Pen & Sword titles please contact

PEN & SWORD BOOKS LIMITED
47 Church Street, Barnsley, South Yorkshire, S70 2AS, England
E-mail: enquiries@pen-and-sword.co.uk
Website: www.pen-and-sword.co.uk

Or
PEN AND SWORD BOOKS
1950 Lawrence Rd, Havertown, PA 19083, USA
E-mail: Uspen-and-sword@casematepublishers.com
Website: www.penandswordbooks.com

Contents

List of Maps

Introduction

The unity of the United Kingdom of Great Britain and Northern Ireland has been under threat for the past generation, and in the matter of Ireland for very much longer. Constant agitation by a vocal minority in Scotland who wish for independence, and by the even smaller number in Wales who wish for the same, has convulsed these islands repeatedly from 1970. But for a clear majority in Scotland, the great majority in Wales and – though they have never been consulted – probably virtually all of those in England, the internal unity of the archipelago is more acceptable than any conceivable division.

It took well over a thousand years to unite the countries of the British Isles, even without including the Roman period. It was a millennium during which, as a preliminary, the four countries were one by one united as separate states, and only then did they join into a union between them. It was not a tidy, inevitable process, nor was it one which has always been fully accepted by the populations of the constituent countries – notably by a majority of the Irish. It is, however, one of the longest-lasting unifications of states anywhere in the world, and that by itself means that the process by which it was achieved is worth studying.

The first part of the process was the construction of unified states in England and Scotland out of a whole collection of minor kingdoms, and this process is the subject of Part I of this book. That this unification did not take place in Wales and Ireland provides a useful contrast and requires explanation. Further, it becomes clear in considering how the two successful unions were actually achieved that it was a process which took a long time, and one which was arrived at only in stages, some of them difficult and painful. The exercise of English power was a result of the unification of the southern part of the main island, and it involved some serious attempts to use that power to capture the rest of the islands. These attempts failed, and the actual unification of the archipelago eventually came about, after violence had failed, by legal processes involving negotiations and Acts of Parliament. While there were variations, and attempts at conciliation were made, it was not wholly a matter of conquest. It is this series of agreements and Acts which are now under threat.

The Scottish referendum of 2014 was a scandal of lies and misre-presentation, a populist nightmare of unfulfillable promises, unattainable dreams – nightmares to the pro-unity supporters - and wildly distorted historical references; a misuse of history on a grand scale. The apparent decline in support for the dissolution of the English–Scottish union since then rather suggests that a degree of common sense is returning in Scotland. The general incompetence of the inexperienced Scottish National Party when in government, in such matters as education and the administration of the health service, and its lack of clarity on the issue of more independence referendums – a classic case of fudge and prevarication – has clearly suppressed any temporary enthusiasm for independence among non-members.

This book is written from the viewpoint that the union of England, Scotland and Wales has been of substantial benefit to the inhabitants of both countries and will continue to be so. The intention is to examine the processes in the past whereby, after many attempts and failures, the union eventually occurred. (Ireland, of course, is a different matter, and its history had been crafted in a very different way, though its unity with the bigger island necessarily brings it into consideration in a book like this.)

The near disaster, from the point of view of the British government, of the Scottish referendum did not dissuade the Conservative government from another similar adventure, with the result that the European Union referendum of 2016 was 'lost'. What has happened to the sovereignty of Parliament? It is to discuss these very matters – Scottish independence, membership of the European Union – that the population elects its MPs, yet the MPs shrugged off the responsibility they were elected and employed to shoulder and handed it back to the people, who were then subjected to misleading and occasionally lying campaigns by the combatants – the same people who agitated for the referendum. But the defeat of the European Union referendum has pushed the question of Scottish and Welsh independence out of sight for the present, apart from occasional pronouncements from Edinburgh of a generally oracular impenetrability. What the separation from Europe should do, of course, is bring the three countries closer together in the face of an extremely difficult problem. For, geopolitically, the result will be to unite an increasingly monobloc European continent against the United Kingdom, and, should relations turn hostile (and that is the implication of the referendum result), the 'Leavers' will have accomplished something only Napoleon and Hitler had, very briefly, achieved.

Chapter 1

The Roman Legacy

The first attempt to unite Britain and Ireland into a single state came with the Romans. This was, in the event, hardly a sustained attempt, and indeed no serious effort was ever made towards invading Ireland, though it was discussed. Yet the Roman presence in Britannia had a serious and lasting political legacy, which was never far from the minds of ambitious English - though not Scottish or Irish – politicians.

The Roman Empire extended its power, as is all too well known, as far north as the valley, between the mouth of the River Tyne and the Solway Firth, which separates the Pennine mountains of northern England and the Southern Uplands of Scotland. The boundary was marked by the wall ordered to be built by the Emperor Hadrian in AD 122 and garrisoned by Roman soldiers for almost the next three centuries. It was a structure which included a paved road south of the wall, providing a means of relatively rapid travel between east and west. This was originally for the soldiers, but it could easily be used by everybody else. There were also frequent gates incorporated in the wall for those travelling between north and south, so it is best interpreted as a boundary rather than a fortification, a customs barrier for regulating peacetime traffic and collecting duties; even fully garrisoned it could have been very easily crossed by an enemy force which concentrated by surprise on a single section. It actually has all the appearance of an imperial vanity project – Hadrian was liable to invent work for his soldiers – and it does not seem to be an effective military installation.

Occasional attempts were made to extend Roman dominion further to the north from the line of the wall. Even before it was, the Governor Cn. Iulius Agricola (AD 78–85) made a serious invasion of the north, reaching into the Highlands. His forts have been located as far north as the Moray Firth. He was unsuccessful despite winning a great battle; afterwards the troops were gradually withdrawn southwards, and the line of the wall became the occupation limit by about AD 100.

Then in the 140s, by order of the Emperor Antoninus Pius, at a moment when the wall of Hadrian was just about finished, a new and more permanent

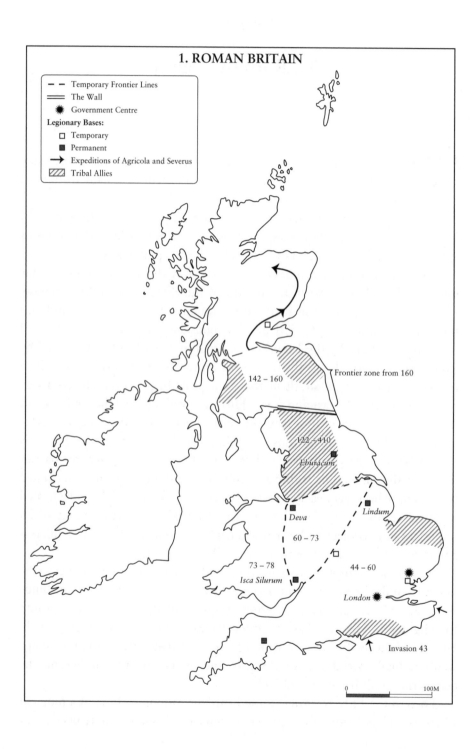

1. ROMAN BRITAIN

Temporary Frontier Lines
The Wall
Government Centre
Legionary Bases:
Temporary
Permanent
Expeditions of Agricola and Severus
Tribal Allies

Frontier zone from 160

142 – 160

122 – 410

Eburacum

Deva   Lindum

60 – 73

73 – 78   44 – 60

Isca Silurum

London

Invasion 43

0   100M

move northwards was made, which pushed the boundary forward to the Forth-Clyde line, and there another, slighter wall – a rampart-and-ditch construction with forts – was built. This frontier lasted about twenty years, and when the Emperor Septimius Severus mounted a personal campaign north of both walls in 209–11, he reached as far as Agricola had, according to the evidence of the temporary forts his army used, but this attempt at expansion also failed. It is not clear just what Severus' aim was in this war. He was a proven conqueror in the East, where he had conquered and annexed Mesopotamia as far as the border with modern Iran, but in Scotland it looks more as if it was either a pre-emptive campaign or a punishment for earlier raids from the north, though a campaign lasting three years seems more serious than that. What stopped the war was not the local resistance, but Severus' death. His quarrelling sons could agree that they were no longer interested in conquering the cold and wet Highlands, though on little else. Instead, Rome beckoned. The army withdrew to the line of Hadrian's Wall once more, where it settled for the rest of the Roman occupation. A properly organized frontier system was now arranged, with the forts on the wall acting as the base for forward projections of Roman power in the form of alliances with some of the tribes to the north, several advanced forts to control the roads and travelling scouts to spy out possible threats. Perhaps on other occasions there were Roman invasions which we do not know about; certainly there were raids into the north, just as there were raids from the north into the richer south, but the permanent frontier lay along the wall.

None of these attempts at further conquest were successful in the long term. The withdrawals provided those living to the north of the wall – yet to be called Scots – with preliminary celebrations of independence, even if they had suffered casualties and a nasty ravaging, and the Roman Britons south of it now had the illusion of safety from invasion. Even though the Romans were generally victorious in the fighting during these expeditions, they had always failed to hold the ground they had apparently conquered in the north.

It is, in fact, not at all certain that these expeditions were really attempts to conquer the whole island. The knowledge that the Romans had seized only the southern two-thirds of Britannia probably stimulated Agricola to move further north, and his development of a legionary base at Inchtuthil in Perthshire would imply an intention to make a permanent occupation at least as far north as Fife, but the land further north was territory which was unproductive from a Roman point of view. Agricola's forces were pulled back south to the line of the future Hadrian's Wall once more serious problems developed elsewhere in the empire. Antoninus' move north was still less an attempt at serious conquest, but probably more a gesture to the Roman expectation that an emperor, even so unmilitary a one as Antoninus, was expected to extend the bounds of the empire by conquest. Septimius' expeditions were stopped when he died, so his long-term aim is unknown. Apart from Agricola's failure, none of the Roman activities in the north seem to have been aimed at permanent conquest.

These campaigns, from Agricola to Severus, took place over a period of more than 130 years. The conquest of the retained province had been similarly intermittent. Again, the intended extent of the new province as projected by the imperial government when launching the invasion in AD 43 is not known, but several possible frontier lines have been suggested – along the line of the Fosse Way from the Wash to the Severn estuary, the Humber-Mersey line and perhaps the line between the River Tees and Morecambe Bay, and these seem to have marked the stages of the conquest of the southern part of the island. The conquest of Wales did not even begin until the 70s. So the province between 43 and 122 (when Hadrian's Wall was built) repeatedly changed in size. The campaign into the lands north of the wall were thus continuations of that erratic process. The arrival of a new emperor on the throne in Rome several times started up the process again – Claudius' original invasion, Nero's reaction to Boudica's rebellion, Vespasian in Wales, Domitian in the north, Hadrian and his wall and Antoninus with his advance to the Forth-Clyde line. It is almost as though the northern part of Britain was left unconquered so that an emperor could arrange a minor campaign, claim a conquest and a victory, and then sit back.

No serious attempt was ever made by the Romans to extend their power into Ireland, although Governor Agricola did claim that he could have conquered the island by using a single Roman legion (plus auxiliaries, of course – which would make the force around 10,000–12,000 men). The boast suggests that he knew little about the island, which, after all, is larger than England, and as damp as Scotland. Nevertheless, there was a good deal of Roman influence in Ireland, and occasional claims are made to have found evidence for a Roman military presence, though they are never verified. What evidence does exist is generally the result of trade between Ireland and the empire – coins and pottery are signs of the import of other goods and the export of Irish products – of booty acquired by Irish raiders into the larger island, or perhaps evidence of the accumulated wages and souvenirs of Irish mercenaries who served in the Roman army in Britain or perhaps further afield within the Roman Empire, and had then returned to their homeland.

The land which became Wales, of course, was conquered during the process of conquering what became England, a preliminary example of the close relations between the two future countries, but it is also noticeable that the two conquests were separated in time. There is no sign that the Romans recognized Wales as in any way different or separate. It was, of course, more mountainous than the eastern part of the island, and so less amenable to their policy of urbanization, and less productive in the goods they looked for. The two conquests went together as the conquerors moved from the south-east corner of Britannia towards the north-west and the wall they eventually built, so inevitably Wales was only dealt with once southern and central England had been secured; but then, in order to make that security certain Wales had to be conquered.

Britannia as a province was thus always in a sense incomplete, though the conquerors had seized control of the richest part of the archipelago, which they could exploit agriculturally, by quarrying its minerals – silver, lead, copper, coal – and by recruiting, or conscripting, thousands of young men into their army. But because of that incompletion it required a continuing Roman garrison out of all proportion to its importance or size. The size of that garrison may be in part the result of a sense that the province was under continual threat from outsiders, or that the British subjects were fundamentally hostile, or both of these considerations. The original conquest, after all, had not been easy, and it had taken forty years from the invasion until Agricola's eventual failure and the withdrawal to the Tyne-Solway line, while the repeated invasions of the North had never succeeded. The combination and continuation of such difficulties clearly required that a large garrison be maintained.

This is a perfect example of an empire reaching the very limits of its capabilities and only learning of its inability to extend further when it had reached beyond those capabilities, then being unable to withdraw. Agricola's boast about Ireland is belied by his own failure to conquer the North. Yet for two centuries the empire mounted expeditions which, if successful, would have 'completed' the conquest. It was also wholly unwilling to withdraw from a province which was becoming too expensive to hold; eventually, of course, the point was taken, though unwillingly, and from the 270s onwards, withdrawals of military forces from similarly unproductive and militarily expensive provinces took place with increasing frequency – Mauretania, Dacia, parts of Germany and eventually Britannia. Britannia was not 'given' its independence, but was just told to look to its own defence, with the implication that Roman imperial power would eventually return – a vague promise never to be honoured, though there is no reason to assume that the abandonment was intended to be permanent. Following those earlier withdrawals, the abandonment of Britannia should have surprised no one. By the time the abandonment was made official, the Roman army had mostly been withdrawn to deal with emergencies elsewhere.

The Roman imperial mindset insisted that any land which had been Roman remained Roman, even if it was no longer governed by an imperial official or defended by a Roman garrison. So Britannia, despite being told to look to its own defence, still remained a Roman province, subject to Roman laws. In the next generation more than one official, such as Bishop Germanus in 429, arrived to carry out official tasks. Further, any country which was ever subjected to Roman attentions, such as the lands north of Hadrian's Wall, were also regarded as Roman. In the minds of bureaucrats in Rome or Constantinople, therefore, it followed that Britannia had been wholly taken into the empire, from Kent to Orkney (which had been visited more than once by Roman fleets). The alliances and agreements made with the tribes north of the wall – the Votadini of Lothian, the Nomantae and Damnonii of the south-west, even the Picts north of the Antonine Wall – were, by the fact of those agreements, Roman subjects. A Roman could argue that virtually all the island was really Roman, and remained so even after 410.

So, despite the essential and evident eventual failure of the physical conquest which began in AD 43, the Roman imprint on the land south of Hadrian's Wall was deep and profound, if in the very long term only temporary, and the idea of the whole island as a single Roman province faded only slowly. On the other hand, an 'occupation' which lasted more than three-and-a-half centuries cannot be considered to be 'temporary', except at a very long time-distance. The population, starting with the wealthy, spoke Latin and lived as Roman subjects. Eventually this included most of the people of the whole island, for the population north of the wall (or walls) was very small.

A limit on Romanization may be seen in that the people of the province seem to have maintained their native languages all along, while, without the need to communicate to officials and army officers, the use of Latin soon dwindled to the educated and the Church after 410. A Roman way of life in towns and villas, with baths and mosaics, town councils and, eventually, Christian churches, took hold of the wealthiest classes. Thousands of British men were taken into, or voluntarily joined, the Roman Army and served throughout the empire, especially in the first decades after the conquest of the province, when the safety of the conquest required the removal of potentially hostile men who were capable of fighting.

This process of what historians and archaeologists call 'Romanization' was slow, partial and limited, but it did happen, though being only partial there was perhaps a good deal of passive resistance, not to mention a lack of any real Roman interest in pushing forward such a process. By contrast, Gaul and Hispania, which had both become Roman provinces a century or more earlier, were much more urbanized, and their populations largely abandoned their 'native' languages and spoke Latin. The wealthy classes in those lands also participated in the political life of the empire, providing administrators and emperors – but from Britannia we know of no officials, no army officers, and no senators.

Well before the fourth century, when it seems there was considerable wealth in the province, if in relatively few hands, the population probably regarded themselves as not only Romans, but also as citizens of their region, their *civitas*, very like other regions of the empire, and in that century increasing numbers of them also adopted the new Roman religion of Christianity when they were encouraged to do so by the Roman government. However, the enduring use of native languages implies a continuing resistance, even if it was passive, and even if the wealthy classes did take to villa and town life. The villas, though they are archaeologically occasionally spectacular, were not all that numerous, were concentrated in the south-eastern half of the province and cannot have housed more than 1,000–2,000 people in total.

Seen from Rome, this was only a marginal society and a distant province, expensive to protect and probably never paying its way. It always remained partly non-Roman, geographically, socially, linguistically and intellectually. One or two army officers used the army in Britannia as the base for attempting to usurp the empire, but only two were successful for more than a few years – the main exception being Constantine the Great, whose British base was inadvertent, not deliberate. The others came even later in the empire's history: Magnentius in the 350s, Magnus Maximus in the 380s and finally Constantine III, who took the British army to the rescue of Gaul and Hispania; the army was not returned, and this led the Emperor Honorius to write his letter to the citizens calling on them to look to their own defence – a gesture in part aimed at cutting off Constantine's logistical base. When the pressure of the empire became too great, the empire therefore abandoned Britain with scarcely a moment of regret, nor any apology.

So the legacy that Rome left behind after nearly four centuries of ruling half of the main British island as part of the empire, and pretending to control the rest, was first of all a memory of unity; second, some legends centred on usurpers and rebels; and third, the Christian religion, to which many Roman Britons were eventually converted during the fourth century. The religion spread to Ireland and north of the wall in the fifth century, when it was no longer an obvious instrument of Roman power in Britannia. Finally, and this was perhaps the most potent effect, there was a memory of the unity of the southern part of the island, a notion which was passed on to their non-Roman successors.

Such evidence as there is over the next couple of centuries does suggest an attempt was made to maintain the Roman system for a time by those who had been addressed by Honorius' letter, but this broke down soon enough. The adoption of Christianity linked the Celtic inhabitants to the remaining, if diminishing, Roman world. Among the Welsh there remained the memory of their presence as Roman subjects, even if this was mere nostalgia, and the original resistance to Romanization was forgotten.

This was not in fact very much of a legacy, and the evidence – necessarily negative – is that any real memory of being Roman faded rapidly away into legend. The life of those Roman Britons who lived in their villas and reclined in their slave-fuelled hot baths vanished even from memory, though the hot baths at Bath remained in use for some time and became the subject of a notable and nostalgic Anglo-Saxon poem. The villas ceased to be inhabited when the complex economy, based in large part on the presence of a large military market, vanished. Their later inhabitants were no more than occasional squatters, whose fires and scattered remains are sometimes found. Christianity was driven from much of the former province by the arrival of unimpressed pagans from across the North Sea, and survived only amongst those whom these new arrivals dismissed as, ironically, *Wealas* ('foreigners'), that is, Welsh.

Ultimately, almost the only political relic of the Roman period, during which the southern half of the main island had been united into a single polity, appears to have been the occasional use of a royal title, 'Bretwalda', which was a sort of decoration awarded to, or taken by, the pre-eminent Anglo-Saxon king at any particular time. He was usually one who had succeeded in dominating many of his neighbours, though only for a brief time, and it was never hereditary. Meaning 'wielder of Britain', it certainly had implications of the continuing concept of the unity of the old province, or an aspiration thereto, but no Anglo-Saxon king who gained that title could claim to have contributed much to the restoration of that unity beyond the brief conquest of weaker and neighbouring kingdoms, nor does it seem that any such king even aspired to do so. Most only dominated their neighbours, and that only for a few years. When actual unity was being built, by Alfred the Great and his family, the title was never used.

The legacy of Rome to its successors in Britain was thus minimal, amounting to no more than the fugitive memory of unity, a language – Latin – which survived in use among the Welsh because it was that which was employed by the Christian Church, and some ruins, the sight of which could stir Anglo-Saxon imaginations to talk of ancestral giants.

Bibliography

Birley, Anthony, *The People of Roman Britain* (London: 1979).
Breeze, David J. and Dobson, Brian, *Hadrian's Wall*, 4th ed. (London: 2000).
Breeze, David J., *The Northern Frontiers of Britain* (London: 1982).
Hanson, W.S., *Agricola and the Conquest of the North* (London: 1987).
Millett, Martin, *The Romanisation of Britain, an Essay in Archaeological Interpretation* (Cambridge: 1990).
Salway, Peter, *Roman Britain* (Oxford: 1981).
Thomas, Charles, *Christianity in Roman Britain to AD 500* (London: 1981).
Webster, Graham, *The Roman invasion of Britain* (London: 1980).

PART I

Two Unifications; Two Failures

Before it was possible to unite the whole of the British Isles, the four constituent regions underwent their own unifications, and even before this can be described the original conditions of those countries need to be explained. This may seem an elaborate process of accounting for the unity of the archipelago, but it will be seen that accounts of the preliminary conditions are a necessary basis for the discussion of the varied processes of unification which took place in each country.

Chapter 2

The Articulation of
Four Communities of States

Kingdoms and Settlers

The abandonment of Britannia by the Roman Empire, traditionally dated to AD 410, was signified by a brief imperial letter that year to the cities of Britannia. The implication was that the abandonment might be only temporary. But the abandonment, and the instruction to look to their own defences, in effect broke the unity of the province. It had long been divided into a series of quasi-city states, sometimes described as cantonal capitals, or *civitates*. These were, in fact, usually the old Iron Age tribal kingdoms with a Roman-type city planted in each. Thus the Trinovantes of Essex were centred on Camulodunum (Colchester), the Regnenses of Sussex on Regnum (Chichester), the Silures of South Wales on Venta Silurum (Caerwent), and so on. There were perhaps twenty of these centres, spread from Luguvallium (Carlisle), close to Hadrian's Wall, to Durovernum (Canterbury) in Kent and Isca Dumnoniorum (Exeter) in Devon. Each of these had around it, and as part of its territory, a sizeable spread of land. It was these communities which were addressed by the Emperor Honorius in his letter, and which eventually became the independent states of Britannia after the Roman imperial withdrawal. Whatever provincial government system had been left in place by the empire soon evaporated; the senior authorities became the cities, government devolving onto the city councils. There appear to have been attempts for a time to maintain the unity of the province, but these were eventually unsuccessful.

At that time there were also already considerable numbers of German-speaking people in the former province. They had arrived during the century prior to 410 in a variety of ways, official and unofficial. Some had arrived as mercenaries, while others were soldiers who had settled in retirement in the province they had guarded. Some groups came as units, transported by the Roman government to be settled in awkward corners. These arrivals had, of course, been typical of other subjects of the empire ever since the original conquest. There was a doctor from Palmyra in Syria who lived at Corbridge on Hadrian's Wall and was married to a Catuvellaunian woman; a sailor who had been recruited, bizarrely, in the Arabian desert, was buried at Ravenglass in Cumberland; a group of Sarmatian soldiers were settled at Bremetennicum (Ribchester) in modern Lancashire; and possibly a group of Alamanni from Germany were settled in the North.

The arrival of 'unofficial' German settlers may therefore for some time not have been particularly remarked, especially since they tended to settle in areas which were hardly occupied by Roman Britons. It was, however, these last who, collectively, were eventually identified by their descendants as the invaders of Britannia, perhaps because they did not have the taint of having served the Roman Empire.

These two Germanic groups therefore tended to settle in different places. The mercenaries, both those recruited by the imperial authorities before 410 and those who arrived afterwards, were employed by those cities which were looking to their own defence and were taken into the towns as garrisons and guards. The unofficial arrivals settled along the eastern coast from the area of what is now Lothian in Scotland and southward as far as the Isle of Wight on the south coast. Some became called Saxons, others Jutes, but the majority were Angles, who settled along the east coast from Lothian to East Anglia. Their arrival and their presence contributed to the political disintegration of the former province, so that the former city states, as they became independent, were joined by a series of minor coastal kingdoms which were developed by the invaders–cum–settlers. By about 450, the former province had become a mosaic of independent kingdoms.

The process was not necessarily violent. The former Roman population had long been disarmed and had become accustomed to relying on pro-fessional soldiers to defend them, or if they suffered from attacks, to rescue or avenge them. The hirelings were not that different from the Roman forces which had been withdrawn. Given the large number of Germans in the late Roman Army, they were probably no different in language from the 'Roman' soldiers of the empire. This meant that from the beginning the cities were under partial military occupation, or at least protection, and it will not have taken long for the military and the citizens to integrate. Tradition has it that a German king was ruling in Kent by about 450, and this may not have been the only region so affected.

'Kent' was an adaptation of the old Iron Age/Roman name for the people of the area – the Cantii – whose name was also used for the still partly urban centre of Canterbury, 'the town of the men of Kent' (the former

Durovernum). In effect, this may have been a takeover of one of the *civitates* by the mercenary garrison, but there was no doubt a good deal of intermingling of inhabitants, practices and religion in the kingdom. It is hardly surprising that the chief of the garrison should have emerged in control, and as king. Elsewhere, immigrants formed themselves into independent statelets which contributed to the disintegration of the city states into whose territory they penetrated and settled.

Over the next two centuries more migrants continued to arrive and organize themselves as new kingdoms. They pressed on the surviving kingdoms of the centre and west, sometimes seizing the whole territory of a dying city, until by AD 600 or so the former province of Britannia was a mixture of 'Celtic' (that is, ex-Roman) states in the west and 'English' states in the east, which were Saxon or Anglian, imposed on and incorporating the Celtic/Roman inhabitants.

To the north of the disused Hadrian's Wall an analogous situation had arisen, though by a different process. The area which we now call Scotland had been variously affected by the Roman presence and menace, which had at times intruded as far as the Highlands. By the time the Roman province expired, the dominant group of people in the area were the Picts, descended from the earlier inhabitants, including the Caledonians and Maeatae, whose political organizations had been suppressed by the Picts or had perhaps become Pictish. These now occupied the land from the Firth of Forth as far as Orkney. They were a recognizable people, in language and culture, as shown by their carved stones which survive throughout the area, but they formed at first, it seems, several independent kingdoms, traditionally seven in number, centred on such areas as Fife, the Aberdeen region, around the Moray Firth, Orkney and so on. In the next couple of centuries, Angles from Germany arrived in the south-east, occupying part of the land between the two walls, the area which was later called Lothian, where they and the local people formed the kingdom of Bernicia. This is a Celtic name ('Berneich'), and implies that the kingdom already existed when the Angles arrived – that is, these had been another mercenary group who were hired by the local authorities of Berneich, who then integrated with the native ruling group; they established notable centres at Bamburgh and Lindisfarne.

In the west were the Scots, who were originally thought to have emigrated from the north of Ireland, but are now believed to have been indigenous to the west of Scotland, adopting the language of their trading partners across the North Channel. Either theory is plausible, and both may be in part

correct; certainly there were Scots living on both sides of the North Channel
speaking the same Celtic dialect.

There were other kingdoms which we know existed but whose traces are
very thin in the sources of the time. It would seem that after the failure of the
early attempts to hold the old province together, numerous local chieftains
emerged, referred to as kings in the sources, but who controlled only fairly
small areas. Some were based in the Roman towns, others developed their
own centres. Some were relatively powerful, but most were small and weak,
and all of them lived by raiding their neighbours. These are classified by
modern historians by identifying them as Saxon, Pictish or British and
so on, but in all cases the basic population was descended from the citizens
of Roman Britain or the independent region to the north.

Ireland had not been affected in any direct way by the Roman presence
in its sister island other than by trade with the empire, and the personal
connections brought by geographical proximity. It had evolved its own
particular and peculiar system of kingdoms which had little relationship
to the contemporary systems in Britain – though the occurrence of similar
names for kingdoms in both islands suggest more detailed contacts than
can be explained by trade. There were Dumnonii in England and Scotland,
Carnovii in Scotland and Cornovii in England, and Brigantes in England
and Ireland – and of course, Scotti in Ireland and Scotland.

The Irish kingdoms had also developed an intricate relationship with
each other. This included the institution of a High King of the island, whose
position was partly hereditary and partly acquired by ability – which usually
meant victory in war, and so is reminiscent of the 'Bretwalda' in the former
Roman province. There were also regional kings in the five provinces of
Leinster, Munster, Connacht, Ulster and Meath, and beneath that provincial
level, the various clans could be considered virtually independent kingdoms
until compelled to acknowledge and respect the superiority of the provincial
kings. It was up to the latter to enforce their authority, and they were liable
to be overthrown and replaced by an obstreperous subordinate – as were
the High Kings by a provincial king. The system was fully understood in
Ireland, and fully accepted; it did at times mean a frequency of warfare,
which was often little more than cattle raiding – cattle being the main
evidence of wealth.

That is to say, the Irish kingdoms were a community of states with a
continuing relationship with each other, and they operated within that
community and its traditions. This could be expressed in terms of the
fictional – but accepted and believed – descent of the kings, and even of

whole communities, from a usually mythical ancestor, usually the original High King Niall of the Nine Hostages, and by the identification of a common group of family names of men who were thought to be ancestors. These separate states, long-lived and moving in and out of independence and power, expressed their close relationships in a variety of ways, including warfare, trade and intermarriage, but also by acknowledging the primacy of St Patrick as their Christian evangelist. Before their conversion to Christianity they acknowledged a joint belief in a system of gods and goddesses which the incoming Church labelled as pagan and sought to abolish. Their conversion to Christianity in the fifth century did not destroy the old stories of these mythical interrelationships or the relationships themselves. As a result the whole island partook of a particular version of Christianity which was self-consciously Irish, and different from that practiced in the rest of Europe. It was this sort of attitude which emphasized their joint membership as a community of states.

With this as a clue, we can also identify three other communities of states in the British Isles in the post-Roman period, though they took some two or three centuries to emerge, whereas the Irish community of states reached back deep into prehistory. There were the Saxons, Anglians and Jutish, collectively called English, who had come to occupy a large part of the south, centre and east of the larger island, incorporating much of the old Roman province and many of the descendants of the Roman Britons. They were distinguished above all by their language, and by the claimed origin of their kings, which, like the Irish, was from a set of gods and heroes from deep in the pagan past, but also by their Christianity, which was linked to the Roman version, while the rest of Britain and Ireland was for a long time wary of that authority.

The existence of these English states, which by the early seventh century occupied most of the modern territory of England, separated off the surviving groups of Celtic kingdoms. To their west were the Welsh states, who were the survivors of the several cantonal states which had emerged from the defunct Roman province, and were spread from Cornwall (the 'Corn Welsh', that is, from Conrnovii, the Celtic kingdom, and 'Welsh', English for 'foreign') through Wales and into the south-west Scottish kingdoms between the Hadrian's Wall and the Forth-Clyde isthmus. Again, these had a distinct language, British Celtic, and a claimed descent from the Roman province and its *civitates*, and practiced the distinctive Celtic Christianity. The north was occupied by the third group, comprising Scots in modern Argyll and the Picts and their neighbours in the north and east of modern

Scotland. (Strathclyde was a member of this group, as was the northern part of Northumbria, which was also one of the English states.)

The British Isles therefore comprised these four communities of states by about AD 600, when the confusion of the post-Roman period had calmed down somewhat, and when we can discern the new political conditions fairly clearly. The development of each of these communities of states over the next five centuries provides a curiously varied set of outcomes, but from the beginning it is clear that these four groups of states were the origins of the four countries of the British Isles. That is, the potential for the unification of these four countries already existed by 600. The first task now is to identify the four communities in more detail.

The Community of Anglo-Saxon States

The mixture of settlers, mercenaries, and abandoned or conquered peoples who occupied the land south of the Firth of Forth consolidated themselves into a series of kingdoms, most of which at first were only small. The immigrants no doubt linked first with the mercenary groups, and between them, in alliance with the native descendants of the Roman province, they formed a series of vigorous kingdoms. The earliest of these kingdoms lay along the eastern and southern coasts. Kent was the first to be articulated, traditionally by about 450, though this may be too early. It inherited from its Roman predecessors some elements of political organization, and certainly occupied the territory of the Durovernum *civitas*. It definitely emerged relatively quickly as the strongest of the early states. King Aethelberht (*c*.560–616) was reckoned to be the first Bretwalda, and was also the king who welcomed the Roman missionary Augustine in 597. Once converted to Christianity, he was keen to see to the conversion of others, using his power and influence to urge the kings of the East Angles and the East Saxons to convert. This gave him influence, and is the basis of his Bretwalda-ship.

Sussex, the South Saxons, appears to have survived for a time as a Celtic state centred on Chichester. It gradually became Saxon, perhaps by welcoming more Saxon mercenaries. The West Saxons were apparently brought ashore by Cerdic, whose name is actually Celtic, suggesting another type of cooperation between Saxons and local forces. All these kingdoms, initially small, were spread along the south-east coast of the southern North Sea and English Channel, but only the West Saxons had any considerable potential for expansion inland. From the Thames estuary northwards there were the East Saxons (who soon took control of the abandoned site

2. ENGLAND: Before Unification 800 – 850

MERCIA - Kingdoms
Deira - Former Kingdoms
Conquered by Wessex 800 – 850

Bernicia

NORTHUMBRIA

Deira

Lindsey

Middle Angles

MERCIA

EAST ANGLIA

Hwicce

ESSEX

KENT

WESSEX

SUSSEX

CORNWALL

0   100M

of London) and the East Angles – who were formed of two groups of Angles, the North and South Folk, and were probably separately organized at first, but were soon joined into a single kingdom. (The king buried with his treasure at Sutton Hoo was probably Raedwald of that state, a contemporary of Aethelberht.) Lindsey was centred on the old Roman *colonia* of Lindum – the name continued, obviously – and Deira (roughly modern Yorkshire) was also centred on another Roman *colonia*, Eburacum/York. Beyond the Tees was Bernicia, the latest kingdom to become established, only a generation before 600 – another contemporary with Aethelberht, and one of the kings he aimed to convert, not altogether successfully. The prevalence of the use of Roman urban centres as the new kingdom centres – York, Canterbury, Chichester – strongly suggests an early cooperation between immigrant forces and local authorities. As the chiefs of the main force, the German migrants' chieftains understandably became the rulers. In the North, the kingdom of Bernicia was also originally a British kingdom, and would seem to have welcomed a mercenary force as reinforcement and defenders; it was thus basically a Celtic kingdom with an Anglian ruling family, just as the West Saxons may have been a Saxon kingdom with a British ruling family.

Other settlers, either new arrivals or adventurous and ambitious men already present, penetrated inland and formed a series of small states behind – west of – the coastal ones. This movement cannot be called a conquest; it is more likely to have been an infiltration into territories not under any serious control by anybody else, or, as with the greater kingdoms along the coast, alliances between armed bands and local groups needing protection.

These minor kingdoms were spread along the eastern Midlands west of the original kingdoms of Lindsey, East Anglia and Essex. They did not last very long as independent entities, and their existence is only known through a later document called the 'Tribal Hidage'. Their names are known, and their sizes (from the number of hides – areas of farmland – they contained), but the source is late and has to be interpreted, so it is quite possible that we have misunderstood it. But since at least some of the peoples listed were certainly at some point independent kingdoms, it is likely that the rest, no matter how small, were also in that condition.

Some of the names survive as present places: the Spalda, for example, in modern Spalding. Others are known only from this document, such as the Wixna, divided into East and West, the North and South Gyrwa, and the West and East Willa. Some can be located by their names, which survive in various forms – the Cilternsaeta and Pecsaeta in the Chilterns and the Peak District, or the Arosaetna in the valley of the River Arrow in Warwickshire.

Altogether, these names and peoples occupied all the Midlands west of East Anglia as far as the borders of Wales.

A few of the peoples listed in the document were of much greater size than the majority. In particular, the Myrcenas Landes (the basis of the later Mercia) in the valley of the upper Trent, the West Saxons and the East Angles were four or five times larger than any of the others, and a hundred times larger than the smallest. From this it is not difficult to follow what happened next: the larger states swallowed the smaller; in particular Mercia and Wessex gobbled up many of the smaller Anglian and Saxon states, and also expanded at the expense of the British.

So these minor states did not in fact last very long, though many of them survived as local governing units, even as sub-kingdoms – the Tribal Hidage dates from the ninth century, so as units they still existed then. The proximity to the Welsh kingdoms of the western states forced them to develop greater size and power, which allowed them to dominate the many smaller states around them. Their size suggests that they needed to be of considerable power and determination to be founded and to survive in a largely hostile situation. They were by this time taking territory from the states which had emerged amongst the former Roman Britons, some of which were of a considerable size themselves, and had been established for some centuries.

Some of these kingdoms have been noted already, but others can only be guessed at. There had probably been one centred on Carlisle, possibly another based on the old Roman fortress of Deva (Chester); others could have been based on Worcester and Viroconium (near Shrewsbury), and certainly three in the south-west centred respectively on the former Roman cities of Cirencester, Gloucester and Bath. In the generation around AD 600, however, a series of victories by Anglo-Saxon kings resulted in the final conquest of all of the Midlands and some of the south-west, and further Anglo-Saxon penetration into what is now southern Scotland. The Mercians advanced to the border of Wales, in the process enclosing some large Anglian kingdoms – Westerne, Magonsaeten and Hwicce – as their sub-kingdoms. The West Saxons, meanwhile, captured the three city-kingdoms of Bath, Gloucester and Cirencester, and eventually moved against the south-western peninsula into Somerset and Devon.

The process of conquest was on a larger and more organized scale than the early rustling and raiding chieftains of the fifth and early sixth centuries, but only slowly were the conquests transformed into stable states. The institution – though that is perhaps too strong a term for it – of the Bretwalda passed from Aethelberht of Kent to his protégé Raedwald of

East Anglia. Aethelfrith of Bernicia was another of these men. He established his supremacy over much of southern Scotland and northern England as far south of the Humber – the name Northumbria was created for his kingdom. He was overthrown by Raedwald (he of Sutton Hoo), who helped install Edwin, who took Aethelfrith's place and ruled both Deira and Bernicia after him. Edwin in turn was overthrown by the Mercian King Penda, who had refused to convert to Christianity and had established a personal supremacy in the Midlands. It was thus the vigour, ambition and capability of King Aethelfrith which had compelled the other kingdoms to consolidate, then Penda of Mercia secured control of his western and eastern neighbours, eliminating most of the independent kingdoms between the Welsh border and the Fens. During the half-century around AD 600, the 'Heptarchy', the term historians have invented for this period, emerged: Northumbria, Mercia, East Anglia and Wessex were the great powers, with Essex, Sussex and Kent the minor players.

Thus was formed a community of states whom we may now call English. They had a common language, which we call Anglo-Saxon, though divided into dialects (which survive to this day). They had a common history, in that they had all claimed to have emerged from settlements of immigrants who had formed themselves into minor kingdoms and had then conquered lands from their ex-Roman British neighbours – their mercenary origins and the Celtic origin of most of the inhabitants were largely ignored. They also had a common ancestry in their identification with the same mythical gods and heroes from the distant Germanic past, just as the Irish kingdoms claimed an ancestry in Irish deities. This was overtaken, of course, but not suppressed, by their conversion to Christianity, a process which began about AD 600. They eventually all chose to follow the version of Christianity which emanated from Rome, sometimes after much argument and discussion, recorded for Northumbria in the *Ecclesiastical History* of Bede, who was bitter about the failure of the Celtic Christians in their attempt to evangelize their pagan English neighbours. A series of bishoprics and two archbishoprics were gradually organized to enforce this religion.

Besides the common elements identified in the last paragraph – language, myth, history and Christianity – the ruling dynasties constantly intermarried, and, of course, they fought each other, though not all that often once the seven kingdoms settled down; such wars were one of the elements of a community of such states. This system of states was clearly articulated before 650, and it survived intact for the next two centuries, into the mid-ninth century. For much of that time Mercia was the most powerful of the kingdoms, dominating the smaller states in the south-east, though leaving the local dynasties in power, as is also the case in the south-west with the Hwicce. The West Saxons looked westwards, expanding at the expense of the Britons there into Somerset and Devon in the eighth century. The Northumbrians inherited from Aethelfrith and Edwin a supremacy over southern Scotland, and tended to look north towards the system of kingdoms being articulated in Scotland, until defeated by the Picts. The three major kingdoms thus all looked to expand, though only Wessex seems to have succeeded; Mercia, however, could dominate the south-eastern kingdoms.

The ruling dynasties of all these kingdoms broke down during the eighth century. Until about 750, the kingship was inherited within a single royal family in each kingdom, usually passing from father to son. But from then on, in one after another, this ceased: in Wessex by the 680s, in Mercia in the 750s and then again in the 820s, in Kent by the 760s, in Essex in the 740s, in East Anglia by the 750s and in Northumbria repeatedly from about 700 onwards. In all cases an attempt was made to seek out ever more distant members of the old royal families to maintain the succession, but in the end the original dynasty failed. In the ninth century, all the kingdoms were subject to conflicts between rivals for the kingship, so that civil warfare came whenever a king died, and, of course, murder or assassination was the likely fate of any man who actually became king (and those who failed); between 705 and 850, five Northumbrian kings were murdered, two abdicated and six were deposed, while only two kings reigned for more than ten years.

Then, in 829, the king of Wessex, Egbert (802–39), seized a moment of Mercian weakness and conducted a swift campaign which overthrew the Mercian 'supremacy' which had existed for a century, though he did not altogether replace it with his own. The campaign took him as far north as the southern border of Northumbria, whose king quickly indicated his submission before Egbert returned home. This campaign resulted in him being counted as the last of the Bretwaldas, though by that time this was a distinctly antiquated distinction.

Egbert had strictly limited ambitions. He established his own dominance over the south-eastern kingdoms of Kent, Essex and Sussex, who were even given a West Saxon prince as their viceroy for a time. He also added the conquest of the kingdom of Cornwall. The result was a doubling of the size of the West Saxon kingdom and its control over many of the wealth-producing trading ports from Ipswich to Cornwall. East Anglia broke away from Mercia into a resumed independence at the same time, without having a Wessex domination foisted on it. In effect the 'heptarchy' was therefore succeeded by a system of four kingdoms. The minor kingdoms now within Wessex's sphere continued to exist within its domination for some time, but were quietly absorbed during the ninth century. Egbert had destroyed the Mercian supremacy, but did not put one by Wessex in its place.

The destruction of the Mercian supremacy could be put down squarely to the failure of the Mercian kingship. Egbert of Wessex had been king for almost thirty years when he set out on his campaign, and was therefore the only English king with a firm grip on power: all the other kingdoms had disputed successions or were involved in dynastic conflicts. It was the kingship which held these fragile kingdoms together. The old dynasties had relied largely on the prestige of their ancestry and their long inheritance for their authority; when they died out, so did that loyalty. A weak king meant a weak kingdom, and Egbert took advantage. But his ambition was carefully limited, and a new West Saxon hegemony was not his aim. By gaining control over the commercially most vigorous area of England he was, however, placing Wessex firmly in position as potentially the most wealthy, and therefore most powerful, of the English states.

The system of states in Anglo-Saxon England as established in the mid-seventh century had thus been resilient, and it was capable of absorbing blows, such as that inflicted by Egbert, with only a relatively minor change. Over the four centuries and more since the evaporation of Roman rule, the many small kingdoms had been consolidated into seven, and then into just the final four which were of political importance. In 850 the system still stood with only minor alterations from what had existed two centuries before; Egbert had rocked the system, but had not broken it. He passed his kingship on to a capable son, while the other kingdoms continued with their dynastic disputes. It would take a rather greater shock than a mere temporary military victory to upset the English system.

The Community of Welsh States

The country which has become called Wales was inhabited by the surviving remnants of the subjects of Roman Britain, most of them descended from the Iron Age inhabitants; others were more recent arrivals, refugees from Anglian invasions. Like most other native inhabitants of that province, they spoke a Celtic language which developed into Welsh, though Latin was also in use. The Welsh language contains a considerable number of Latin loanwords embedded within it, and it is clear from a variety of sources that

Latin continued to be used amongst the inhabitants of Wales for centuries after the Roman province had disappeared, no doubt largely because the population had become Christian, though it does not seem that Latin usage was confined to churchmen. What made this country 'Wales' was the fact that the rest of the old Roman province was conquered by the Anglian and Saxon states, and to them the Welsh were foreigners – which is what the word Welsh meant in Anglo–Saxon English. Wales was therefore the remnant of the old Roman province, and fully conscious of that inheritance.

Wales as a distinctive country existed from about AD 600, when more or less simultaneous advances in the north and south isolated the Welsh of Wales by land from the other parts of former Roman Britain which were inhabited by peoples speaking British Celtic – the south-west peninsula and Strathclyde. In the north, the capture of the old Roman city of Chester by King Aethelfrith of Northumbria in 604 can be taken as the definitive separation of the Britons of southern Scotland from Wales; in the south, the earlier conquest of the three cities of Gloucester, Cirencester and Bath by a king of Wessex in 577 performed the same function by interposing a Saxon wedge between the Welsh and the Corn Welsh. Communication between them continued, of course, not least by sea, for the Irish Sea and the English Channel were always busy waterways, but the English advances and the establishment of a clear boundary within which Wales was confined was as much a psychological as a physical change, defining Wales for the next millennium and a half to the present day.

Curiously, though, these conquests were not followed up by either Northumbria or Wessex by further advances into Wales, though Wessex went on to conquer Somerset and Devon (but not until the eighth century) and to dominate Cornwall, which was annexed by Egbert in 838, but had its own king as a Wessex subordinate for another century at least. The Northumbrians secured Lancashire and Cumbria and parts of southern Scotland. Instead, it was Mercia which now became the main Welsh enemy across their mutual boundary.

It is perhaps anachronistic to speak of a country called Wales, though it was always certainly a country inhabited by people speaking what became the Welsh language. The sixth and seventh centuries were the time when a series of Welsh poets celebrated their language and their kings, no doubt a reaction to the defeats being suffered. As in the rest of the former Roman Britain, there had emerged during the two centuries or so after the end of Roman power in the province a series of independent states – the Welsh were no more a united people than their enemies. The Wales which

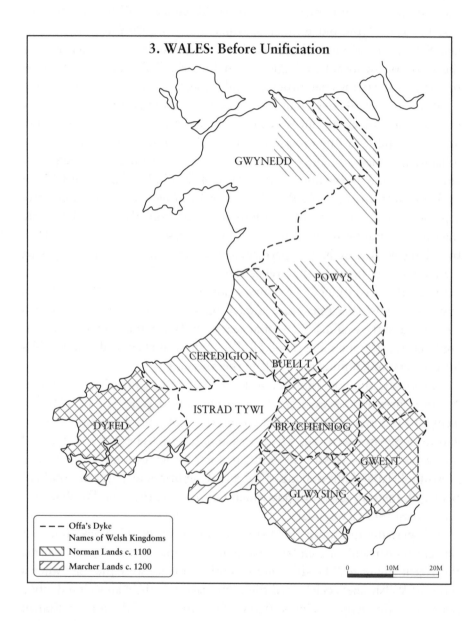

3. WALES: Before Unificiation

GWYNEDD

POWYS

CEREDIGION   BUELLT

ISTRAD TYWI   BRYCHEINIOG

DYFED   GWENT

GLWYSING

- - - Offa's Dyke
Names of Welsh Kingdoms
Norman Lands c. 1100
Marcher Lands c. 1200

0   10M   20M

confronted Mercia from about AD 600 onwards was a country of kingdoms whose boundaries reflected the mountainous geography of the land, and which to agriculture-based states, such as those in England, seemed to exist in poverty. As in Ireland, cattle and sheep were the means of wealth and currency. The imprint of the Roman city-state system had been much lighter in the mountains than elsewhere in the province – though parts of the South Wales coastal area had been fairly well developed. It was therefore the old tribal system from the Iron Age which had been in large part utilized and frozen in place by the Roman administration, and which formed the bases of the new Welsh states, rather more clearly than had happened in the future 'England'.

From north to south, the first of these kingdoms was Gwynedd, the largest, and always the most powerful. Based on part of the Iron Age and Roman *civitas* of the Ordovices, it occupied the Snowdon area and the agriculturally wealthy island of Mon (Anglesey). It was possibly originally centred at the Roman military camp at Caernarvon (Segontium), though the Christian bishopric was established at Bangor, not far away. Its founding myth claimed that its ruling family descended from a refugee aristocracy from the Votadini of Lothian in south-east Scotland, and that they had arrived late in the fourth century; their leader supposedly gave his name to the kingdom. To the east was Powys, which stretched along much of the Mercian border, and so therefore was usually the first target of Mercian raids. At some point in the eighth century a boundary was constructed to separate the two kingdoms. This border acquired the name of Offa's Dyke, from the Mercian king who may have overseen its construction; examination of its layout and route suggests that it was a mutually agreed boundary rather than a fortification like Hadrian's Wall, though it was perhaps the wall which was the dyke's inspiration. The dyke itself started from the northern coast at the Dee estuary and ran as far south as the River Wye. It is assumed that the river then formed a non-dyke boundary, but in fact the Welsh kingdom there was not Powys but Gwent, and earlier Ergyng, so if the boundary was laid out by mutual agreement it was between Mercia and Powys only.

The southern half of Wales was more divided than the north. In the south-west was Dyfed (later Pembrokeshire, the former Demetae), which included the primary Welsh bishopric at St David's. Along the Irish Sea coast between Dyfed and Gwynedd was Ceredigion (which the English named Cardigan), whose northern boundary lay at the estuary of the River Dyfi. The area north of this became called Merioneth, named after a king who came to rule it when it was separated off from Gwynedd. The south-east was divided into several kingdoms, including Istrad Towy, east of the Towy River and including the agriculturally productive Gower peninsula, centred on the fortress of Dinefwr. To the east was Glywysing (the former Silures), which later became called Morgannwg, named from a later king (the modern Glamorgan), and Gwent (modern Monmouth/Gwent), which included the early kingdom of Ergyng which has produced a useful group of charters, and the former Roman legionary fortress at Caerleon. Finally, there were two small upland kingdoms, Brycheiniog and Buellt, between these coastal kingdoms and Powys. All these kingdoms were subdivided into smaller areas called cantrefs, which were the basic administrative units – Merioneth and Buellt were originally no more than cantrefs themselves, and Brycheiniog comprised two cantrefs.

Of these kingdoms only Gwynedd stands out as wielding much power at any time, though Powys was not wholly incapable. Gwynedd was also in a sense protected by the fact that it was relatively distant from the English lands, and was mountainous enough to be difficult to conquer. Powys and the south coast kingdoms were very vulnerable to English raids, which could penetrate along the coasts and several inland routes. Dyfed and Gwynedd had also suffered from Irish raids in the past.

These Welsh kingdoms had a permanent existence from at least the late sixth century, yet a certain tentativeness and instability is suggested by the practice of naming and renaming them after prominent kings – Glywysing, named after Glywys, was later renamed Morgannwg. Political change in this set of kingdoms came about largely by inheritance, so that at times kings inherited more than one kingdom. Conquest was not the usual system for increasing a king's power, though raiding and looting were. Such political unions tended to be only for the lifetime of the particular king, mirroring their original foundation myths, which insisted on their independence, so any unions usually broke up at the death of the unifier. The exception was the union of the kingdom of Ceredigion with that of Istrad Towy, which formed the kingdom of Seisyllwg in an unusually permanent arrangement – the uniter was King Seisyll of Ceredigion – which lasted for a couple of centuries. But when Rhodri Mawr of Gwynedd (844–78) succeeded in uniting his kingdom with Powys and Seisyllwg, bringing most of Wales under one king, that unity immediately dissolved upon Rhodri's death. Hywel Dda of Dyfed (909–50) similarly united his kingdom with Seisyllwg and Gwynedd but, again, this unity lasted only about a decade, and broke up when he died. And so on; it is evident that the individual kingdoms were thoroughly set in their ways.

It will be seen, therefore, that these occasional unifications, temporary though they were, did indicate that the several states recognized that they were 'related' to one another – this was the message of the founding myths and was promoted by the poets – but unifying the country by royal intermarriage and the inheritance of kingdoms was not a workable scheme. The various kingdoms continued to exist even in such unions, and when the inheritor died they resumed their own individual identities and independence: the inheritance system insisted on separation once more. They all spoke the same language, listened to and applauded the same bards, practiced the same religion and, if threatened, were perfectly capable of fighting in alliance. Far more perhaps than amongst the English, or the kingdoms of Scotland, this Welsh community of states was an active and self-conscious one, based on their inheritance of the Christian religion from the Roman period, a common language and culture, and an antipathy towards the Anglo-Saxons. They shared a pastoral lifestyle and a similar pattern of government; the royal families intermarried. All these elements brought the kingdoms to consider themselves a particular community of states.

Christianity in Wales was inherited from the final phase of the Roman occupation, and had been continuously practiced while the early Anglo-Saxon kingdoms were pagan. This would be one of the unifying factors in the face of the early Anglo-Saxon pressure from the east. The main four kingdoms each had their own bishopric, and these dioceses had existed from a very early period. They were also distinct and independent of any outside ecclesiastical authority, with the possible exception of the very distant Pope, who probably scarcely knew of their existence; their practices, after the centuries of isolation (from the Roman point of view), were inevitably at variance with those of Rome. The failure of St Augustine, the evangelist of the English, to stand when greeting a group of Welsh bishops who had come to visit him was long remembered and was taken to symbolize a clear distinction, even hostility, between Welsh and Roman Christianity. The common background and history of the Welsh bishoprics was thus another element convincing the Welsh to regard themselves as forming a distinct community of states and a distinct nationality. There was also an active tradition of monastic foundation, resulting in a large number of Celtic-type monasteries all over the country, something which again distinguished Wales from the Anglo-Saxons.

This community of states had existed from the end of Roman Britain onwards and lasted much longer than other such groups of states in the

British Isles, except perhaps in Ireland. The original community had presumably included the Romano-British kingdoms which had emerged after about 450, but had since been suppressed by the Anglo-Saxon invaders – the memory of the northern Welsh kingdoms was a staple in the repertory of the Welsh poets. The community had then been much larger before those conquests. At least some of the Welsh kingdoms can be seen to have existed from the fifth or probably even the fourth century AD, and there was little geopolitical change, apart from the brief unifications of such kings as Rhodri Mawr and Hywel Dda, until the eleventh century, when political conditions altered, though some of the very earliest kingdoms, like Ergyng, did disappear. Attacks were suffered from England, and at times from Ireland, but only in the form of raids. This was a stable political system, in which change was always superficial.

The Community of Scottish States

The political geography of Scotland at the time of the Roman Empire is obscure, and was apparently constantly changing as tribes and leaders gained a temporary predominance – which implies that many kingdoms were barely established, and existed only during a king's lifetime. There are glimpses of tribal states, one of which, the Caledones, gave its poetic name to the region, though quite possibly the most powerful of these temporary political formations was that of the Maeatae in the Central Valley in the fourth century. By the time that something reasonably certain and permanent is visible in the sources, about the end of the Roman province to the south, these early states had largely disappeared and the country which later became called Scotland was divided into four or perhaps five kingdoms. In the south-west was the British/Welsh kingdom of Alt Clut (later to become the kingdom of Strathclyde). It was centred on the stronghold of Dumbarton and was Welsh-speaking, but was separated by land from its fellow Welsh kingdoms after the Northumbrian conquest of the Irish Sea coast of Lancashire about 600. Saints Mungo and Kentigern were the kingdom's religious founders. The kingdom was not large, and there were several even smaller kingdoms in the Southern Uplands. Along the Irish Sea coast was Galloway, a region whose political status is generally unclear, but was probably normally independent: it included the site of Whithorn, the centre of Christianity for the region.

To the north and west of the Clyde estuary was the kingdom of the Scots, whose ruling group was related to one in the north of Ireland.

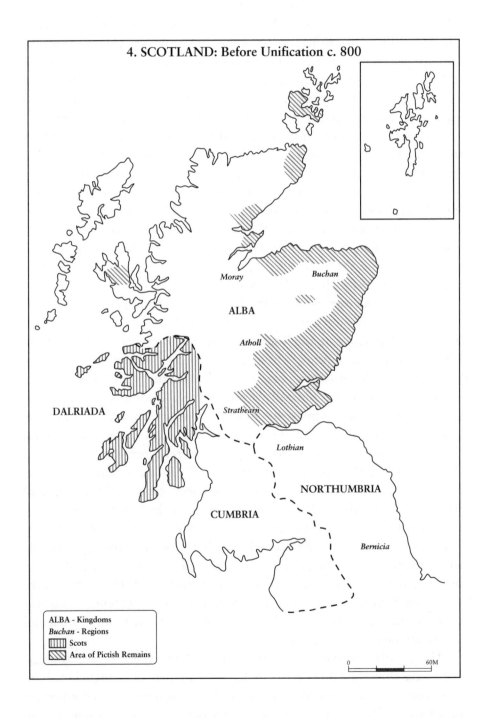

4. SCOTLAND: Before Unification c. 800

Moray   Buchan

ALBA

Atholl

DALRIADA   Strathearn

Lothian

NORTHUMBRIA

CUMBRIA

Bernicia

ALBA - Kingdoms
Buchan - Regions
Scots
Area of Pictish Remains

0   60M

It was formed of three related kingdoms, centred on Kintyre, Lorn and Islay. Its territory was essentially the modern counties of Argyll and Bute and Arran. Its main political centre in the early years was at Dunadd on the Kintyre peninsula; its main religious centre was at Iona next to the island of Mull, founded in part by the missionary Columcille, or Columba. None of these western kingdoms was especially powerful, each had developed separately and each had an important religious centre within its territory.

The south-east, between the Forth and the Tyne, had included kingdoms in relations with Rome, notably the Votadini, who became the Gododdin, and Berneich, later Bernicia. The latter accepted the help of Anglian mercenaries, and the joint peoples became the base for Aethelfrith's aggressions. When united with Deira, modern Yorkshire, centred on the old Roman city of York, Bernicia, based at the great coastal fortress of Bamburgh, became the most powerful kingdom in Britain. The Gododdin fell to Northumbrian conquest in the 640s, under Aethelfrith's son, Oswiu, whose power was such that he was referred to as the 'King of the North'.

The north and east, north of the Forth and east and north of the great mountains, was the territory of the Picts, one of the few continuing tribal names which dated from the Roman period. Their territory extended from Fife to Orkney, and appears to have been divided into a number of separate areas which might have been separate kingdoms at times, and at others were co-ordinated by an exceptionally vigorous king. Traditionally there were seven of these areas, supposedly attached to the seven sons of Cruithne (which is Pictish for 'Pict'). This was another of those founding myths, like that of the Welsh kingdoms, but it also reflected the geographical divisions of the Pictish lands. One of these ('Fib') was centred on Fife, another ('Circhen') lay along the east coast north of Fife, a third ('Fidach') was around the Moray Firth, with a fourth in the Buchan area ('Ce'); Caithness ('Cat') was a fifth. The Picts also moved into Orkney, which at one point at least was a Pictish sub-kingdom. Two regions occupied the southern interior – west of Fife was the land of 'Fortrenn', and to the north of that was the land of 'Fotla', in modern Perthshire. The degree of the political separation of these territories, however, remains unclear for these early centuries; probably they were very liable to unification and separation on the Welsh pattern.

These early kingdoms are rather shadowy presences in our sources, but by the time they do become visible they are part of a single kingdom. One reason for this seems to have been wars fought against the Northumbrians in which the Picts were eventually victorious once they became united, notably at the Battle of Nechtansmere in 685. The experience of attacks forced the Picts to unify, and as a result that kingdom became the most powerful in the north, and also came to dominate the Scots kingdom. This unification was a process which paralleled that being performed in the English Midlands with the contemporary growth of the Mercian kingdom, similarly in reaction to Northumbrian power and aggression.

There were thus at least four or five kingdoms comprising the northern part of Britain, and earlier there were probably several more. Unlike those which appeared and disappeared during the Roman period, they were relatively stable, in the sense that they all appear to have lasted for a considerable length of time; visible in the sources as a group during the sixth century and continuing in existence until the ninth. They were competitors, allies and rivals, and at the same time formed a clear and obvious community of states. Bernicia was for a time the most powerful of them, and its kings campaigned to subdue Galloway, Alt Clut and the Picts in the seventh century, though without ultimate success. The relationship of the several kingdoms is illustrated partly by their intermarriages and partly by the strange custom of adopting members of each other's royal families as their kings, possibly originally a Pictish practice – but this is a very obvious indication that they were self-consciously a community of kingdoms. Thus several of the Pictish kings came from the Scots royal family, and the same later with the kings of Strathclyde. It is not clear if the Angles of Bernicia participated in all these practices – though some Northumbrian kings did marry ladies from the north; the unification of Bernicia with Deira to form Northumbria brought a much stronger emphasis on the joint kingdom's English identity, and greater interaction with the kingdoms of the south.

There was also the matter of religion. Columba's version of Irish Christianity was successful in converting the Picts (and of course the Scots), whereas the Northumbrians, after seeming for a time to accept that Irish version, decided to adopt the Roman practices – a decision based on the assessment of the power of the competitors, and perhaps on the greater distance of Rome from Northumbria, and therefore its lesser likelihood of exercising that power locally, where the Church would be dependent on the king's favour. Meanwhile the Christian centre at Whithorn had had an independent origin at the end of the Roman period, though it fell under strong Northumbrian influence later. This northern group of states therefore included a whole series of important religious centres – Iona, Whithorn, monasteries such as Lindisfarne and others which are slowly being revealed, for example that on the Dornoch Firth at Portmahomack, but they all owned to a different origin. Whether this caused enmity between the royal sponsors of the different centres is not altogether clear, but the adoption of Roman customs did emphasize the separation of Northumbria from the rest of the northern kingdoms. The emphasis of the Christian organization, though limited amongst the Celtic lands, tended to emphasize the wider community of states, and acted as a stimulus to kings to expand their authority. The Church was a potent element tending to unity.

The community of states in the north, therefore, consisted of Strathclyde, the Scots, Galloway, Northumbria and the Pictish kingdom. They had in common their interrelationships among the royal families and their participation in wars with each other. But they all spoke different languages – Scottish, Welsh, Pictish, English – and they had diffident religious traditions. Further, the Northumbrians certainly shifted away from a participation in northern affairs in favour of England, especially when threatened by the power of Mercia, while the Britons' connections were also with the Welsh kingdoms. Nevertheless, despite these differences, they can be counted as a community of states largely because of their royal families' relationships, their religious origins and their geographical proximity, and this turned out to be the crucial element for the future.

The Situation of Northumbria

Northumbria is worth further consideration. Geographically it was the largest kingdom in the islands, reaching from the Humber and the Mersey to the Forth. It was capable of sending armies to Anglesey, to the Isle of Man and Ireland, to Galloway and the Firth of Clyde, into Mercia and once against the West Saxons, as well as deep into the Pictish region. But the accumulation of enemies was too much for it; Northumbria was defeated by the Picts in 685 at Nechtansmere, its expeditions to Anglesey and Man were unproductive, as was that to Ireland, and it was defeated by Mercia. To cap it all, the succession to the kingship was repeatedly disputed even while it was at its most powerful.

Weakened by defeat and internal disputes, the kingdom held out for a century or more in independence, though its king submitted briefly to Egbert in 829 as soon as he arrived at its borders – hardly the action of a powerful king – and it was under serious threat from its northern and southern enemies all the time. Nevertheless, it was always the major British power after Mercia, and a possible future was that it would hold onto its lands from the Forth to the Humber while the kingdoms to the north united, as they did in the ninth century, as the new kingdom of Scotland (or Alba), and those to the south would similarly unite, led by either Wessex or Mercia. There would then have been three kingdoms in Britain – Scotland north of the Forth, Northumbria and England south of the Humber; Wales could well then continue in independence. The collapse and division of Northumbria in the late ninth century (see next chapter) prevented such an outcome, and both English and Scots kingdoms secured parts of the kingdom so that for the next eight centuries the boundary between them was in constant dispute. One small area of the border is 'The Debatable Land', but such a description could well be applied to the whole land from the River Tyne to the River Forth, which was constantly fought over from the ninth century onwards, a legacy of the original enlarged Northumbrian kingdom.

The Community of Irish States

The Irish states are the easiest of all four of the countries in the British Isles to characterize as a community, and this has been discussed in some detail already in the first part of this chapter. As far back as can be discerned, and certainly from the time of the end of the Roman province in the larger island across the water, from which time a reasonably coherent account can be made of the country's divisions, the island of Ireland was subdivided amongst a large number of tribes or clans. The island has five major sections, or provinces – Ulster, Leinster, Meath, Connacht and Munster (in English terms) – which are marked by a degree of geographical separation by the existence of bogs, hills, lakes and other physical barriers. These regions were in fact of only intermittent geopolitical importance, though each of them at times had forceful kings who established a local supremacy. Instead, what counted were the numerous clans, none of which had any large or real political power. In this, of course, Ireland was really not much different from Scotland and Wales in the centuries after the Roman Empire, or indeed England, as the old Roman provincial system broke down into tribal kingdoms after the Roman withdrawal. But in Scotland, Wales, and England, these many kingdoms were soon replaced by larger versions, which consolidated into larger and more powerful units. This did not happen in Ireland, and the extreme division of the island continued.

There was, of course, no reason for the Irish to alter this situation, as the Picts and Midland English had done under Northumbrian pressure. Irish warfare tended not to involve conquest, only dominance and the acquisition of loot, and in a largely pastoral society the prize of victory tended to be capture of slaves and animals rather than the occupation of land. The High Kings were a similar institution to the Bretwalda, and were generally similarly intermittent and ineffective. None of the High Kings was able to establish his authority over the whole island, and none was able to pass on any real power to his biological successors. The office tended towards being hereditary, but shifted between different branches of the O'Neill family, which came from a variety of different clan kingdoms.

Power therefore remained centred on the chiefs of the clans. The emergence of a man of particular ability might bring together several clans into what might be termed a kingdom, but as with the High Kings and the brief unity of the Welsh kingdoms under Rhodri Mawr and Hywel Dda, these kingdoms rarely lasted long before dissolving back into their constituent clans and tribal areas. From the fifth century additional centres of power developed as the country was converted to Christianity, and the bishops and abbots wielded a different sort of power, but they usually did so in large part as members of their clans. Their existence and influence was often as intermittent as that of any temporary king, though just as political. Therefore, though the Church was an Irish-wide institution, it was so much a part of the local communities that the pressure towards unity was very much less than in England or Scotland.

These Irish kingdoms had a common language, of course, and a similar way of life, their royal families intermarried, they all had a common system of myths of royal and clan descent, and they had a common attitude to the Christian religion, with their particular traditions of anchorite monks, mobile bishops and small local churches. It was clearly a community of like-minded and related states, as would be expected in a circumscribed and relatively isolated island, but there was no indication that much would change without a serious challenge from either inside or outside the island.

Conclusion

The four regions of the British Isles therefore had already formed themselves into distinct countries and political groups by about AD 600, if not earlier, and these had become distinct groups of states, which are referred to here as 'communities'. At first they comprised many small and weak states, but, in England at least, from the seventh century onwards they began to coalesce into larger polities, a process which was absent in Wales and Ireland, but which was developing in Pictland. However, even though related in various ways, there was no sign that they were likely to become united. That would take a much greater pressure than any single one of the states could exert; and yet the fact that they formed clear and distinct communities was the first stage in that unificatory process.

Bibliography

The sheer quantity of books on these four countries is nothing less than daunting. I list here only a few which have been exceptionally helpful.

England:

Adams, Max, *The King in the North, the Life and Times of Oswald of Northumbria* (London: 2013).

Carver, Martin (ed.), *The Age of Sutton Hoo, the Seventh Century in North-western Europe* (Woodbridge, Suffolk: 1994).

Carver, Martin, *The Sutton Hoo Story, Encounters with Early England* (Woodbridge, Suffolk: 2017).

Hill, David, *An Atlas of Anglo-Saxon England* (Oxford: 1981).

Kirby, D.P., *The Earliest English Kings*, 2nd ed. (London: 2000).

Loyn, H.R., *Anglo-Saxon England and the Norman Conquest* (London: 1962).

Mayr-Harting, Henry, *The Coming of Christianity to Anglo-Saxon England* (London: 1972).

Stenton, Sir Frank, *Anglo-Saxon England*, 2nd ed. (Oxford: 1947).

Yorke, Barbara, *Kings and Kingship of Early Anglo-Saxon England* (London: 1990).

Scotland:

Carver, Martin, *Portmahomack, Monastery of the Picts*, 2nd ed. (Edinburgh: 2016).

Clarkson, Ian, *Columba* (Edinburgh: 2012).

Clarkson, Ian, *The Men of the North, the Britons of Southern Scotland* (Edinburgh: 2010).

Fraser, Ian (ed.), *The Pictish Symbol Stones of Scotland* (Edinburgh: 2008).

Fraser, James E., *From Caledonia to Pictland, Scotland to 795* (Edinburgh: 2009).

Grigg, Julianna, *The Philosopher King and the Pictish Nation* (Dublin: 2015).

McNeill, Peter G.B. and MacQueen, Hector L., *Atlas of Scottish History to 1707* (Edinburgh: 1996).

Smyth, Alfred P., *Warlords and Holy Men, Scotland AD 80–1000* (London: 1984).

Wales:

Charles-Edwards, T.M., *Wales and the Britons, 350–1064* (Oxford: 2013).
Davies, Wendy, *An Early Welsh Microcosm* (London: 1978).
Davies, Wendy, *Patterns of Power in Early Wales* (Oxford: 1990).
Rees, William, *An Historical Atlas of Wales from Early to Modern Times* (London: 1972).

Ireland:

Byrne, Francis J., *Irish Kings and High Kings*, 2nd ed. (Dublin: 2004).
Charles-Edwards, T.M., *Early Christian Ireland* (Cambridge: 2000).
Cosgrove, Art (ed.), *A New History of Ireland, vol. I, Prehistoric and Early Ireland* (Oxford: 1990).
O Croinin, Daibhi, *Early Mediaeval Ireland, 400–1200* (Harlow, Essex: 1995).

Chapter 3

The Viking Effect

The four regions of the British Isles in which distinct communities of states had developed since the end of the Roman Empire were all assailed in the ninth century by the overseas raiders from Scandinavia whom we refer to as the Vikings. It was these attacks which compelled two of those communities to begin to unite into single states; the fact that it did not happen in the other two communities is partly due to the fact that the Viking attacks were less concentrated, and also that the individual states of those communities were clearly much more resilient. It was England and Scotland who suffered enough to be driven to unify; the Welsh and Irish kingdoms survived the assaults without being compelled to make major political changes (see Chapter 4).

The attacks came in different ways. The earliest, after the original explorations, brought Viking settlers to Shetland and the Faeroes, and then to Orkney, during the eighth century. Then there came raids along the mainland coasts, particularly aimed at coastal communities and monasteries, and probably launched from the new settlements by the immigrants. Settlements from Norway in particular were made all through the northern and western coasts and islands of the British Isles. After half a century of this, serious military campaigns began, and these came largely from Denmark rather than Norway, first into various parts of Western Europe, and later into England, where a strenuous attempt at conquest was made. All the British regions experienced these Viking effects in different ways, with different combinations of their activities; the result was a varied reaction.

The Viking Assault: Scotland

From about AD 800, Viking raids began to affect the coastal areas of the kingdoms of the north. For a time they were confined to the coasts. The habits of Columban Christianity in establishing monasteries on isolated islands and promontories rendered them extremely vulnerable and provided the Vikings with easy pickings – Iona was ransacked several times, and the archaeological evidence at Portmahomack on the east coast appears to show that the monastery there was also destroyed by a raid. Lindisfarne on its island was another early victim. Life along the coasts, particularly the western coast and the Hebrides, became especially uncomfortable.

This early period of raids was accompanied by, and succeeded by, a deliberate migration and settlement by the Norse out of western Norway. Shetland had been discovered from Norway by about 700, and these islands were settled from there in the face of only a few Picts and Christian hermits who had chosen to live there. From Shetland it was relatively straightforward for competent seamen to reach north to the Faeroe Islands by perhaps 800, and then to Iceland by 870 – where they found more Christian hermits already there. Some settlers went to the south, where they could reach Orkney and the Scottish mainland. Irish or Scottish hermits had reached and lightly settled in all these islands, including Iceland, before the Norseman colonized them; Orkney had been inhabited for several thousands of years, and was a Pictish sub-kingdom in the sixth century. It is likely that it was knowledge gleaned from these original settlers which led the Norse ever further afield.

The Norse migrants and the raiders were, of course, the same people. From Shetland and Norway, migrants moved into Orkney, where they subdued the Pictish inhabitants – unlike Shetland, Orkney was already well populated, and had been for millennia. The joint Norse-Pictish population provided the human basis for a flourishing Norse earldom. In this, the experience of both groups replicated that of the Britons and the Angles and Saxons in England. The migrants sailed on to the north Scottish coast and into Caithness and Sutherland – clearly a Viking name – and round westwards into the Western Isles as far as the Isle of Man. This settlement was by men and their families who were searching for land and new homes, either because they had become politically unacceptable to the authorities in Norway, where local lords were developing their power, or because they simply wanted somewhere else to live. This was, therefore, partly a peasant movement led by a few lords or commanders. From their base in Shetland and Orkney, it was possible to raid along both the eastern and western coasts of Scotland. A notorious raid which struck the monastery at Lindisfarne in Northumbria in 793 presumably came from these migrants based in Shetland or Orkney. Raids also struck at Pictish coastal communities. After a time their most diligent attention was directed at Ireland, where the divisions in the country encouraged their attacks.

These raids were nothing out of the ordinary for the victims. There are scattered notices of seaborne raiders active in western Scotland in

Columba's time, three centuries earlier, and Irish raiders had been known to attack Wales. Raiding was the preferred form of warfare for most kings and commanders throughout the early centuries of Anglo-Saxon England, notably by Mercians into Wales, and Northumbrians and Scottish kingdoms against each other. Apart from ecclesiastical outrage at the attacks on the coastal monasteries and the theft of ecclesiastical treasures, there was little that was unusual in these raids, other than their origin and perhaps their ferocity.

The migrants formed themselves into states, on the pattern of those which were emerging at the same time in their homeland; the earldom of Orkney was formed soon after 850. The earls were a conquering set, and established their domination of Shetland as well as Orkney and the nearby Scottish coast, where Caithness became part of the earldom. The settlers who spread through the Western Islands also briefly organized an earldom, but it was never strong enough to resist the better-organized earls of Orkney, and later the Norwegian kings. They took control of the Hebrides, and most of the islands of the west coast as far south as Kintyre – the kingdom of the Scots thus suffered cruelly. In the Irish Sea, the Isle of Man became a longstanding Norse kingdom, an ideal base for seaborne raids along the coasts of the Irish Sea. Settlers moved into Galloway and the Cumbrian area, though their organization there is not known. They sailed and raided around the coasts of Ireland, seizing bases for their raids and eventually founding city kingdoms at Dublin, Waterford, Wexford, Limerick and other places.

The kingdom which probably suffered the most was that of the Scots. Iona was sacked in 795, 802 and 806; the abbot then moved the surviving treasures to a new foundation at Kells in Ireland. The kingdom was under Pictish domination and the main Pictish kingdom was not so badly damaged at first. It was able to direct resources to developing a new church and bishopric at Dunkeld, and another at St Andrews, actions which imply that no serious threat was apprehended. On the other hand, the mixture of Norse settlements in the islands and raids along the coasts continued for much of the ninth century. The Picts met disaster in 839, when a major Viking raid fought a large Pictish force in Fortriu (on the south coast of the Moray Firth), probably the centre of the Pictish state. The result was a Viking victory which destroyed a large part of the military aristocracy of the Pictish kingdom. That it was really no more than a large raid is implied by the fact that no immediate political result came from this massive Pictish defeat. We may presume that the raiders had also suffered serious casualties, and they then contented themselves with looting the inland territories of the North before returning home, perhaps to Orkney or Caithness.

The disaster provoked an interesting and creative reaction. The community of states in the north came together, though to some extent this was inadvertent. The practice of interchanging kings and royal intermarriage helped to promote cooperation. The Scots had already suffered seriously from the Vikings, losing control of their coasts and islands (and western seas), but the destruction of many of the Pictish nobility opened the way for the accession to the Pictish throne of the Scots king Kenneth MacAlpin, which took place a few years later in 842.

The casualties in the Fortriu battle had included numerous members of the Pictish royal family. Kenneth (Cinead) was a distant member of that group, and was already king of Dalriada (the Scots kingdom). The Scots had recently been a sub-kingdom of the wider Pictish state, so Kenneth's accession was not a revolution, but was quite in line with earlier Pictish practice. It was decisive, however, in bringing a vigorous man to the throne, establishing a new royal family in power and uniting the remnant of the Dalriada kingdom with the damaged Pictish state.

Much of the surviving Scots' aristocracy also seems to have shifted into Pictish territory, perhaps taking the place of the badly reduced Pictish lords. For example, the new religious centre of the joint kingdom was now in Fife, at St Andrews, Iona being hardly habitable any more in view of the ubiquity of the Norse in the west and the frequency of their attacks on the monastery. It is curious that the richest parts of the Scottish lands, which was the territory along the eastern coastlands from the Moray Firth to Lothian, were so much less affected by the raids than the north and west – few raids or attacks are recorded in that area. It seems to have been perfectly acceptable that the new religious centre at St Andrews could be perched on the very seaward Cape of Fife and still be expected to be safe. On the other hand, there was a great raid during Kenneth's reign along the valley of the River Tay as far as the new ecclesiastical centre at Dunkeld, so the Vikings were clearly active in the Scottish North Sea. It may be that the Picts of the east and the men of Fife had proved to be too tough an enemy even for the Vikings, at least until the disaster of 839. The coast north of the Moray Firth, however, was under Norse control or domination from Caithness, to the extent that a local Thing, or law assembly, was located at Dingwall.

The united Scoto-Pictish kingdom, now called Alba, had, in fact, lost plenty of territory in all directions. The western seaboard, which had been the Scots kingdom, came very largely under Norse control and partial

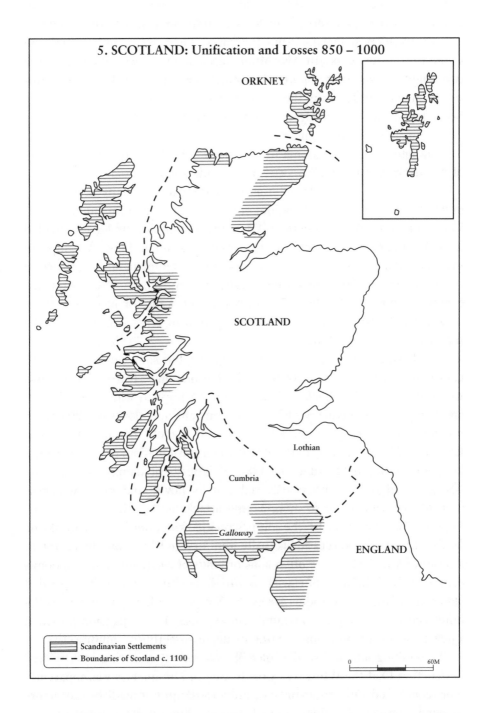

5. SCOTLAND: Unification and Losses 850 – 1000

ORKNEY

SCOTLAND

Lothian

Cumbria

Galloway

ENGLAND

Scandinavian Settlements
– – – Boundaries of Scotland c. 1100

0   60M

settlement, much of the north was subject to the earldom of Orkney, and Caithness was thickly settled by Norse immigrants, who spread south as far as the region of Dornoch and Inverness. There seems to have been no suggestion, after Kenneth MacAlpin's acceptance by the Picts, that the two kingdoms should separate once more; the value of a larger state was surely obvious, and anyway, the Norsemen had control of most of the former Scots kingdom. The newly united kingdom was much smaller than the two originals in combination.

The fates of the kingdoms to the south - Alt Clut, the northern part of Northumbria and Galloway, if it was independent - demonstrated the virtues of a larger state. Alt Clut as a kingdom was virtually destroyed in much the same way as the kingdom of the Picts. In one tremendous raid in 871, led by Olaf the White, the Viking king of Dublin, the kingdom ruled from Dumbarton was virtually destroyed in a single blow. A campaign through its territory ended with the siege of the Dumbarton fort, the royal centre. In this fighting much of the British royal family and aristocracy eventually died, in battle or by massacre; the king, Arthgal, was taken prisoner, to be killed in 872 'at the instigation of King Constantine', the son of Kenneth MacAlpin.

The Irish chronicle notice of this is sparse, but some suggestions as to Constantine's motivation may be made. He may have feared that Arthgal would be returned to his kingdom as a Viking puppet, which would place another powerful Viking kingdom on Constantine's doorstep. His sister was married to Arthgal's son, Rhun, and with the old man out of the way, Rhun could be made King of the Britons, as a sub-kingdom of Constantine's kingdom, and thus exclude the Vikings. The great damage suffered by Arthgal's kingdom had seriously reduced its power and in its weakness it would be vulnerable to more Viking attacks and perhaps settlements. A period of protection by the joint Scot-Pict kingdom of Alba would be useful to both. The succession actually went first to Rhun, and then through a series of kings who were often sons of kings of Scotland. The kingdom's centre shifted inland, but with Scottish encouragement it expanded along the Clyde Valley and as far as the Solway Firth and Cumbria in the ninth century, largely at Northumbrian expense. This expansion provided a new name for the kingdom – Strathclyde, or sometimes Cumbria.

This Viking attack, like that of 839, was mainly a looting raid, if very destructive. Olaf the White was already king in Dublin, and was apparently more concerned with loot than land, and no attempt was made by the victors to retain control. But this cannot have been known at the time, and the decisive actions of Constantine, following those of his father, did result in a much tighter control over all three of the related kingdoms in the North. Given the curious inter-relationship between the royal houses of the North, and their lateral modes of succession, it was always possible to find a king for Strathclyde from amongst the Scottish royal family, usually in the form of a son of one of the Scots kings, and this was what happened for the next century or so. Strathclyde therefore for a century became essentially a vassal state of Alba, and was eventually incorporated into that kingdom in the eleventh century. Galloway escaped, in part because it became an area of fairly dense Norse settlement, as was Cumbria, on the other side of the Solway Firth. Galloway was ruled by a line of 'Lords'; it was far too small to survive for long in real independence, and the line of Lords of Galloway eventually ended in 1161. In these slow events was the beginning of the unification of these northern kingdoms into a single state. For from 843, and then 871 and Olaf the White's raid into Alt Clut, we can date the beginning of the united Kingdom of Scotland; the later extensions of the kingdom to north and south were un-united fragments, so its unity was only partial, but we may say that the kingdom existed from 843 with Kenneth MacAlpin's accession to the Pictish kingship.

The Norse who had conducted the earlier raids into the kingdoms of the North, that of 839, of Olaf the White in 871 and of another raider, Halfdan, who came up from campaigning in England in 876, did so from an existing base elsewhere in Britain or Ireland. Olaf was already king in Dublin, Halfdan was based at York and became king in Dublin after his Scottish raid, and the raiders of 839 probably came from Orkney or the Western Isles, where they already had homes. The result was that, after each raid, the raiders left the devastated country and returned to their home bases. Possibly they met strong resistance – the fighting in Fortriu and at Dumbarton was clearly tough, and even if the Vikings won they no doubt suffered heavy casualties – and this made further raids less than profitable. They had also so devastated the country they traversed that it was not worth their while staying.

The unification of the Scottish states had therefore taken place under considerable Viking pressure. The result had been to preserve the independence of the survivors, so long as they huddled together as a single state, shorn of the coastlands all the way round from the Moray Firth to Cumbria. At the same time they could create a reorganized community of states in the North, a large Scoto-Pict kingdom of Alba and its satellite Strathclyde, a combination which was only loosely integrated, with other sub-kings here and there, and which was surrounded by smaller powers.

This community of states consisted now of the joint Scot-Pict-Strathclyde kingdom which we can call the kingdom of Scotland, plus Galloway in the south-west and Orkney to the north, which eventually became subject to the king of Norway, and, depending on its status, whatever state operated in control of the Hebrides, which sometimes was an independent earldom and in others was part of the earldom of Orkney, or the kingdom of Man. By 1100, the islands were beginning to emerge as the nascent Lordship of the Isles.

The fifth of the original set of northern kingdoms, Northumbria, had been destroyed by the Viking invasions of England. A remnant, Bernicia, was governed by an ealdorman from Bamburgh, and continued in a precarious independence, but it was too weakened to constitute any sort of threat to the newly united kingdom to the north. In fact it became a region into which the Scots kings felt they could profitably encroach during the tenth century.

This new political situation was very different from the earlier version. It was not a series of kingdoms of almost equal size and strength, which had been the case earlier, even if the Pictish kingdom had been dominant; instead, there was now one major kingdom, Scotland, which was surrounded by other less powerful states and fragments of states. One of the more or less constant, if intermittent, aims of Scottish kings in the future would be to bring those marginal kingdoms under their rule. The newly united Scotland therefore spent much energy over the next centuries in incorporating these margins; that is, the unification of Scotland might have been begun in 843 with the accession of the Scots king to the Pictish throne, but it was by no means complete.

The Great Army in England

Viking raids against the Anglo-Saxon kingdoms were a nuisance for seventy years, but they did not happen frequently enough, nor on a sufficiently large scale, to create any serious alarm. The sacking of the monastery of Lindisfarne in 793 caused a shock amongst religious groups; the monastery at Monkwearmouth was attacked the next year; a landing in Dorset at some time in the 790s perhaps originated from Ireland. This was the sort of raid which took place – small, sudden and over quickly – and such raids could be borne.

The most serious early attack in England came in 835, when a Viking army camped for the winter on the Isle of Sheppey in Kent, and then went back to the continent in the spring. For the most part the Norsemen were concentrating on Ireland or the Low Countries, and raids in England, like that at Sheppey, were often by-blows from elsewhere. In 841 and 842, several places on the east coast, along with London and Hamwih (modern Southampton) – both relatively wealthy ports – were raided, and across the Channel in the same period, the town of Rouen and the port of Quentovic near Boulogne were sacked. These raiders were in fact Danes, not the Norse who raided in Scotland and Ireland, and the expeditions were sometimes entrepreneurial expeditions organized by Danish kings. Their intentions were clearly primarily to acquire portable wealth. The size of their raiding forces allowed them to penetrate somewhat further inland than had been the case with the Norsemen, who had so far raided in relatively small bands along the coasts.

Governments of all sorts found it very difficult to cope with these raids. Charlemagne on the continent had organized a coastal system and had built fortifications. His son, Louis the Pious, had maintained the system, but after Louis' death in 840 the great Frankish Empire broke up and indulged itself in dynastic wars; a division of this sort was always a condition which attracted the Vikings. A couple of raids on the Arab Caliphate in Spain provoked the government there to begin a major process of coastal fortification and fleet building, which effectively deterred most Viking activity in subsequent years. But these governments were rich and powerful; the kingdoms in Britain were, by comparison, small and poor. Of course, being rich meant that one became a greater and more interesting target, but it could also mean for the invaders hard knocks and defeats. Eventually, as governments began to become more effective in defending their territories, the aims of the raiders shifted once again. They had begun by attacking coastal communities, then they had moved onto major trading centres; their next aim was conquest and settlement.

In the 850s there was a heavy concentration of Danish campaigning along the rivers of France and the Low Countries. One Danish army campaigned along the River Loire for three years, and another army ranged along the Channel from Kent to the Rhine. Twice, at Thanet in 851 and Sheppey in 855, this army camped for the winter in England, choosing these offshore islands where they could more easily rest and refresh and defend themselves. London and Kent were raided at the same time. But by the 860s, as the defenders became tougher and more organized, the several bands tended to coalesce into considerable armies. Between 856 and 865, a Danish force, which was in effect a continuous army, campaigned from the Netherlands to south-west France, camping at a different place each year and looting the surrounding territory before moving on. The response in France, where the kings proved unable to stop most attacks, was a heavy concentration on local defence and defensive castle-building, with the counts of the local government areas leading the defence and then assuming local political authority – it was the legacy of the effective disintegration of the West Frankish kingdom, and pushed that process on further.

In all this time the English kingdoms had largely been ignored, no doubt because there were richer pickings on the continent, except for the occasional raid by one of the Continental armies or an island used as a winter camp. But the long and detailed Viking attention and campaigning had ensured that northern and western France and the Low Countries had been heavily looted, and so provided few further incentives for raids. The local defences were also becoming more effective, as castles were built, local forces organized and fortified bridges built across the rivers they used. But England was now a tempting target, never seriously raided and divided amongst several weak kingdoms.

Compared with the continental kingdoms, the English kingdoms may well have appeared weak, but the leaders of the Viking army which assembled in East Anglia in 865, and which the English called the 'Great Army', had done their research, and they understood clearly enough that the land was divided between kingdoms which were antagonistic to each other, and had never been known to cooperate. On the other hand, it was by no means an easy task to attack any of the three greater kingdoms, each of which might be able to put into the field a larger force than the Great Army itself – they might thus be faced by the same sort of local defences which were making their work in France so much less rewarding. That is to say, the invasion by the Great Army which gathered in late 865 struck quite deliberately at the weakest and most vulnerable of the kingdoms, East Anglia.

Not only that, but the Great Army seemed at first to be present only temporarily, perhaps reminding the English of the earlier over-wintering at Sheppey and Thanet. Food was extorted from King Edmund of the East Angles and his subjects, and the Vikings then took no offensive action for some time; it might have seemed that it would soon go away. When it did move, however, it struck at the heart of the kingdom, and the king was defeated in battle. A new agreement was made that the Great Army would be supplied with horses, food and equipment, and that it would then leave the kingdom. With all this the Great Army could begin its deliberate and conscious campaign of conquest.

For this army had evidently developed the intention of taking control of as much of England as it could. King Edmund became a Viking vassal. The occupation of East Anglia was not just a raid, not even a campaign of looting; the Army was making a deliberate attempt to conquer territory and impose itself on a subjugated population. This was a new development in Europe as a whole, but evidently it was the product of the experience of the Viking armies on the continent over the previous generation. It was probably a decision arrived at during the camp at Thetford over the winter, and the next events show that they had considered their strategy in that time as well. It is hardly surprising that none of the English rulers appreciated this change in Viking strategy for a while, and it may well have taken some time for anyone outside the Viking headquarters to appreciate the change.

The leaders of the Great Army appear to have been three brothers, sons of Ragnar Lothbrok called Halfdan, Ivar and Ubbi. Having gathered their horses and supplies, and compelled King Edmund to acknowledge their suzerainty, they surveyed the condition of the other English kingdoms and chose the weakest as their next point of attack. The Viking army had become mobile both by land and sea. On the horses they had taken from the East Anglians, the soldiers rode hard for Northumbria. They could have sailed, and their ships certainly made the voyage from East Anglia to the Humber, but instead they chose to ride, a journey which took them through eastern Mercia, probably as an exercise in bravado and as a test to see if King Burgred of the Mercians was capable of reacting. So far as we know he was taken by surprise, and failed to do so. He might well have been relieved to find that someone else was the target.

The decision of the Great Army to attack Northumbria indicates clearly that they understood exactly what they were doing. For the Northumbrian kingdom was going through a crisis of royal succession, and a dynastic war was in progress between King Osberht, king since 851, and a challenger, Aelle, currently in control. The Great Army arrived, seized York and promptly allied with Aelle. Together the new allies defeated Osberht, and then, of course, Aelle became dispensable and was killed as he 'rebelled' against his new masters. A new Northumbrian king, Egbert, was selected and installed as the puppet of the Vikings, holding his throne only at the Great Army's convenience, and no doubt subject to the same extortions as Edmund and the East Anglians had suffered. Within a year of arriving in East Anglia, the Great Army had therefore subdued two of the four kingdoms of the English.

The message for the other two kingdoms was perfectly clear and instantly understood. As it happened, Mercia and Wessex were linked by a marriage between the two royal families, and, faced by the obvious threat that one of them would become the Great Army's next target, they cooperated. A joint army commanded by the two kings, Burgred of Mercia and Aethelred of Wessex, met the Great Army when it moved south out of Northumbria in spring 867 to attack Mercia. The Great Army was besieged during the winter of 867–68 in Nottingham, and in the spring accepted that it had not succeeded and agreed to return to York, where its puppet king was deemed unsatisfactory and was replaced by another, a man called Ricsig. The Wessex-Mercian alliance continued to operate through the next year while the Great Army ravaged Northumbria before returning to the camp at Thetford in East Anglia for the winter of 869–70.

King Edmund objected to their renewed presence in his kingdom and the Viking army had to fight to secure itself for another winter. Edmund was defeated in battle at Hoxne and died in the fighting. Another puppet king, Oswald, was put in his place. Such men were clearly not reliable, and the 'rebellions' of Egbert and Edmund may well have been encouraged by the Viking defeat at Nottingham, and quite possibly by promises of help from Mercia and Wessex, though there is no record of any such help being offered or supplied. It would be in the interests of both Wessex and Mercia, however, to see that the Great Army was fully occupied in someone else's kingdom.

It is worth noting that this was the same time that Olaf the White was campaigning in Scotland, and in 871 captured Dumbarton. The establishment of puppet kings at York and in East Anglia might well have been a factor in King Constantine's reactions to the capture of King Arthgal; his reaction, of course, was to install his own puppet king.

In the spring of 870, riding once more through Mercian territory, and moving too quickly to be intercepted, the Great Army seized and camped at Reading on the northern border of Wessex – and on the Thames, which allowed them to bring their ships well inland. The Vikings were no doubt pleased to discover that King Aethelred received no assistance from King Burgred of Mercia – unless he blockaded them from the north bank of the river. On the other hand, they also discovered that King Aethelred was intent on fighting them, rather than paying them to go away as several kings had done in the past (and as in fact Edmund of East Anglia had done in 865). Several times in the next year or so battles took place in Wessex, near Reading and at Englefield, Ashdown, Wilton and Basing, as well as at Reading itself.

Each side could claim victories, and in the spring the Great Army moved out of Wessex and took up its camp for the next winter at London. This was technically a Mercian town, but was on the borders of Mercia, Essex and Kent; no doubt all these areas suffered from the Great Army's attentions.

During the war King Aethelred died, but not apparently in battle. He left at least two sons, but both were children. The kingship therefore went to Aethelred's younger brother, Alfred, as the last adult male of the royal family. It was clearly far too dangerous for a kingdom to have children as kings in the circumstances. Alfred had taken part in the fighting at Nottingham, and in the clashes in the previous year; in addition he was married to a lady, Ealswith, who was a member of one of the Mercian royal families. The marriage had taken place in 868, the year of the Wessex-Mercian alliance and of the siege of Nottingham.

News of a new rebellion against, or by, their puppet king Ricsig in Northumbria took the Great Army north again; Ricsig was removed and a third puppet king, Egbert II, was installed in his place. As a result of the preceding hard-fighting campaign against Wessex, the next target had now become obvious: Northumbria and East Anglia were already puppet kingdoms of the Viking army, Wessex had fought too well to be attacked again, at least for the moment, and there had probably been an agreement between Alfred and the Danish leaders after the fighting around Reading that they leave Wessex, an agreement which for the moment they cared to honour. Mercia was therefore the obvious next victim.

Having dealt with the situation in York, the Great Army marched into Mercia once again. A certain degree of caution is evident this time, just as it had been in the attack on Wessex. The first camp was at Torksey in Lincolnshire, quite close to a possible refuge in Northumbria if one was needed, and if the Mercians fought as well as the men of Wessex. The next year they camped at Repton, again not very far into Mercia from Northumbria. Both of these places were on the River Trent, once again providing relatively straightforward water transport for their ships. The evidence is thin concerning this campaign, but it seems that King Burgred fought but was defeated. He then abdicated, possibly as a result of an ultimatum from the Great Army. Burgred left his kingdom and went to Rome, never to return.

The Great Army then broke up into two parts, evidently having disagreed on what to do next. Another puppet king, Coelwulf II, was installed in Mercia, but he had authority only over the western half of the kingdom. The eastern part, from the Humber to the Thames, was taken over by part of the Great Army for itself. The other part of the army took Yorkshire for itself, but then this contingent divided again, between those who stayed in Yorkshire to take over the land and form a Viking kingdom, and those who wished to continue fighting and conquering. This group was led by Halfdan, who may be considered as the first king of the Viking kingdom of York, but he then led his section of the army north to camp on the lower Tyne and raid over the northern part of Northumbria – Bernicia – which had not apparently been touched so far, and then into Scotland and finally into Ireland. Halfdan became king of Dublin, where his brother, Ivar the Boneless, had already been king for a short time. The puppet King Egbert II of Northumbria disappeared.

Those Vikings who had had enough of the fighting took over estates in Yorkshire and the eastern part of Mercia which no doubt had earlier belonged to Northumbrian and Mercian lords who had perished in the wars. It seems that others also did so in East Anglia at about that time; no doubt the puppet king Oswald now disappeared, like Egbert. This southern part of the Great Army, which had taken over East Anglia and eastern Mercia, also divided, like the Yorkshire army, between those who had settled down and those who wished to go on fighting. These latter had, as it later proved, no objection to settling on some dead Englishman's land, but some of them clearly realized that so long as Wessex remained undefeated and unconquered they would not be safe in their new homes. Also, no doubt, their effective defeat in the Reading campaign rankled, and some of the army at least would hope that in a second round against Alfred of Wessex they would be victorious.

The Great Army spent the winter of 874–75 camped at Cambridge. There it split between those who wished to settle in eastern Mercia and those who wanted to make another attempt on Wessex. The leader of the latter group was a man called Guthrum. In the spring or early summer, he took the Viking army right across Wessex to a new winter camp at Wareham in Dorset, while no doubt the ships sailed round to join the land army. How many men he led in the invasion is unknown – the size of the Great Army itself is a matter of dispute – but it was surely a major gamble to attempt a new campaign with an army much smaller than one which had already been defeated in Wessex. However, he may also have been reinforced by incomers from the continent or Denmark.

The attack seems to have come as a surprise, at least in its timing, for it was surely obvious to Alfred and his captains that they were very likely to be the Vikings' next target. An attack in winter, however, was unlikely.

King Alfred called up the army of Wessex and laid siege to Wareham, reviving the strategy which had succeeded at Nottingham by denying the invaders the opportunity to raid the local area. The Great Army broke out and went to Exeter – another river port where the fleet could join it. Again it was besieged and harassed; again it broke out and moved to a new winter camp, this time at Gloucester, in Coelwulf's kingdom of remnant-Mercia. This was outside Alfred's boundaries, and Alfred may well have believed that he had succeeded in defeating the attack and driving the Vikings out of his kingdom.

This campaign had already lasted for two years. Wessex was still intact, if somewhat damaged, but so was the Great Army. In the winter of 877–78 its leader, Guthrum, brought it south in a surprise attack, from Gloucester into Wessex, and smashed the resistance. This was the moment when Alfred was forced to take refuge in the marshes in Somerset at Athelney, around which stories gathered, describing his initial despair, and the revival of his spirit by the scolding of a peasant woman over her burnt cakes. But his time in a swampy refuge lasted only a few weeks. Alfred sent out the word once more for his army to gather, and then it was his turn to initiate a surprise attack.

The Great Army had camped at Chippenham in Wiltshire, which gave it effective domination of the central part of Wessex. Alfred was separated from that country by the great Selwood Forest, which formed the boundary between Somerset and Wiltshire. It was still winter and the Great Army was short of provisions; also, the territory west of the great Selwood Forest, Somerset and Devon, was still free. Alfred's own forces emerged from out of the west, gathered the local forces from Wiltshire and Hampshire, and first defeated the Great Army in open battle, then laid siege to it yet again, blocking it up in its camp at Chippenham. This time it was no longer possible for the Vikings to escape, for they had severed contact with their ships; they were also no doubt in dire need of provisions by this time. They accepted defeat.

Guthrum and Alfred met and concluded a treaty of peace, one of the clauses of which was that Guthrum should become a Christian; this would presumably be intended as an example to the rest of the Great Army, would allow the evangelization of the pagans and let priests minister to the surviving Anglian inhabitants. For Guthrum and his army had decided to follow the example of their earlier colleagues and settle down. It was also a move which might help to divide that army yet again, since no doubt some would feel annoyed and disgusted at Guthrum's giving in. The boundary between Alfred's and Guthrum's territories was agreed to be along the River Lea north of London, then in a straight line to Bedford, and then along Watling Street, an old Roman road heading into the north-west Midlands. Alfred was clearly speaking for western Mercia in this as well as his own kingdom. Guthrum took his army into East Anglia and settled himself and them on the land with himself as king, the successor of Edmund and the vanished Oswald.

The New Condition of England

This was not the end of the Viking wars in England, but it was clearly the end of the first stage. Some of the Great Army had still not had enough of campaigning and went off to the continent once more, where they campaigned in Flanders and the Rhineland in northern France, with much less success than before. A decade later, in 892, another army tried again in England, commanded by a leader called Haestan, and for three years it campaigned back and forth, mainly in the Midlands, until it eventually dispersed, a clear sign that it had been defeated and that many of its men had at last had enough. Signficantly, it was able to use Danish territory as its base, but even more significant was that it was unable to penetrate into Wessex after its first landing in Sussex, though it raided into English Mercia. Much of its campaigning was done within the territory taken over earlier by the Danes, and no doubt it was as unpopular amongst these new settlers as it had been amongst the English, though it is clear that some of them joined the campaign. Haestan arrived in Sussex at the same time as a seaborne force landed in Devon, and another landed to attack Chester. The army's preliminary negotiations were evidently as complex as the early plans of the Great Army.

This had been a dangerous crisis, but by this time major political developments within England had made this new Viking attack, though unpleasant and destructive, a much less serious threat. The campaigns of the Great Army between 865 and 879 had resulted in the destruction of three of the four English kingdoms. East Anglia, the smallest, had been taken over complete and had a new king in Guthrum. The kingdom of the East Saxons was added to it, as was a section of south-eastern Mercia, and these formed an expanded East Anglian kingdom. Northumbria had been broken up, with the richest part, the future Yorkshire, excised to make the new Danish kingdom of York. The northern section, north of the River Tees, had been ravaged by Halfdan when he went off to campaign in the north, but had survived under a local ruler, the Ealdorman Eadwulf, who ruled from his impregnable castle at Bamburgh. Halfdan became king of York, and when he made himself king of Dublin he began a fateful connection between the two kingdoms.

Mercia had similarly been broken up. The western part, west of the boundary of Watling Street, was ruled from Worcester by the Ealdorman Aethelred, who had apparently displaced the Danish puppet king Coelwulf II; he was married to King Alfred's daughter, Aethelflaed, his eldest child, a most formidable lady. The eastern part of Mercia, from the Humber to Guthrum's boundary, resolved itself into a series of Danish towns which acted as independent states – Lincoln, Nottingham, Peterborough, Stamford, Leicester, Northampton, Cambridge and others. These are usually referred to as the 'Five Boroughs', though there were generally more than this number.

The political geography of the England of the 'Heptarchy' had thus been smashed by the Danish campaigns, and had been resolved into a completely new formulation (as, of course, had Scotland). The most important element was now the alliance, symbolized by the marriage of Ealdorman Aethelred and the Lady Aethelflaed, between Wessex and the surviving half of Anglian Mercia (a revival, in a way, of the earlier alliance of Burgred and Aethelred). In this the directing brain was that of Alfred, the king of the more powerful of the two parties. The fact that, unlike his short-lived brothers, Alfred lived on and ruled as king for nearly three decades (871–99) was clearly crucial to the development and survival of the allied kingdoms, a condition which evolved into a joint kingdom.

The overall effect of the Viking wars had thus been to drive two of the English states together for mutual defence; their alliance had been shown to work in the 890s, preventing Haestan's army gaining any territory or indeed any victories. Meanwhile, the Danes who had campaigned and then settled in England had made the mistake of taking up their conquests as separate units, of which there were now two kingdoms and more than half a dozen independent towns. That is to say, in power terms, the English had emerged from the fire of these wars tempered and beaten into the beginnings of a unified kingdom. Kent, Sussex and Cornwall were now part of Wessex without demur; they were far too small to survive in the new conditions. The unpleasantness of the Danish wars had convinced both the surviving Mercians and the West Saxons that they must join together. On the other hand, the Danes had been so successful that they had evidently become over-confident and believed that they could survive in separation and disunity. Haestan's failure should have disillusioned them.

Superficially, it might seem that two new communities of states had therefore emerged from the Viking wars: the Danish group and an English one. It would be better to see the whole as another version of the original community of English states, but one in which there was now one predominant kingdom – Wessex-Mercia – with two lesser kingdoms (York and East Anglia), a weak ealdormanry (Bernicia) and several even weaker Danish towns. But there was also a strong antipathy between English and Danes. The parallel with Scotland is instructive, especially in view of the succeeding events: in each case the wars had forced the survivors of two remnant kingdoms into uniting to form the most powerful state in the new grouping, with several much weaker states, several of them under the rule of uncertain kings and earls, around it. But the situation in Scotland, a kingdom with lesser resources and a much smaller population than Wessex-Mercia, was difficult to move. It was a century before the new united Scottish kingdom could make any serious advances, whereas in England the sequel saw the elimination of the minor powers by the greater.

The discrepancy in power between Wessex-Mercia and the several Danish states was such that there was probably little danger of any serious attack by the Danes disturbing Wessex-Mercia. But Haestan's campaigns indicated that Danish hostility remained and continued, and that an outside intervention might tip the balance in the Danes' favour. There were two major possible sources of such an intervention. Haestan or a successor from the continent was one; the other was intervention from Dublin. Either of these – or even a descent from Denmark or Norway – could so reinforce local Danish military power that the Wessex army might be beaten.

This new English situation was therefore clearly unstable in the long term. Apart from possible outside interventions, there were any number of elements internal to England which might bring about a change, and any particular change anywhere in the system might well precipitate others elsewhere. The alliance of Wessex and remnant Mercia might fail; the independent Danish boroughs might fall to Guthrum's kingdom, whose enlargement would be dangerous, or to Wessex, the Danish kingdom of York or a reviving Mercia; the kingdom of York might expand, reviving the old Northumbrian kingdom, or it might collapse; if it united with Dublin it might become a formidable power. The renewed Viking wars in the 890s did tend to cement the Wessex-Mercia alliance, but they might also have encouraged the Danish states to band together.

Of these possibilities, the Danish kingdom of York in the event proved to be thoroughly unstable, being the object of repeated ambitions by

Danish rulers from Dublin. The kingship at York was, after Halfdan, taken by a succession of unrelated men, each of whom ruled only briefly. But if they united with the Norse Dublin kingdom, making a coalition which commanded the Irish Sea, York could be turned into a powerful state. Guthrum in East Anglia was succeeded when he died in 890 by his son, Eirik, and an established succession was one of the guarantees of stability; without it any kingdom was liable to disruption. There had been plenty of cases of that in Anglo-Saxon England.

Alfred spent the period of peace in the 880s, between the end of the Great Army's campaign in 879 and the arrival of Haestan's army in 892, constructing a defensive system which operated well against it. This consisted of a series of fortified centres, 'burhs', some of them towns, some of them simply available for the local population in an emergency. They were spread throughout his kingdom more or less equidistantly. Individual burhs could certainly be seized by the invaders, as Guthrum's army had seized Wareham and Exeter, but when properly manned they denied an easy refuge to the invaders. The system worked tolerably well in the 890s against Haestan, to such a degree that he scarcely attacked Wessex at all. It was supplemented by a well-understood military system, in which half the men of any particular area were called up to serve in the army for a limited period and were later replaced on campaign by the other half. Thus Alfred could count on defenders of his new burhs, and at the same time have at his disposal a field army. The universality of the defensive system was a strong impulse to consider the whole land as a single state.

When Alfred died in 899, he had accomplished more in his lifetime than most kings ever achieve. His inheritance was safe, and had been expanded. He had won several wars against an enemy which had overthrown three out of four of the English kingdoms. He had reorganized and refortified his kingdom so that it was for the moment almost invulnerable. There can be few kings who had done as much.

He had, however left more than one problem for his successor. The two sons of his brother who had been put aside when he was made king in 871 could expect to be considered for the kingship once he was dead. They were given inheritances out of Alfred's territories in his will. The elder of the two, Aethelwold, was, however, unsatisfied and appears to have made an attempt at a *coup d'etat* before Alfred's own son, Edward (the Elder), was installed as king. When that failed, he managed to get himself chosen as one of the brief kings in York, where he maintained his position for a couple of years. By that time Edward's position in Wessex was strong enough for him to ignore Aethelwold's attempts, but the question of the succession recurred later in his reign.

The Preliminary Unification of England

The Wessex field army was also available for an offensive war, as it proved. Alfred's success had been mainly in preserving his kingdom and forming the political alliance with Aethelred and Mercia; his son and successor, Edward (899–924), maintained the alliance with his brother-in-law until the latter's death in 911, and then continued it with his sister, Aethelflaed, who proved to be as successful a ruler and warrior as her father and her brother, and perhaps more so than her husband. Between them, from 912–18, brother and sister conducted a series of careful, aggressive and well-planned campaigns to conquer the Danish territories in eastern Mercia and East Anglia. By the time Aethelflaed died in 918, all the Danish territory south of the Humber and the Mersey had been taken. The Danish kingdom of East Anglia had been extinguished and the Danish boroughs in the East Midlands had become part of Edward's kingdom – and none of them had been seriously assisted from the continent, or from Dublin or York. This success provided another impulse towards continued Wessex-Mercian unity, for there are few achievements like a victorious war to convince the winners that they are all one people.

Aethelflaed's death in 918, however, created a difficult situation for Edward. She and her husband had been Lord and Lady of the Mercians, not king or queen, but their position had been in effect regal, and there are signs that Aethelred was regarded as king within Mercia. It was, of course, an hereditary position, and the distinction between Wessex and Mercia had been maintained, if not emphasized. The dispatity in power was shown, however, when Aethelred died, for Edward then arranged the transfer of London and the south-east Midlands from Mercia to Wessex, a change which divided the frontier against the Danish territories more or less equally between Wessex and Mercia.

Aethelred and Aethelflaed had only one child, a daughter, Aelfwyn. If Aethelflaed could rule the Mercians as their Lady, then so could her daughter, who would presumably marry and whose husband would therefore become a new Lord of the Mercians, or king. This would, potentially at least, derange the alliance with Wessex which had proved to be so successful in both defence and attack over the previous thirty years. Acceptance of the succession of Aelfwyn as Lady of the Mercians threatened the new unity of the joint kingdom.

Edward took rapid measures to ensure that this separation did not happen. He quickly moved to Tamworth, where Aelfwyn was living, and removed her to Wessex, where she was thrust into a nunnery. By this *coup*, he therefore made himself Lord of the Mercians as well as king of the West Saxons. Combined with his control of the conquered Danish territories, Edward had now created a kingdom of England, stretching from the Channel to the Humber. This was, however, no more than a preliminary unification; there was still a lot of work to do.

This is the moment when we may start to refer to a kingdom of England, just as from 843 we may speak of a kingdom of Scotland. From now on Edward and his successors commanded the most powerful kingdom in the British Isles, and over the next three decades their work consisted of uniting the pieces together into one state and extending that kingdom to take in the rest of the old community of Anglo-Saxon states.

The Problem of Northumbria

There were sufficient external problems facing this new kingdom to persuade all sides to accept the union of the 'Southumbrians' into a single kingdom, though there was still some resentment in Mercia at Edward's high-handed actions, and no doubt some Danes mourned their lost independence. The king's acceptance of the Danish land settlement (by 918 this was forty years old) would have reconciled the Danish land-owners to the new political regime; they also retained their own legal system.

There was a difficult problem for the next thirty or forty years over relations between the English state and the kingdom of York, which could threaten the new unity achieved south of the Humber. Edward's successor, his son Athelstan (924–39), succeeded for a time in conquering York and bringing Bernicia into the kingdom under its ealdorman, but he had to fight hard to do so, and after his death York was recovered by the Norse kings of Dublin. These wars included invasions of York by the English, and invasions of England by the Norse rulers – both events which encouraged the Southumbrians to remain united. York was an independent kingdom, or united with Dublin, for most of the period from 876–954, though at times under Athelstan it was controlled by the Wessex king. It was not until the latter date that it was successfully and permanently united with the Southumbrian kingdom. This thereby also gained greater control over the Ealdormanry of Bamburgh further north. By that date it looked as though a kingdom of England had been created which stretched from the English

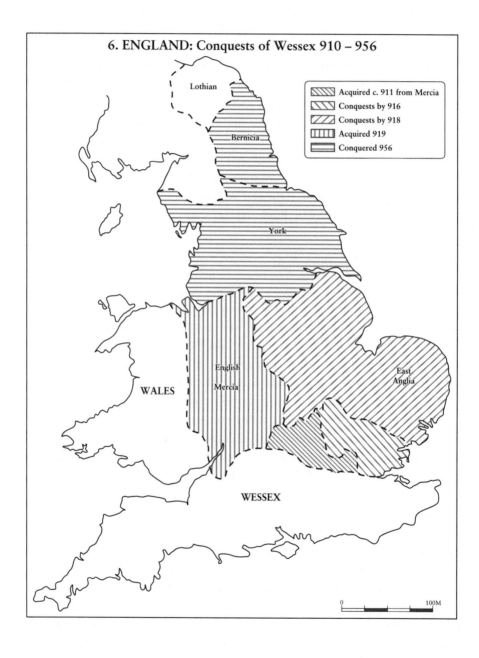

6. ENGLAND: Conquests of Wessex 910 – 956

Channel to the Firth of Forth. This expansion of the Southumbrians to the borders of Scotland frightened other powers into attempting to drive Athelstan's power southwards again. In the campaign which led to the Battle of Brunanburh in 937, he faced a coalition of York, Dublin and Scotland. He won the battle, but could advance no further. When he died his conquests fell away once more, and soon York reverted to control by a king of Dublin.

This unity achieved by the English was therefore only superficial. At one point during the York wars, King Olaf Guthfrithsson of York and Dublin succeeded in wrenching the territory of the Five Boroughs (from the Humber to the Wash), as well as York, out of English hands. This alienation did not last longer than Olaf's brief rule (940–42), but it was an indication that it would take more than a mere military conquest to enforce a unification of all these various and disparate territories.

For another decade York remained separate from England as either a kingdom on its own or united once more with Dublin. The last king, Eric Bloodaxe, was an intruder from Norway. This may well have been too much even for the Danes of York, and when Eric was killed by his Northumbrian subjects in attempting to escape them, it became possible for the king of England, in this case Edred, Edward the Elder's third son, to seize control. Between 939 and 954, when Eric Bloodaxe died, the kingdom had had eight kings, a sequence which was far too unsettling to be acceptable. In effect the kingdom of York faded away, and its people accepted the English king. Even then it was not necessarily the end of the story, and one of the measures taken to conciliate the possibly insubordinate Danes of York was to guarantee their autonomy under an earl of their own. The unification of South and North was strictly limited.

The New Organization of the New Kingdom

The essential long-term problem for the kings of England was that their own political and economic base remained Wessex and little more. Kings depended upon their own estates to sustain them, and their lives were spent in moving more or less regularly between estates which were part of the royal patrimony and where they could live on their produce. Surplus production was rarely sufficient to allow them to remain in one place for long, and the transport infrastructure was not efficient to allow the movement of goods for any distance – unless by sea. All the kings in the tenth century, from Edward to Aethelred II, held essentially the same estates as Alfred had received when he inherited Wessex in 871 – that is, almost all of them were south of the Thames. It does not seem that any of the kings acquired any royal estates in their new territories to the north of Wessex, probably because these – the estates of the former Mercian kings especially – had already been alienated to Danes and to other Mercians. The itineraries pursued by the tenth-century kings as they moved about the kingdom are therefore almost entirely within the ancestral Wessex kingdom, with occasional forays northward, usually on military campaigns. This meant that royal authority north of Wessex was difficult to enforce, since it was the presence of the king in person which was necessary for government.

Certain measures were taken to mitigate the problem, which was very obvious to all involved. The old system of local government in Wessex, in which several areas had been governed by ealdormen who were appointed by the king, was extended to the conquered territories. These were the shires, of which Hampshire and Wiltshire were perhaps the originals, while Dorset, Somerset and Devon became others during the conquest of that area in the earlier years. Into this system the south-eastern kingdoms of Kent and Sussex could be fitted easily enough, as could the Danish boroughs, for all of these were roughly the same size as the Wessex originals, and were territories which were small enough to be governed by a single mobile ealdorman. In English Mercia, a system of defence modelled on Alfred's burhs had been created during the time of Aethelred and Aethelflaed, by which fortified centres controlled the surrounding land. These territories easily became shires – Gloucestershire, Warwickshire, Shropshire, Worcestershire and so on – but the artificiality of these counties is easily demonstrated by considering the central position of the county towns, and the regular size and shape of the shires.

This system helped to enforce some royal authority outside Wessex, but it also allowed local lords to achieve local hereditary power, for the ealdormen quickly established themselves as the new local aristocracy. This system was probably in place by the 930s. The local applications of the system are evident in the varying sizes of the new shires: large units in the east – Norfolk, Suffolk, Lincolnshire, Yorkshire – compared with the more artificial shires of the West Midlands, where they are of a uniform size. That is, the system was only imposed where a useful local unit did not exist, and where something approximating to it did exist this was used. The permanence of these shires, and the affection with which they are generally regarded, is a testimony to their effectiveness.

The imposition of this shire system on the lands outside Wessex is one indication of the development of a national administration. Another is

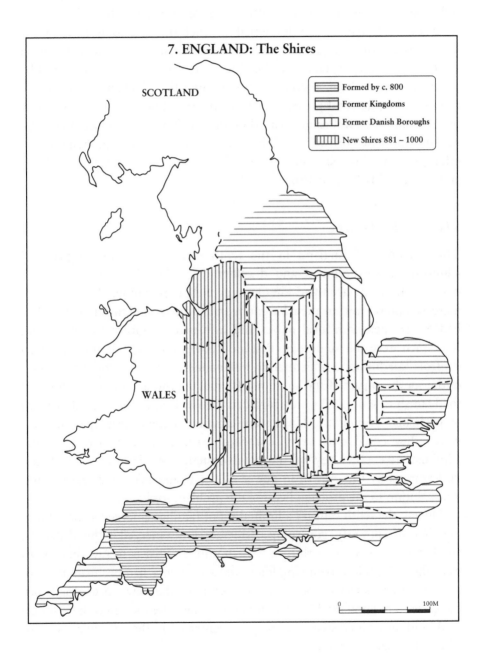

7. ENGLAND: The Shires

SCOTLAND

WALES

Formed by c. 800
Former Kingdoms
Former Danish Boroughs
New Shires 881 – 1000

0   100M

the spread of mints which produced coins in the names of the kings, a system which eventually developed into a regular re-coining every few years, a clear indication of the operation of an effective governmental system. Similarly, a royal administrative system developed in which the king could issue 'writs' in his name, addressed to ealdormen or to the sheriffs of the shires, requiring a specific action to be taken, so the king could operate at a distance and by proxy. To some extent, therefore, this negated the problem of the lack of resources for the royal presence outside Wessex. This might also be a way of bypassing the local ealdorman, though usually it was the local man who was the addressee of the writ. The result was a fairly comprehensive and effective royal administration, certainly by the time of King Edgar (959–75) and Aethelred II (978–1016).

The New Earldoms

The kingdom of England in the tenth century was thus a place of administrative experiment and development, which was clearly in part designed to create a unified kingdom, as well as providing the kings with increased power within their kingdom and in their foreign relations. They had to use men with local power and influence to govern for them, and these men were able to develop that local power into local dominance, even control. Northumbria thus fitted in well enough to the developing situation in the southern part of the kingdom. By making these men earls (a form of the Danish title of 'jarl' which replaced the old English title of ealdorman) of particular regions the kings were creating regional principalities over which they could only exercise control with great difficulty. Thus the administrative efficiency of the royal system was simultaneously being undermined by the growth in power of a new and hereditary aristocracy. The solution to the problem became the problem itself.

During the tenth century a limited set of families emerged as hereditary members of a powerful governing aristocracy. One emerged in the Midlands, another in Wessex and a third in Northumbria. That is to say, their bases were the old Anglo-Saxon kingdoms whose existence had been submerged, but which had survived beneath the overlay of the new shires. In theory the earls were appointed by the king, but in fact their strength lay in their land holdings, which were generally concentrated in the particular areas of which they had become earls.

Using their wealth and position, the families could acquire further estates and more local influence. For example, the family of Leofric, Earl of Mercia, had lands which were particularly concentrated in Shropshire, Staffordshire and Cheshire. The family extended its power into the North, with lands in Yorkshire, and became Earls of Northumbria. The family of Godwin, which eventually produced King Harold II, who seized the throne in 1066, had lands which were heavily concentrated in Wessex, Essex and Herefordshire. The point was that, just like the kings, these families required local concentrations of estates for their support as they moved about their areas of responsibility – but this also gave them a local power which could negate or compete with that of the king.

These men were more than local magnates; they had become virtually independent princes. They could defy the king and run their own internal and foreign affairs, as Harold did before 1066, even though he was only an earl and so technically a loyal subject of Edward the Confessor. The Earl of Northumbria, Sigurd, could similarly conduct a foreign policy of his own with regard to Scotland.

That is to say, England had only been superficially united by the conquests of Edward the Elder and Athelstan. It was under these kings that the later provincial magnates' families had begun their growth in power and wealth. By the reign of King Edgar (957–75), the process had gone so far that it was too late to change it, and from his reign onwards these magnates operated in an increasingly independent manner. England therefore retained the old kingdoms – Wessex, Mercia, East Anglia, Northumbria – in their new guise as provincial earldoms. The much-divided eastern Midlands mirrored this process, and remained much divided among a group of less important earls. (In a way this was a revival of the older and much fragmented political system of minor, tribal states which had developed in the early Anglian expansion, and which had been overridden by the Mercian conquest; the Danish 'Five Boroughs' had been in the same area.) The unification achieved in the conquest years was sufficiently weak that it was possible – in 940 and 957 – to separate off parts of the kingdom to solve a dynastic war; it was to happen again.

Foreign Threats – Danish Kings

A new set of Danish wars began in the 990s with increasingly determined invasions by Danish armies. At first this was a resumption of the coastal raids of the ninth century, but eventually they became full-scale invasions commanded by Danish kings, first Svein, later his son, Knut. This imposed a major strain upon the precariously united English kingdom.

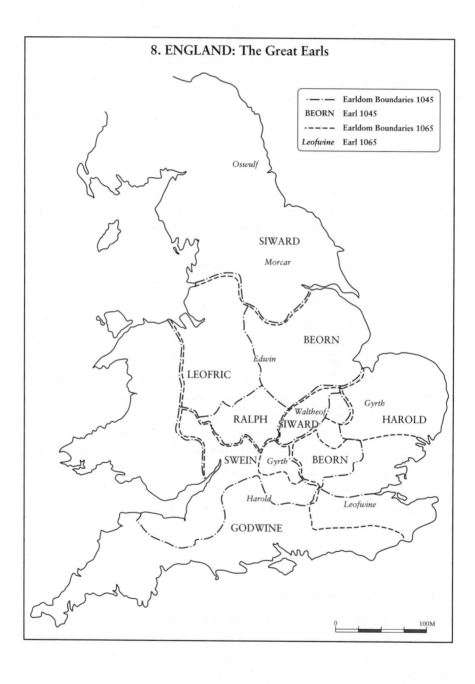

8. ENGLAND: The Great Earls

·—·—·	Earldom Boundaries 1045
BEORN	Earl 1045
·----·	Earldom Boundaries 1065
Leofwine	Earl 1065

Oswulf

SIWARD

Morcar

BEORN

Edwin

LEOFRIC

RALPH   *Waltheof*   *Gyrth*
        SIWARD   HAROLD

SWEIN *Gyrth*   BEORN

Harold   *Leofwine*

GODWINE

0   100M

King Aethelred II (978–1016) may have been a less than competent ruler, but he was always handicapped in taking any action by the possible enmity of the great earls of his kingdom. In the end, in 1014 the king fled overseas, but then returned when Svein suddenly died. Finally, the Mercian Earl, Eadric Streona, deserted his successor, Edmund Ironside, and joined with Knut. This facilitated the eventual Danish victory. In the final action of the war, Edmund Ironside agreed to another division of England with Knut, the latter taking all but Wessex as his share, while Edmund took Wessex. English unity was again shown to be superficial, and it could be broken easily. Edmund's death a few months after the treaty allowed the country to be reunited under Knut, but the continued existence of the mighty earls indicated that it remained fragile.

The final crisis of the Anglo-Saxon kingdom, which came in 1066, was essentially a continuation of the problems of royal succession and of the power of the earls who had dominated affairs for the previous century (see Chapter 5).

Foreign Threats – Scottish Ambition

It cannot be said that the process of the unification of England under Alfred and his successors was at all easy, and for a long time it was clearly incomplete. The same may be said for Scotland. The united country was still subject to Norse raids until about 900, and from then on the Scots contented themselves with pursuing their own internal quarrels over the royal succession. Gradually these were resolved into the acceptance of the succession within a single family, but it was still never sure just who the heir of a king was. This problem lasted until the end of the eleventh century, and even beyond in a minor way; Strathclyde continued with a separate king for much of the tenth century, though most of those kings were imported from the main Scottish royal family, while Galloway was intermittently independent.

Yet the kingdom was vigorous in a political sense, and aimed to expand both northwards at the expense of the earldom of Orkney and south at the expense of the old kingdom of Northumbria. The problem for the kings was that they ruled a small country with few resources and only a small population. Aggressive warfare was scarcely possible under the circumstances, though cautious advances, taking advantage of weaknesses among the targets, remained possible. The suzerainty established over Strathclyde was an example. The Bernician region (from the Tees to Lothian) had been separated off from the southern half of Northumbria when the Danish kingdom of York had been excised from the old kingdom in 876. York eventually succumbed to English attack from the south, but only after a long struggle during which it remained possible for a time that York could be united as a sort of sea-kingdom with Dublin. Only in 954 was the last Viking king of York driven out.

During this time the Scots nibbled away at Bernicia's northern regions. King Indulf (954–62) gained control over the rock of Edinburgh, which also gave him control of the southern coast of the Firth of Forth. It is significant that this fortress was seized by the Scots king just at the time when the York kingdom finally succumbed to English conquest, almost as if Indulf felt the rising pressure from the south and needed to enhance his defences. In 973, King Edgar ceded all the Lothian territory as far as the River Tweed, it being out of his reach anyway. Forty years later, at the Battle of Carham in 1018, Indulf's successor, Malcolm II, defeated the new Danish ruler of England, which confirmed his possession of the whole Lothian territory from the Forth to the Tweed. By this time Strathclyde had expanded its control into northern Cumbria. Malcolm II's son, Duncan, was installed as king in Strathclyde, but that was the last item in its pseudo-separate existence.

Much less progress was made by the kings of the Scots in the north. The earls of Orkney held onto the northern mainland as far as the Dornoch Firth, and were able to send seaborne expeditions into the Irish Sea. Yet the main point about these expansions to the north and south by the Scottish kings is the ambition they demonstrate that the whole of northern Britain, from at least the Tweed to the Pentland Firth – if not also the further islands – should become part of the single kingdom of Scotland. It was probably also recalled that Orkney and the Western Isles had been Pictish before the Norse arrived. The difficulty of achieving this expansion was that Scotland could never afford a large armed force; its kings found it difficult to enforce their authority far beyond their own presence. In many ways it was a similar situation to that of the kings of Wessex who became kings of England without acquiring the population and material resources to make their kingship effective throughout their kingdom. Lothian, therefore, was really out of the reach of the English kings, but its comparative wealth was a major boost to the power of the Scottish kings.

The kings of the Scots were similarly trapped, in that their royal resources were concentrated in the south-east, in Fife and the Lothians, as was the bulk of the population. Even the Church was not much of a help;

its monasteries and bishoprics helped to expand royal power in the rest of Europe, but these scarcely existed in Scotland before about 1100. At that point Scotland was still only very partially united, with a substantial fringe of independent lands to the north and west. Like England, its unity was a work in progress; the Normans would change that.

Conclusion.

Both the communities and states in England and Scotland had come through the Viking wars battered and broken, and had responded by putting the parts back together into two new and united kingdoms, more comprehensively in England than in Scotland. But the union in either case was still not wholly convincing. The Scottish kingdom had brought in Strathclyde and had conquered – or been given – the Lothian part of Bernicia, but had made little progress in the north against the Orkney earldom or in the west along the shores of the Hebridean seas, and Galloway was still clearly semi-detached. The English kingdom had shown a regrettable tendency to be all too readily broken up by its kings for temporary purposes, and to permit the development of over-mighty earls, who were all but independent.

It remained quite possible that both kingdoms might be dismantled once more. In both there were repeated and serious disputes over the royal succession, disputes which could well lead to further divisions – the Scots kingship was disputed between two lines of kings; England was subject to three separate ruling dynasties in the eleventh century. In both kingdoms the death of a ruling king was always followed by a contest for the succession, in effect a series of *coups d'etat*. Nevertheless, the breaking of the old community of states by the Viking attacks had led to new political developments which had been impossible under that old system, and in each region a single dominating kingdom had emerged. It might even be said that the destruction of the old political system was necessary if unification was to take place. It remained to be seen if further unity could be achieved by internal developments, or if another period of political destruction would be necessary.

Bibliography

Some of the books listed in the bibliography for Chapter 2 – Hill, Loyn, Stenton, MacNeill/McQueen and Smyth – are also relevant in this chapter. In addition there are:

The Vikings:

Haywood, John, *The Penguin Historical Atlas of the Vikings* (London: 1995).
Jones, Gwyn, *The Norse Atlantic Saga, being the Norse Voyages of Discovery and Settlement in Iceland, Greenland, America* (Oxford: 1964).
Loyn, H.R., *The Vikings in Britain* (London: 1977).
Sawywer, P.H., *Kings and Vikings* (London: 1982).
Sawyer, P.H., *The Age of the Vikings*, 2nd ed. (London: 1971).
Wainwright, F.T., *Scandinavian England*, edited by H.P.R. Finberg (Chichester: 1975).

Scotland:

Barrow, G.W.S., *Kingship and Unity, Scotland 1000–1306* (London: 1981).
Crawford, Barbara E., *The Northern Earldoms, Orkney and Caithness from AD 872 to 1470* (Edinburgh: 2013).
Oram, Richard, *The Lordship of Galloway* (Edinburgh: 2000).
Woolf, Alex, *From Pictland to Alba, 789–1070* (Edinburgh: 2007).

England:

Blackburn, Mark A.S. and Dumville, David N. (eds), *Kings, Currency, and Alliances, History and Coinage of Southern England in the Ninth Century* (Woodbridge: 1998).
Brown, Michelle C. and Farr, Carol A. (eds), *Mercia, an Anglo-Saxon Kingdom in Europe* (London: 2001).
Campbell, James, *The Anglo-Saxon State* (London: 2000).
Duckett, Eleanor Shipley, *Alfred the Great, the King and his England* (Chicago: 1956).
Foot, Sarah, *Athelstan, the First King of England* (New Haven: 2011).
Higham, Edward N.J. and Hill, D.H. (eds), *Edward the Elder, 899–924* (London: 2001).
Hill, Paul, *The Age of Athelstan, Britain's Forgotten History* (Stroud: 2004).
Lavelle, Ryan, *Ethelred II, King of the English, 978–1016* (Stroud: 2002).
Lawson, M.K., *Cnut, the Danes in England in the early Eleventh Century* (Harlow, Essex: 1993).
Mason, Emma, *The House of Godwine, the History of a Dynasty* (London: 2004).
Richards, Julian D., *Viking Age England* (London: 1991).
Stafford, Pauline, *Unification and Conquests, the Political and Social History of England in the Tenth and Eleventh Centuries* (London: 1989).
Walker, Ian W., *Mercia and the Making of England* (Stroud: 2000).

Chapter 4

Failures to Unify – Ireland and Wales

England and Scotland both went through an awkward and protracted series of events which eventually produced recognizable early versions of their later national states, though in neither case had they become fully united by the eleventh century. By contrast, Wales and Ireland did not undergo such processes, even though both countries faced broadly similar political dangers and invasions. It is always difficult to explain why something did not happen, but in an account of unifications in Britain, the difference between the two pairs of countries needs necessarily to be explained.

The compulsion to unite which produced the kingdoms of Scotland and England in the ninth and tenth centuries came from the clear threats of Viking attacks and invasions, and the political and human destruction they caused. The more successful of the unifications, in England, was clearly due to the greater threat posed by the Viking Great Army, which aimed at the conquest of the whole country, section by section, kingdom by kingdom, an intention which gradually, over several years' campaigns, became clear to the victims. In Scotland, conquest does not seem to have been the Viking aim, but it proved all too easy for Viking armies to penetrate deep into the centre of the country in destructive raids, and into kingdoms to destroy the governing (and military) aristocracy, as in Fortriu in 839 and at Dumbarton in 871. To survive such raids and ravages the Scottish kingdoms had to resist them, and the only way to do so proved to be to unify the Picts and the Scots. The difference in the size of the threat can be measured in the scale of the response: in England the reply was a major, sustained and successful effort to drive the invaders either out or down; in Scotland the response was largely defensive, unity being developed to deter further attacks, but little effort was made to 'reconquer' the lands taken by the invaders, at least not for several centuries.

The experiences of Ireland and Wales were different, and it is these differences which help to explain the differing outcomes of the Viking attacks. Not only were the initial conditions in the two countries different from England and Scotland – and from each other (as noted in Chapter 2) – but the scale, nature and purpose of the Viking warfare were different also. The result in both countries was that no unification at that time took place. This chapter therefore discusses something which did not happen, but since unification did happen in England and Scotland, and since the Vikings attacked all four countries, there is clearly an issue to be explained.

Ireland

The experience of Ireland in the Viking period was difficult enough, more similar in many respects to that of Scotland than England, and as intense as both of these. The division of Ireland amongst a large number of tribes or clans was a condition of affairs which would inevitably attract Viking raiders, for it appeared to be a condition of disunity which always attracted raiders (as in Northumbria in 867 or in the Frankish empire after 840). As in Scotland, the local Church's habit of establishing monasteries on offshore islands and promontories, and then rewarding them with rich gifts, provided ready-made targets for the looters.

At the same time the extreme political division of the island meant that it was very difficult for any Viking group to establish any real authority over more than a small segment of the population. The more organized English kingdoms such as East Anglia and Northumbria had a political structure which permitted their conquest as a result of their defeat in battle – the removal of the king allowed the Vikings to put their own man in the royal office, and Oswald in East Anglia, Egbert I and II and Ricsig in Northumbria and Coelwulf II in Mercia all seem to have been accepted by their subjects. All three kingdoms had seen repeated dynastic changes in the recent past; a new king was hardly a novelty. The emplacement of a new king was therefore in several cases all that was required, and the Viking armies could then seize power by simply removing their puppet, then putting one of their own in as king. (One of the strengths of Wessex therefore would seem to have been the existence of a dynasty of kings in place for the previous three generations.) But such organized kingdoms simply did not exist in Ireland.

Not only that, but the small and numerous Irish states were belligerent, and in many ways were organized for warfare. Their chosen form of war was the same as that of the Vikings: the raid for cattle and slaves. By the same token, the population was adept at countering such raids and at escaping from their attackers. The Vikings had hard fighting on land as soon as they went ashore.

At first the Viking presence amounted to a few raids devoted to the accumulation of loot, mainly along the north and east coasts. These grew in size and range, the fleets of tens of ships mounting raids inland. Later, from about 840, they began to base themselves at fortified camps – called 'longphorts' – near or on the coast, camps which were originally purely temporary. The first two, established in 841, were at Linns in County Louth and at Dublin. And yet certain groups of Vikings soon settled down and formed their longphorts into proto-towns.

These raiders and settlers were in fact Norsemen, men originating from Norway, and by the 840s from Orkney or the Hebrides as well. Their experiences in the Scottish islands had been exactly the same as in Ireland – isolated raids, then greater raids and the establishment of central bases from which to trade or raid, whichever was the most likely to produce a profit.

The places they chose as their camps were always on the coast or beside rivers with easy access to the sea. Dublin was founded as a town by about 851, and along with Waterford is the most notable example, though there were half a dozen others – Limerick, Cork and Wexford, for example. These places became the vigorous centres of a widespread maritime trade, connecting Ireland with the British Isles, Muslim Spain and Scandinavia, and through Scandinavia with Russia and Central Asia. This was a development which had taken place earlier in a smaller scale along the south-eastern coast of England and the North Sea and English Channel coast of the continent. The Vikings had in fact travelled in many cases along existing seaways and trade routes; their presence significantly boosted activity along those routes, hence the success of the towns.

The initial raiding parties grew in size as Irish opposition continued and the riches to be stolen were slowly appreciated. This in turn stimulated increased resistance by the Irish. Actual settlement by the Vikings in Ireland was very limited; their towns remained small and at first were merely temporary. Warfare between Vikings and Irish became endemic, but then in Ireland it always had been, if on a less intense scale, and neither the Irish nor the Vikings proved to be capable of establishing large and powerful political units, even though the Viking armies grew in size, as they did on the continent. An army arrived in the 830s with a fleet which stayed on Lough Neagh for three years, and another army commanded by 'Turgeis' campaigned inland – if this man and his raid is not an invention. This became the pattern in Ireland, though none of the armies was able to hold on to any conquests, while causing plenty of damage. No part of Ireland escaped their attentions.

The several Viking towns which survived and developed were scattered around the coasts; each had their own kings, but had only small extents of territory under their control. The several Irish regions similarly had their own kings, but again their territorial sway was always limited by the existence, and sometimes the recalcitrance, of subsidiary clans or surrounding enemies. In the wars kings might be killed, but the Viking forces seem to have made no attempt to secure political control, no doubt because of continuing Irish enmity and their own limited military resources.

Here was the initial contrast with events in England, after the similarities of the raiding parties in temporary camps. The substantial forces deployed by the 840s in Ireland were never big enough to achieve widespread conquest. In such circumstances the achievement of political unity, or even an approach to unification by either the Irish or Vikings, proved to be quite impossible; indeed it was probably not even considered worth attempting. The invaders of England in the Great Army in the 860s (and those campaigning in France and its neighbours for twenty years beforehand) were mainly Danes. Those who raided in Ireland and Scotland were mainly Norsemen. The latter were less numerous than the Danes, and had different political experiences and expectations: Denmark was tending towards achieving its own political unity during the ninth century, but Norway was less 'advanced' in this respect, so that the Norse concept of a political entity tended to be a much smaller, less ambitious unit – a town or an earldom, rather than the kingdom. These Viking kingdoms became so domesticated into the Irish scene that intermarriage and political alliances between the two 'sides' became widely practiced. The Vikings in Ireland were operating in a political environment they found familiar, very like that of their homeland, just as Viking behaviour was much the same as Irish.

Any victory by either side proved to be purely temporary. For example, in 902 Dublin was conquered by an alliance of the local Irish kings of Leinster and Brega. Yet the city was back in Viking hands within little more than a decade, and the new kingship of the city was even more vigorous than the old; presumably a mixed Norse-Irish population had contrived to continue to inhabit the city all through its vicissitudes. Dublin was already the main urban centre of Ireland by that date, and its kings were certainly among the most powerful of the invaders, which were prime reasons for the Irish kings to seize the city. They were acting in much the same way as the Vikings in their raids, aiming for the richest prizes for the purpose of collecting loot.

Yet the city's kings also tended to turn away from Ireland – Olav the White, for example, raided in Scotland, and later kings from Sihtric II

Caoch from 921 onwards became fixated for the next forty years on gaining control of York. This turning away from Ireland is an obvious sign of the effectiveness of Irish resistance, and perhaps of the greater wealth of the English lands. That the Irish remained disunited meant that it was impossible for any Viking army to secure control of any large territorial area. It was not possible, for example, to gain control by killing the whole Irish aristocracy, as the Viking army did in Fortriu in Scotland in 839 or at Dumbarton in 871, or if they captured or killed the king, as in East Anglia and Northumbria, because the Irish kings rarely gathered together in alliance, and there was always another man to take over a vacant kingship.

One further explanation for the limited success of the Vikings in Ireland must be that they were simply not numerous enough to have a large effect. Their armies were perfectly capable of ravaging territory, though when confronted by a determined Irish army they were beaten as often as not. Their shortage of numbers must be put down to their origin in Norway. Many of those who sailed out of Norway settled in Orkney, Scotland or the Western Isles. Those who went on to Ireland were thus those who did not wish, at least at first, to settle down. These were inevitably only a fraction of those who had originally left Norway; they could not therefore sustain the numbers needed for a decisive and prolonged invasion.

In the 840s, a second group of 'Vikings' arrived in the south of Ireland. They were probably a group of Danes who had been raiding in northern France and southern England and decided to try Ireland. They arrived in 140 ships ('seven score'), which is regarded as a very large force – certainly larger than most Norse fleets in the Irish Sea until then. If we can accept the suggested figure of thirty men per ship, this would only produce an army of about 4,000 men – and that is if none of them were left to guard the ships. Given Irish conditions, a force of this size would scarcely affect the balance of power in Ireland in any serious way, though they could seize and hold a base and conduct raids.

But there is another aspect which must be considered. It would seem that the decision in England to attempt a conquest rather than simply looting came during discussions within the Viking Army which had camped in East Anglia over the winter of 865–66. Here it would seem that the crucial element was that the three sons of Ragnar Lothbrok – Halfdan, Ivar and Ubbi – had emerged as leaders of the army; men the Anglo-Saxons regarded as 'kings'. Perhaps they had been instrumental in recruiting the army in the first place. Halfdan certainly looked to securing a kingdom, and Ivar was apparently similarly ambitious. It may well be that this was the decisive moment, the step change in the intentions of the army which converted it from an assembly of raiders into the Great Army which the English had to fight for the next dozen years, and that this was particularly due to the presence of these three men, their ambition and their leadership. No such leaders emerged in Ireland except in the case of the kings of the cities, and in those cases only Olaf the White at Dublin became seriously important – and he was succeeded as king in the city by Ivar the Boneless Ragnarsson, whose dynasty were kings of Dublin for the next two centuries, and intermittently at York for almost a century.

Irish and Norse and Danes became familiar with each other, intermarried and traded together. It became steadily more difficult to distinguish between the several groups. By the eleventh century, the Viking city-kingdoms were well integrated into the Irish political system, and most of them could no longer pretend to full independence. Indeed, the hero of what the Irish tend to regard as the climactic battle of their Viking wars, the High King Brian Boru at Clontarf, had a daughter who was married to the Dublin King Sihtric Silkenbeard, and Sihtric's mother had as her second husband Brian Boru himself; in the battle itself Norse and Irish contingents fought on both sides. Wars thus became not so much fights between Irish and Norse, but a type of dynastic conflict, usually between alliances with both groups on each side, a process familiar in Ireland for centuries. This may be taken to typify the domestication of the Vikings into Irish society – and it was Irish society which proved to be the stronger, most resilient and more adaptable.

It is also clear that the Viking settlers saw no need to consider making widespread conquests. They were relatively few in number, and their original purpose in leaving Norway or Denmark (or Orkney or the Hebrides) had been either to raid for loot or to settle in towns and become merchants and traders; their settlements in a series of port cities around the Irish coast proved to be perfectly adequate for their needs. Dublin was probably the largest, and controlled the land to about 5 miles from the city to the west, inland, and rather more along the coast to north and south, though this again tended to vary with the raids which the Dubliners and their neighbours conducted against each other. The other ports were no doubt smaller in area.

By political alliances and intermarriage and by residence, these city states had become in effect Irish kingdoms – Irish-Norse or Norse-Irish, in historical parlance. It is unlikely that they would ever have been able to conquer any more territory than they could dominate from their cities. Conquest, in other words, was never the Vikings' aim in Ireland, though their presence proved to be for several centuries an extremely uncomfortable one. In this they resembled the Vikings in Scotland, from whom indeed they originated in many cases, where settlement and raiding had also been the aims of the settlers-cum-migrants-cum-raiders.

The Irish political system was therefore quite capable of creating effective military alliances at need, as in the conquest of Dublin in 902, and the Irish kings do not seem ever to have feared that they were in danger of being conquered by the relatively small Viking armies, though their raids and campaigns were damaging. The culmination of the Irish-Norse wars came in 1014 in the Battle of Clontarf (next door to Dublin), in which the Irish High King, Brian Boru, defeated a large Viking army led by the king of Dublin (his stepson) and several other Viking kings. The result seemed to replicate that of the contemporary war in England, where the Danish invasions had culminated in the flight of King Aethelred II to Normandy and the installation of Svein of Denmark as king in his place in that same year. But Clontarf had no clear political consequences, and in England King Svein died after a few months and his coalition of Danes and English allies fell apart. Aethelred returned, and Svein's son, Knut, fled in his turn. It looked as though on both sides of the Irish Sea the Viking conquests were failing.

If ever there was an occasion when some sort of political unity might have developed in Ireland it was therefore at this crisis, and in fact Brian Boru's descendants did lay claim to a dominant political role for themselves for some time afterwards on the strength of the victory, though this was never widely accepted. In a sense, of course, the fact that the Irish technically won that battle meant that they could not see the need for any sort of permanent political unification – after all, their political system had largely survived without resorting to unification, and it had won the victory.

No real measure of unity therefore developed in Ireland. But if a lesson from overseas was needed it came from England. Knut tried again after his father died. King Aethelred also died, and the contest was therefore now between a divided England and a determined Danish king. The result was to divide England for a brief spell between them, and then the invader gathered it all together as a united Danish-ruled kingdom of England.

Of course, Clontarf was not a purely Irish-Viking conflict – the two sides were, as usual, mixed alliances, with Irish and Norse kings on both sides. But Clontarf was indecisive in Ireland because England and Ireland were not alike: the defeat of the Viking kings was due as much to their lack of numbers, and their internal divisions, as to Irish expertise, and to the fact that in effect Clontarf was a civil war between Irish and Norse on both sides. In England, the fight was clearly between English and Danish invaders. So Ireland remained as divided in the aftermath of Clontarf as it had been before.

Wales

The Welsh kingdoms existed for a long time, with some of them dating back to the end of the Roman province; they were clearly stable political entities. Political change in Wales came about largely by briefly uniting kingdoms under kings who inherited both kingdoms, not by conquest. These unions were almost always merely temporary, expiring with the king who had acquired them. Attacks on Wales came out of England, but only in the form of raids conducted against individual Welsh kingdoms, not usually against all of Wales; this was not a sufficient threat to force the Welsh into any sort of unity. The construction of Offa's Dyke provided a legal recognition for much of the mutual boundary, and its existence seems to have blocked any English attempts at conquest. Other raids could come by sea, and a certain amount of Irish settlement can be traced in the early period after Rome, but these settlers were quickly absorbed.

Viking armies attacked Wales, sometimes viciously. They were, however, usually only raiders, and they rarely made any attempt to settle, normally being based elsewhere in the British area. These Vikings tended to come from Ireland or from the Isle of Man, both of these being countries in which they had already settled. To the Welsh there was little to distinguish them from the English, for both attacks came in the form of raids searching for wealth. The general poverty of Wales as a whole, together with its forbidding mountainous topography, were the greatest discouragements for such raids.

The Vikings' attacks were therefore very similar to those mounted into Ireland or Scotland, and there was never any systematic attempt at conquest as there was in England. Nor was there any permanent attempt by Vikings to settle in such places as the port towns they had founded in Ireland. There were possible Viking settlements in Dyfed and the Gower Peninsula in South Wales, but both could be quickly absorbed by the local population. Viking raids were occasional, temporary and limited, if annoying. At times the Viking armies were utilized by Welsh kings as hirelings in their own conflicts. The more consistent enemies of the Welsh were the kings of Mercia, who had, until the destruction of the kingdom by the Vikings, exercised their own overlordship over the nearest parts of Wales. Then the kings of England, beginning with Alfred, aimed to exercise the same influence. Ealdorman Aethelred of Mercia, Alfred's son-in-law, conducted very destructive raids into South Wales, perhaps as a deterrent to Welsh exploitation of English difficulties, one result of which was that the targeted Welsh kings applied to Alfred himself for protection. No doubt Aethelred's aim was deterrence; he did not want to have to face a joint Welsh and Danish invasion from west and east simultaneously. Alfred's protection would have also prevented Welsh raids.

Yet attacks by English kings were merely occasional, temporary and limited. They occurred occasionally throughout the later Anglo-Saxon period, right up to the last years of Edward the Confessor's reign. Wales was scarcely a wealthy enough country for the kings of either Mercia or England to wish to extend their power over it, and it seems that the Vikings had much the same reaction.

None of these threats were strong or persistent enough to stir the Welsh political system into change. The series of brief unifications which had happened since Rhodri Mawr in the ninth century were repeated without any long-term results. Maredudd ap Owain of Dyfed-and-Seisyllwg briefly ruled Gwynedd and Powys in the 990s, but not the small kingdoms of the south-east. A generation later, Gruffydd ap Llywelyn of Gwynedd-and-Powys succeeded in conquering both the southern kingdoms and those in the south-east. He was assisted by an alliance with two successive Earls of Mercia, but when he seemed to be becoming too powerful (and his ally was dead) he was attacked by Harold, Earl of Wessex (the future king). When the English army reached Snowdon, Gruffydd's Welsh conquests and allies fell away, and Gruffydd was murdered. Success in this campaign was one reason why Harold could lay claim to the English throne three years later. Wales reverted to disunity.

Gruffydd's career was the closest anyone had so far come to creating a unified Welsh state. But as its collapse, when he was defeated and killed, showed, just conquering was not enough, any more than was a personal collection of kingdoms. He had made little attempt to create a Welsh administrative system which would bind the several kingdoms into one – he had hardly enough time – and the fact that he was operating with an English ally demonstrated his essential political weakness. As soon as the Mercian alliance ended with the death of Earl Aelfgar in 1063, Gruffydd was vulnerable, and the speed of the secession of the conquered lands showed the unpopularity, outside his own kingdom, of his work.

The Lack of a Viking Effect

The effects of the Viking settlements, invasions and raids on Wales and Ireland therefore differed radically from what had been the case in England and Scotland. The Irish experience, where Viking raids continued for two or more centuries and ranged widely over the whole island, was surely a traumatic one, but it did not compel the Irish to develop any real political unity. Indeed, by multiplying the number of political units – adding the Viking towns to the innumerable Irish kingdoms and clans – any sort of unity was pushed further away than ever. The nearest attempt, the alliance which won at Clontarf, became a victim of its own success, and, like Gruffydd ap Llywelyn's conquests, it led nowhere, especially since the victor, Brian Boru, was killed in the fighting.

The Welsh experience was much less serious, though unpleasant raids were widely experienced, particularly in Anglesey and Gwynedd, and in the south-west around St David's – a prime target (like Iona and Armagh), being a relatively wealthy church close to or on the coast; it was sacked by the Vikings at least four times in the tenth century, and later once by the English. But if the heavier and nastier Irish raids were not sufficient to compel the Irish to unity, the lesser Welsh experience would clearly not do so either.

One reason for the failure of the Irish experience to bring the Irish to some sort of unity – other than cultural and religious – which would have been the obvious reply to foreign invasion, was that their own society had been similarly violent, and their wars were not materially different from the Viking raids. The same may be said of Wales. At the same time, Irish society was sufficiently resilient to absorb the Viking settlements and adapt to their presence. One of the early Viking raids reached the monastery at Clonmacnois, but this had already been sacked and many of its monks murdered two years before by a nearby Irish king. Viking raids were thus often no worse than those conducted by Irishmen on each other. In addition, of course, the violence of Irish political society bred in Irishmen a skilled military ability, which proved quite adequate to combat Viking armies in the field. The Vikings therefore could be seen as perhaps little more than a nastier version of the normally violent political activity of the country, and could be fitted easily enough into the general pattern of Irish political life. Their political and military pressure was constant for several centuries, but these pressures were never powerful or threatening enough to demand a strong and decisive political response from the Irish rulers, who felt, rightly, that an individual military response was generally sufficient. And if another kingdom was damaged by a raid, they would not worry too much.

In Ireland, furthermore, the enormous variety of political units, Irish and Viking, all relatively small, was a constant obstacle to any sort of unification. If such a change was to take place it would have to be built around an existing kingdom which was large enough to provide a basis for a powerful defence against attack and strong enough to conquer, the role taken in England, that is, by the Wessex-Mercian alliance. None of the High Kings controlled a large enough kingdom or a wide enough alliance to perform this function, and their leadership was that of an alliance of many small kingdoms, none of which were prepared to subjugate their independence into a larger whole for any longer than was required by the immediate crisis which had brought them together. In Wales it could have been possible for Gwynedd, for example, to lead the country into a unity, as in fact Gruffydd ap Llywelyn attempted to do in the eleventh century, but it seems clear that the Viking threat was simply not powerful enough to engender the need amongst the Welsh for unity. For the Welsh, the major threat was always from England; but for the English, Wales was not a sufficiently powerful threat to concern them, most of the time. The intermittent nature of the Viking raids did not justify any decisive precautions being taken.

Conclusion

The differing responses of the Irish, Welsh, Scots and English to the threat posed by Viking attacks was thus in large part the result of the differing pressures exerted on their states and societies by the Viking attacks. These differences were in turn the result of the differing geographies and societies which the Vikings faced. England, as the richest of the countries, clearly merited conquest and conversion into Danish kingdoms, and the divisions between the several kingdoms made it very obviously vulnerable. Scotland and Wales could be raided and their few treasures looted, but widespread conquest was not worth the effort in either case, especially since the islands of the Scottish coast were clearly congenial to Norse settlement while the mountainous mainland was not. But the power of the raids into Scotland and the destruction they perpetrated compelled the Scots' and Picts' kingdoms to join, and then to establish a suzerainty over Strathclyde, a process which fitted well with the traditional mode of royal succession in those kingdoms. The unity the Vikings imposed on Scotland was thus in a sense accidental. Ireland was clearly far too difficult for the small Norse forces to conquer; the Irish response to the Viking arrival had been partly vigorous resistance, but also an acceptance of the Viking presence and the absorption of their towns into Irish society.

However, history being the record of the activities of human beings, another essential difference is that the force attacking the English kingdoms, the Great Army, held together under permanent leadership for much longer than any other Viking force which campaigned in Ireland or Wales. Only England was subjected to a systematic attempt at conquest by a major force over a period of over a decade. This must be due in a large part to the quality of the leadership exercised over that Great Army by the sons of Ragnar Lothbrok. This was the achievement of Halfdan Ragnarsson and his brothers, and it evoked a comparable response from the kings of Wessex to create a unified English kingdom, and to develop a strong administrative system with which to hold it together. Such a challenge did not exist in the other three British countries, though in Scotland the danger was clearly apprehended, and a Scottish solution was arrived at.

Bibliography

In addition to the books of Byren, Charles-Edwards, Rees, Cosgrove and O Croinin noted in Chapter 2, the following have been useful:

Ireland:

Hudson, Benjamin, *Viking Pirates and Christian Princes, Dynasty, Religion, and Empire in the North Atlantic* (Oxford: 2005).
O Corrain, Donncha, *Ireland before the Normans* (Dublin: 1972).
Smyth, Alfred P., *Scandinavian Kings in the British Isles, 850–880* (Oxford: 1977).
Smyth, Alfred P., *Scandinavian York and Dublin, the History and Archaeology of two related Viking Kingdoms*, 2 vols (Dublin, 1979).

Wales:

Charles, B.G., *Old Norse Relations with Wales* (Cardiff: 1934).
Davies, Wendy, *Patterns of Power in Early Wales* (Oxford: 1990).
Davies, Wendy, *Wales in the Early Middle Ages* (Leicester: 1982).
Loyn, H.R., *The Vikings in Wales* (London: 1976).

Chapter 5

The Norman Effect

The Norman invasion of England in 1066 had great and deep repercussions, for the well-being of the people, for the English aristocracy and in the government of the kingdom. It also had a large effect in the three other countries of the archipelago, though later, less drastically and differentially. But the net effect was to increase in power the kingdom of England, so that, given an appropriate king, the possibility now existed of uniting the four countries into one by force.

The Norman Hammer: the Definitive English Unification

William the Conqueror grew up as an orphaned illegitimate child (he became known as 'William the Bastard'). His father died when he was 7, and had not been married to the boy's mother; and yet at that age the boy was made Duke of Normandy. His life in Normandy as a child and a young adult was precarious and exceedingly difficult; that he survived at all must be counted as a major surprise and his first major political achievement. He became duke only because no other male member of the ducal house existed. He saw at first hand the anarchy to which an uncontrolled aristocracy could reduce a kingdom, and his first task upon reaching adulthood was to reduce that aristocracy to some sort of obedience. He did so in part by a brutal conquest of the duchy, but also by directing the aristocracy's energies against territories outside Normandy. As a result he secured effective control over Maine and domination over Brittany, becoming the dominant political force in northern France and a figure of European importance.

One of the areas to which William's attention was directed was England. Several Norman lords had been recruited by King Edward the Confessor (1042–65) of Alfred's dynasty; he was also the successor of the expired Danish dynasty, and had a Norman mother. The imported Normans were supposed to give the king a source of independent political and religious support separate from the overbearing earls, such as Godwine of Wessex and his several sons, and successive earls of Mercia. Presumably for the same reason, Edward, who had no children, gave William to understand that he regarded the duke as a potential heir to the throne, which, given their rather distant relationship, could be plausible. He really had no right to do this, and it seems unlikely to have been a serious offer, given that he had a more plausible heir in his nephew, Edgar, and that his brother-in-law was the overbearing Earl Harold of Wessex, son of Godwine, who thus could also lay a claim to the throne. But Edward's game was evidently to enlist others who might hold the Godwinessons in check, and by keeping several claimants close, to balance them against each other. That the aristocracy in England was capable of playing the same game becomes clear when Earl Harold, on a visit to Normandy, gave Duke William to understand that he supported him in his claim to the English throne. Given Harold's relationship to King Edward, this must have counted strongly with William. Harold was never serious in this, any more than Edward had been in his offer to William, for he had his own designs on the kingship. Being on the spot, he clearly had a much better chance of seizing the throne when Edward died than anyone else.

This he did. Edward died on Christmas Day 1065. Harold made himself king, being crowned on the Twelfth Day of Christmas, thus executing the same sort of *coup d'état* as Edward the Elder had at Tamworth in disposing of his niece, Aelfwyn. This seizure of power was in fact the normal method for the English succession. However, there was only a limited set of people who were regarded as eligible; descent from King Alfred seems to have been the crucial element. This factor had been broken already by the intrusion of four Danish kings – another claimant was the king of Denmark. Harold, though not of the direct line, was at least married into the royal family.

Harold was an experienced commander and administrator, and for ten months he wielded the royal authority with some success. At the same time he did not have the full support of his rival earls, earlier his equals, so he was in danger of falling victim to the very division which had assisted his own rise. At least three competitors felt that they had much the same rights to the throne as he did, and they were quite prepared to fight for it. William spent much of 1066 gathering support – military, naval and diplomatic – in preparation for an expedition to England, though his caution was almost self-defeating. The Norwegian King Harald Hardrada had only the vaguest of claims, and was even more of an adventurer than William, but he might just succeed in a programme of conquest, which had worked for Svein and Knut fifty years before. He linked up with the Earl of Orkney and with Harold's estranged brother, Tostig, who wanted to return to his former earldom of Northumbria, from which he had been expelled by his subjects. These allies managed to launch an invasion well before William was ready. The Danish King Svein Astridsson, a grandson of Knut and so of the royal house which had ruled in England between 1016 and 1042, also made preparations. Edgar the Aethling did not make a public claim; he was in Harold's power and presumably feared for his life. Edgar was the last male descendant of the Alfredian house, being the grandson of King Edmund Ironside, and was Edward the Confessor's step-nephew. If primogeniture and male descent were the main criteria, his claim was the best. But it was clear by the early summer of 1066 that legal, moral or royal claims did not count. The issue would be settled, as Harold had indicated from the first, by force.

When the crisis finally came, in the autumn of 1066, the first to move was Harald Hardrada, who invaded Northumbria along with Tostig. York, of course, had an old tradition of accepting Norse and Danish kings, though he was opposed by the local army. Harald seized the city, but then waited to be attacked. King Harold marched north to deal with this unwelcome invasion and succeeded in eliminating Hardrada and much of his army, but at the cost of many of the warriors from the Midlands and the North who had been provided by Earls Edwin and Morcar, respectively of Mercia and Northumbria, of the rival Mercian dynasty. They were Harold's brothers-in-law, and clearly had no wish to be ruled by such as Hardrada. Harold then had to march south again to deal with William, who had taken the opportunity of Harold's absence in the North, and of a favourable turn of the weather, to cross the Channel and make a landing. There followed Harold's defeat and death in battle near Hastings. Edwin and Morcar were not present, since they had lost many men already, and Harold, over-confident, did not wait for their forces.

During the next few years the old English aristocracy of earls and thanes was steadily eliminated by William, now king. Harold and two of his brothers, both earls, died at Hastings along with a large proportion of the English thanes from the south of England; others had died fighting Hardrada. Edwin and Morcar at first submitted to William, but then they rebelled, were defeated and died. Earl Gospatric, Morcar's successor as Earl of Northumbria, rebelled later and also died.

This was standard procedure, and had happened in East Anglia, Northumbria, Mercia and in Fortriu in the Viking invasions. These men stood in the line of battle, leading by example, and they frequently died in battle. The victor then took over the lands of the dead men. The general population in most of England had been unmoved by the changes of rulers in the past. The Danish invasions of Svein and Knut had hardly stirred any popular opposition, except perhaps in London, though Danish ravaging had been widespread. William had perhaps expected the same muted reception.

This time these aristocratic rebellions spread further throughout the rest of society and became something approaching popular rebellions in the North. William did not have the manpower to plant large controlling garrisons, so his only means of combating such widespread popular rebellions was to devastate the land and kill the male population. It was in fact a similar reaction, but on a much greater and more brutal scale, to the methods he had used to gain control of his Norman inheritance. Huge areas of the North of England, the Welsh borders and parts of eastern England were rendered depopulated, or as the later survey put it, they were made 'waste'.

By 1075 the old English aristocracy had largely ceased to exist, along with a large proportion of their subjects. This was not only the case with the earls, but also with many of the less prominent men, who were simply fairly large landowners. Those not killed had fled, Edgar the Aetheling to Scotland, for instance, and the Byzantine emperors recruited their imperial guard from the English exiles for the next generation. The lands of these men were distributed to William's men, or were taken by them. The situation clearly became confused, and the ownership of estates, and so also the liabilities for tax and military service, were uncertain. William therefore eventually commissioned his 'Domesday' Book survey to investigate and document the new landowning situation – it was this which provides the detailed evidence for the devastations. This record demonstrates quite clearly that the whole old Anglo-Saxon ruling class of England, from the king down to virtually all the landowners of any size, had been eliminated, replaced by a variety of incomers from several parts of northern France. One of the few to survive was the man who, had he been installed and supported as king by the earls (including Harold) after Edward the Confessor died, might have been able to avoid all the killing: Edgar the Aetheling.

This decade of conquest, killing and destruction between 1066 and 1075 was the true and final unification of the English kingdom. This was not, presumably, the actual intention of King William, who was intent most of the time on surviving and on beating down the main sources of opposition, but the effect of his warfare and his destruction was to eliminate all the Anglo-Saxon opposition – and in some cases his own Norman followers

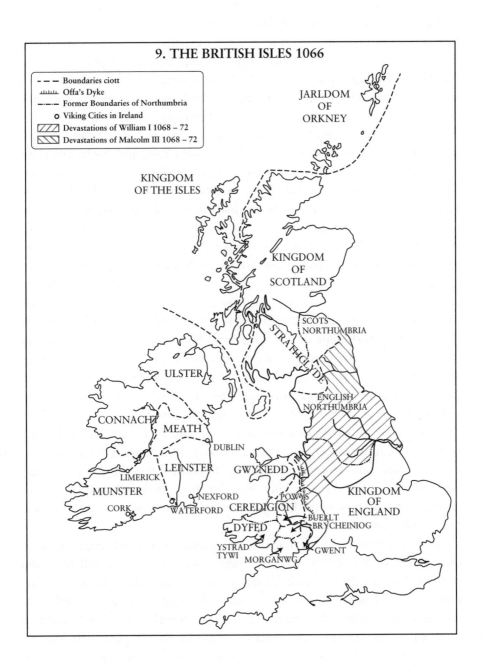

9. THE BRITISH ISLES 1066

- – – Boundaries ciott
- Offa's Dyke
- –·–·– Former Boundaries of Northumbria
- o Viking Cities in Ireland
- Devastations of William I 1068 – 72
- Devastations of Malcolm III 1068 – 72

JARLDOM
OF
ORKNEY

KINGDOM
OF THE ISLES

KINGDOM
OF
SCOTLAND

STRATHCLYDE

SCOTS
NORTHUMBRIA

ULSTER

ENGLISH
NORTHUMBRIA

CONNACHT

MEATH

DUBLIN

LEINSTER

GWYNEDD

LIMERICK

MUNSTER

POWYS

KINGDOM
OF
ENGLAND

NEXFORD

CORK

WATERFORD

CEREDIGION

DYFED

BUELLT
BRYCHEINIOG

YSTRAD
TYWI

MORGANWG

GWENT

who were less than keen to support him – so that the semi-unity which had been the condition of the kingdom until 1066 was destroyed, and a much tighter royal grip was imposed. William had found it necessary to massacre large numbers of Englishmen to achieve this; the clearest indication that the English as a whole were unwilling to accept his new dispensation, and that they had a profound loyalty to the old kingdoms-become-earldoms such as Northumbria. But having perpetrated these massacres, William's new dispensation was perforce accepted; opposition was a losing choice.

William did not replace the eliminated great earls with men of his own, at least not on the same scale. After all, it was the earls and the loyalty their earldoms had inspired which had formed part of the continuing opposition to him, and yet powerful military men were needed on the borders. The Welsh border had become unusually disturbed, and had suffered almost as much destruction as Yorkshire, so the traditional defences against Welsh attack were much weakened – the kings of Powys took the opportunity to mount a raid into Shropshire and Cheshire. Major earldoms were created at Chester, Shrewsbury and Hereford. These were sensibly smaller in area than the old Anglo-Saxon earldoms, and were much more directed to exploiting the border situation and less to seeking to control or subvert the central government of the kingdom. Similarly, the Scottish border required a powerful guardian – King Malcolm of the Scots had conducted an unpleasant invasion – and a Northumbrian earldom, smaller than before, was developed to control the area north of the Tyne, along with a militant palatine bishop based at Durham. The most powerful of the earls was William's own half-brother, Odo, who as a churchman (Bishop of Bayeux) could scarcely establish a dynasty; he became Earl of Kent, in case invasion came from the continent, to control the county, which had rebelled once. The French king was also now an inveterate and active enemy. The borders were thus guarded by warriors whose attention was firmly directed outwards.

This was another lesson William had learned in the fighting against his own Norman aristocracy, who themselves were now rewarded by being presented with wealthy English estates, though none of them were of any great size, and only those on the vulnerable borders were geographically concentrated. Quite a few men did acquire several estates, well scattered to avoid too powerful or influential a presence in any particular locality, and only the border earls had concentrated power – another lesson from the immediate past. They would thus be unable to acquire a major landed interest out of which to form their own principalities. This did not prevent men from rebelling, of course, but it did mean that they were less likely to be successful.

The Anglo-Saxon kings, with their shires, their writs, their sheriffs and their coinage, had established a viable and workable administrative system, possibly the most effective in Europe at the time, and William was able to take over this system wholesale and make it work, no doubt employing the same clerks as had served the Anglo-Saxon kings – William's writs were issued in English for several years after he became king, only shifting to Latin from 1070. Those Anglo-Saxon kings had, of course, operated the system, but their control of the country had been impeded by the existence of the great earldoms, where the earls could intercede to prevent royal orders being implemented and prevent royal taxes from reaching the king, and could avoid military service simply by finding an excuse not to turn up. Furthermore, they had been too powerful to be disciplined, except at the cost of a civil war. Harold had been reduced to making a marriage alliance with the Mercian earls by marrying their sister, though this would scarcely have prevented them from rebelling had they wished to do so. The removal of the earls and their earldoms also removed these obstacles to good administration; the king could now be rather more confident than his predecessors for the previous two generations that his orders would be obeyed, and that tax revenues would flow into his treasury.

William's devastating conquest had brought into his hands many forfeited estates to add to the royal estates he had acquired as the successor of Edward as king and as earl, and these provided him not only with wealth but power, to add to his control of the royal administration. His royal power therefore penetrated throughout the kingdom, not just, as Harold found, into certain areas, such as the traditional Wessex. Harold, and before him the earlier kings of Alfred's dynasty, had been essentially earls of Wessex with the royal title, whereas William was the first true king of all England, the first king who could claim to be the ruler of the whole country without serious impediments from any over-mighty subjects. The destruction of the Anglo-Saxon aristocracy which he accomplished at Hastings, and in suppressing the subsequent rebellions, was the means by which he created a united England. King Edward the Elder had laid the groundwork by his conquest of the Danish territories in the east – he had deliberately confirmed the existing Danish land settlement he found in place – but the royal patrimony which he inherited from his father and passed on to his descendants was never enough to allow him or his successors to dominate the rest of the country properly. William was able to do this, because he had acquired the land and resources to make his kingship effective and had destroyed the intervening intermediaries. This came, however, as a by-product of his devastating conquest and at the expense of vast casualties.

The removal of the provincial earldoms and their replacement by men whose estates were fewer than those of the former earls, and might be spread throughout the country, combined with the king's acquisition of estates in all parts of England, reduced the administrative competence of the aristocracy and increased the penetration of royal power into all parts of the country. The instrument for this was the royally appointed sheriffs. These officials had already existed in Anglo-Saxon England, but as subordinates of the provincial earls; now they were appointed and supervised by the king. The sheriffs were assisted, if that is the right word, by local assemblies – shire moots and surveys and juries – who constituted in a small way a restriction on the local power of the sheriffs and therefore more distantly on the king's power. These groups, sworn juries often, were the primary agents of law and justice, and usually worked in consultation with the sheriffs and/or royal representatives, but only on local affairs and local crimes, and based their authority on local collective memory.

The proof of William's concoction lies in the contrast between, first, the century-and-a-half separating the reign of Alfred from that of William and, second, the ten centuries which have followed since William's reign. Under the Anglo-Saxon dynasty of Alfred, even though it seemed that England had been united into a single kingdom, it had been regularly broken up into sections which could easily become independent, or at least separate, for a time. This happened regularly with Northumbria, it happened when the Five Boroughs were taken away in the 940s, it happened in the 950s and it happened again with the Danish conquest in 1016, when Wessex was separated off from the rest of the kingdom. These episodes of partial dismemberment were only brief, but that they happened indicated, as much as the existence of the giant earldoms, that English unity was liable to be broken up fairly easily. These were only the most obvious cases, for the growth of the power of the great earls in effect caused a disintegration in which the earls, not the kings, controlled their own regional principalities. That is to say, between 900 and 1066, England had been only a partially united state, despite the victories of Alfred and his family. The kingdom could be broken up all too easily, and the king was the only institution which promoted any real unity.

Compare the period since 1066. No serious attempt has been made at any point in the last ten centuries to break up England since William the

Conqueror's hammer blows forged its new unity in the heat of his conquest. Occasional attempts have been made by great lords to establish their pseudo-independence, but it has rarely been difficult for any king to suppress these movements. One of the most curious cases came in the reign of the usurper Henry IV (1399–1413), when an agreement, the 'Tripartite Indenture', was made between Owain Glyndwr, the insurgent Prince of Wales, Henry Percy, Earl of Northumberland, and the Marcher lord Edmund Mortimer, by which the Anglo-Welsh kingdom was to be divided into three parts, each man taking one section. The plan died the first time the alliance attempted to fight, and one of the reasons for their defeat was that the plan became public knowledge. Only along the Scottish and Welsh borderlands has it been possible to develop any sort of aristocratic independence or to promote some element of separation, and in both regions the authority of the lords was almost always directed outwards, as William intended with his appointment of the first Marcher lords. William the Conqueror had united England so tightly that this unity has been unbreakable for over a millenium.

The Pattern of Unification

Before considering the continuing Norman adventures in other parts of the British Isles and the effect they had, it is worth stopping to consider what has been revealed by the successive episodes of unification which England went through. The history of England provides a particularly clear example of the pattern of change which any country goes through during the process of unification – a pattern which can be traced in the histories of virtually all the countries of the modern world. First of all, there exists a group of states who form a clear community, in which they are related to each other by proximity, by language, by repeated warfare with each other, by religion, by the intermarriages of the royal families or in some other way; often by several of these elements. In England this was the group of Anglo-Saxon kingdoms which were established after the evaporation of the Roman Empire. These states, many of the earliest of which were small and weak, were gradually consolidated down to a few, usually by conquest by some of the others; in England the survivors of this process were seven (the 'Heptarchy') for a century and more but they were reduced to four after the campaign by Egbert of Wessex in 829; despite his victory, the four were roughly equal in strength, and formed an international balance of power.

This balanced group will continue until a crisis of some sort arises by which that system of states is destroyed. King Egbert's campaign in 829 rocked the old system, but it settled down again as the set of four replaced the original seven when he withdrew back to Wessex. In England it was the invasion and campaigns of the Danish Great Army between 865 and 879 which broke that early system. Three of the four kingdoms were conquered or destroyed. The resulting fragments were then reassembled into a unification of the whole by conquest of the others by the strongest of them; this was the work of Alfred and Edward the Elder.

This, however, was only a partial unification. This initial unification would seem to be quite sufficient for any king to achieve, even in a long reign, and establishing a viable and unifying administration is something which takes much longer than a single reign or a single lifetime to achieve, even if the conquerors saw the need. So this early period of unification was one of only partial, even tentative, unity, which, in the case of England, lasted from about 880–1066. It was marked by occasional fragments being hived off into independence – York especially – for shorter or longer periods, and by the growth in power of the semi-independent earls, partly occasioned by the still limited reach of the royal government. This was the condition of England between the reigns of Alfred and Harold II.

The final stage of unification came with the cathartic crisis of the Norman Conquest between 1066 and 1075. In that time all the semi-independent elements in the period of partial unity were destroyed and the fragments were welded together, in the heat and fire of warfare and destruction, into a wholly unified state. In England this process was sufficiently brutal to produce a unified state which has lasted for a thousand years. It will be seen that, once the processes of unification in the other states of the British islands have run their course, this pattern is repeated in the cases of all three others of the communities of British states.

The pattern of unification may be reduced to a brief list:

1. formation of a community of states;
2. reduction of the original set of states to a small number;
3. a crisis in which the states are unified in part;
4. a final crisis which welds the parts securely together.

The time-scale for these processes is flexible, and there is no guarantee that every country will either start or complete the course, though most which begin the process do complete it, even if they take a long time to do so. For England the timing of these stages has been:

1. the formation of the community of states, $c.550$–650;
2. the heptarchy, reduced in the end to four states, $c.650$–865;
3. the crisis of 865–80 led to partial unity from 880–1066;
4. the crisis of 1066–75 produced full unity from 1075 until the present.

In Chapters 2 to 4, the early condition of the other countries in Britain and Ireland has been delineated. In the pattern as discerned in English history, both Ireland and Wales were, at the end of the eleventh century, still in stage 1, the community of states, though Wales seemed at times to be tending towards stage 2, the reduction of the numbers of states, but it had not happened by 1066. Neither country had evidently reached the stage of a decisive crisis which would convince the kings and the people to become united.

Scotland, however, had faced that crisis during the Viking attacks in the ninth century, and had entered the condition of partial unity even before England. The Viking raids had destroyed the ruling aristocracies of both the Picts and the Britons of Strathclyde; the Scots of Dalriada had by then lost control of much of their territory; and Northumbria was broken into fragments. These events saw the destruction of the old system of five traditional states which had been roughly balanced in power. Partial unification followed, when the Scoto-Pictish kingdom – Alba – was formed by Kenneth MacAlpin's accession, and his successors came to dominate and control Strathclyde. In this case, however, the partial nature of Scottish unity was not a matter of internal politics, as in England, with the near independent earls, but was due to the actual independence of Galloway, the Orkney earldom, the Western Isles and Bernicia, and the partial separation of Strathclyde into the eleventh century. None of these independent or autonomous sections was a threat to the main kingdom, whose general policy for the future was to gain control of all these weaker neighbours as much by a sort of political osmosis as by conquest. (On the other hand, the near autonomous northern Moray region produced Macbeth, whose successful rebellion enabled him to seize the throne – but the area did become independent.) There was no cataclysmic Norman-type conquest, but there was to be a distinct Norman effect, and so a Norman-type destruction of the partially unified state did not take place.

For Wales and Ireland, of course, the Viking effect had not been strong enough to destroy the political system and so to force the first change in this process. Both countries were to be presented with a further challenge by the Normans, however.

The Further Norman Effect: Scotland

The Norman conquest of England began to have significant side-effects on its neighbours almost at once. In Scotland, King Malcolm III Canmore (1058–93) had received members of the deposed Anglo-Saxon royal family as refugees, including Edgar the Aetheling, and he had married Edgar's sister, Margaret. The wider significance of this new marriage is that this was Malcolm's second marriage; the first had been to Ingebjorg, a Norse lady, the widow of Earl Thorfinn of Orkney, and now he married one from England. This symbolized a switch in political interest in Scotland, if not actually in political friendship, from an attempt to ally with his northern neighbour to an interest in what was happening to his south. The earlier Danish conquest of England had resulted in a war which one of Malcolm's predecessors had won, enabling him to establish full control of Lothian. It is probable that King Malcolm looked to gain similar advantage from the major disturbances taking place in England after 1066, and he and Edgar certainly intervened in the great rebellion in Yorkshire in 1069, but without result. He was thus disappointed. In 1072, William the Conqueror replied to Malcolm's provocations by invading Scotland. He aimed to deter any further interference in England's affairs from the north. His army and fleet penetrated, by land and sea, as far as Fife and the Forth and Tay estuaries. The invasion ended with a treaty signed at Aberfeldy in Perthshire. This had been a severe shock to the Scots; no southern army had marched as far north since the Northumbrians in the seventh century, and before that only the Romans had done so. Eight years later, a new Norman castle was built on the Tyne ('Newcastle'), and ten years after that another was built at Carlisle, so fortifying the English side of the border.

One element of weakness in Scotland was the instability of the royal succession. Every king in the eleventh century died by violence – including Malcolm Canmore, in 1093. The root of the problem lay in the old system of lateral succession, whereby there was a constant tension between carrying the succession to the king's son, or to a distant relative, who would be the eldest male of the royal house. This issue arose again with Malcolm's death and that of his son, in the same ambush. He had complicated the matter by having sons by both wives. The succession went first to Duncan II, his eldest son by Ingebjorg, then, after Duncan's murder, to Malcolm's brother,

Donald Ban, who was also murdered, and so to Malcolm's eldest son by Margaret, Edgar (1097–1107). Edgar had two younger brothers, Alexander (1107–24) and David, who succeeded him in sequence; neither Edgar nor Alexander had sons, which simplified the matter later. This in effect settled the system of succession into one by primogeniture, except that Duncan II's son, William, was thereby excluded. The MacWilliams became an irregular threat to Malcolm's descendants for the next century and more.

David I (1124–53) was educated in England at the royal court and, having married an heiress, became Earl of Huntingdon. From his English estates he derived a useful source of wealth which assisted his control of Scotland. He soon began to welcome an influx of Norman lords into Scotland, often originally his tenants in England, or from the Welsh Marches. Some Normans, indeed, had already arrived, and had been cautiously welcomed by earlier kings. These men were imported as military men to strengthen the kingdom's power in war, for the main enemy was England, which was now fully equipped with such knights. These immigrants had to be rewarded with land, and they brought with them the administrative practices of powerful men in England. The influence of these men became extremely strong, just as the adoption of a version of the English administrative systems, actually by David, contributed largely to the integration of Scotland into a single kingdom. This was symbolized by the transition of Scottish mormaers into earls – there were thirteen earldoms by 1150 – David's work again – and sheriffdoms, whose presence had the same implications of a more effective royal control as in England. One effect was to help make the direct hereditary succession in the Scottish kingship the established custom, since this was the Norman system, which eventually produced a necessary access of stability at the very top of the Scottish political and social system. When, in 1130, David defeated a rebellion by the Earl of Angus (who had a claim to the kingship by lateral descent), he annexed the earldom to the royal estate and installed feudal tenants there.

Queen Margaret became a major symbol of the change in Scotland, notably in her promotion of the practices of the Roman Church, though this activity became somewhat exaggerated in retrospect. The Scottish Church, in so far as it existed in 1100, was still in many parts a Celtic Church, certainly in its monastic practices, and its bishops and bishoprics tended to be of the mobile, unstructured type favoured in Ireland at the same time. The warfare of the Viking times had also wreaked much damage on the Church and its properties, perhaps even more so than in the kingdom as a whole. Queen Margaret had been brought up in the Roman Church

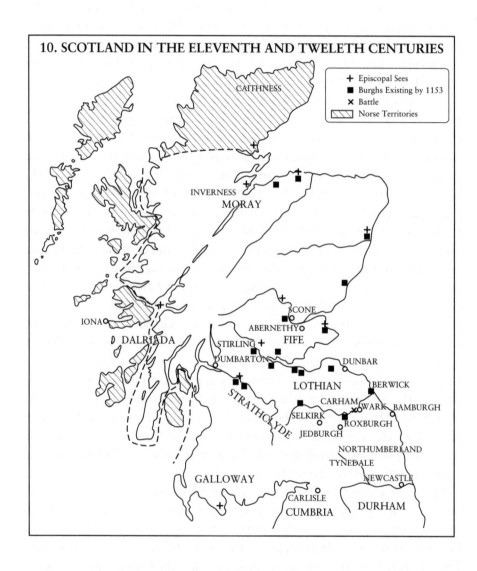

10. SCOTLAND IN THE ELEVENTH AND TWELETH CENTURIES

in England and she observed the Roman Church's practices once she had reached Scotland. She established the first of the monasteries of the Roman Church's Benedictine type at Dunfermline in 1089, importing three monks from Canterbury as the founding community, and this became the model for later Scottish monasteries, though some time passed before further foundations were made. Her work was mainly private, focused on her family, and yet the foundation of a single monastery had a profound, if slow, effect. The work of foundation was continued by her sons, and it spread to the local magnates who could afford to set aside land to endow the new monasteries; again it was particularly the new Norman lords who did this.

The integration of Strathclyde into the Scottish kingdom was finally accomplished under David. It had been used as a sub-kingdom by recent Scottish kings for their sons. Malcolm Canmore had been 'king of the Cumbrians' before holding the Scottish throne, and David had been given that territory while his brother was king. (He had a force of Norman knights at his command, which helped persuade King Alexander to appoint him). By then the old kingdom had been truncated by the annexation of the southern part (the modern Cumbria) by King William II Rufus of England, who fortified Carlisle to block any Scottish attempts to recover the lost land. When David became king he retained the Strathclyde region under his own control; Norman knights were placed there, as they were also to be in Angus.

The autonomy of Galloway was eroding in the same way as that of Strathclyde, but in the end more violently. In the 1150s, King Malcolm IV faced a group of earls in the area who were less than loyal, and about the same time he faced Henry II of England who was asserting his control of lands on the English side of the border. David I had occupied the northern English country as far south as the Tees and Morecambe Bay during the English civil war between the Empress Matilda and King Stephen; Henry II reasserted the English king's control. The threat Henry had thereby produced to southern Scotland was clear, and Malcolm conducted a swift campaign to suppress the dissenters in the district. Galloway thereby became more certainly part of the Scottish kingdom. The diocese of Whithorn was, along with the other Scottish dioceses, freed from the pretensions of York to control during the same century. The process of integrating Galloway was as slow as that of its neighbour Strathclyde had been, but both were gathered into the Scottish kingdom by the end of the twelfth century.

One further aspect of the integration process was language. In England this was only a minor issue: the English spoke English; Norman French overlaid it, but clearly gave way in the end. In Scotland, Gaelic had been the language of the North, Brittonic or British (i.e., Welsh) of Strathclyde, English in Northumbria and Lothian, and Norse in the far north and the islands. By the eleventh century this was changing quickly as Gaelic and Brittonic gave way to English in Strathclyde, which also began advancing into the north-east and Fife.

Meanwhile the repeated attempts by members of the disfranchised branch of the royal family, the MacWilliams, to secure the throne from their northern base, contributed to the continuation of a partial disunity in the kingdom, as did the continued independence of the Northern and Western islands under the Earls of Orkney and, after 1100, under the kings of Norway. The constant instability on the border with England was another factor. This compelled the kings to extend their power into the disaffected areas. It was in the more distant areas of Scotland – Galloway, the Highlands – that these would-be kings gained the support they needed; indeed, it was the fact that these areas were already disaffected that allowed them to support the pretensions of the MacWilliam family.

In suppressing their personal and royal enemies, therefore, the kings of the Canmore dynasty had to campaign into these distant and difficult regions, and to some extent they were able to ensure that their authority was at last felt there. On the other hand, the fact that they had to repeat these campaigns fairly frequently indicated that such areas would have been less than loyal even if there had not been a line of pretenders available to lead them and to give an overarching cause to their disaffection. They were, that is, less than wholly convinced that they should be members of the kingdom, or should be obedient and loyal to the king. Meanwhile, the Norse society in the Hebrides evolved into the Lordship of the Isles, whose lords, beginning about 1100 with Somerled, were distant, powerful, disobedient and expansionist; in effect they were independent, though they might profess a certain loyalty to the distant king, of either Scotland or Norway. The Scottish kingdom still had its ragged and un-united peripheries.

Within the areas generally under royal control, the administrative methods originally developed in tenth-century England were applied – shires and sheriffs, earldoms and lordships. Castles were built, a practice brought in by the Normans. A beginning was made in establishing towns – 'burghs' – as partly autonomous organizations. All this was slow work in a country so much poorer in population and resources than England, but it all contributed to the slow internal unification of the kingdom.

These innovations were in fact geographically limited to the south and east, as far north as the Moray Firth. They were to a large extent dependent on the practice of arable agriculture, which was the essential economic basis for a horse-riding warrior aristocracy, such as the Normans. Ironically, of all these innovations, it was only the castles which could be introduced into the Highlands, where arable agriculture was difficult, so the spread of the Norman aristocracy tended towards the separation of the Lowland arable lands from the pastoral territories of the Highlands.

The curious result was that, when King Malcolm III Canmore gave refuge to members of the old Anglo-Saxon royal dynasty at the time of the Norman Conquest, he opened the way for the later Norman incursion. Queen Margaret's foundation of her new monastery at Dunfermline was done in cooperation with Lanfranc, the Norman Archbishop of Canterbury, who dispatched the three foundation monks from Canterbury; her sons, notably David I, began importing Norman lords into Scotland. So the process, which had been in its initial phases the reception of refugee Anglo-Saxons, and so one of at least potential Anglicization, became one of Normanization and hence Frenchification.

This was all contributing to the slow integration of the kingdom, but by applying only to certain geographical areas, it was not decisively ending the condition of partial unity. Bringing Strathclyde and Galloway into the kingdom was a major step forward, but the western islands and Orkney and Shetland had meanwhile been brought under the suzerainty of the king of Norway – King Magnus Barelegs sailed through the islands enforcing this in 1100–03. Galloway, meanwhile, remained to a degree autonomous, and the border with England was still less than clear. Scotland remained only partly united.

The Further Norman Effect: Wales

The Norman incursions into Wales started differently and had very different effects to those in either England or Scotland. In England, they arrived with the Conqueror and were imposed on a conquered and shattered kingdom, while in Scotland they were invited in by the king and slowly infiltrated into several areas. However, in Wales it was more a matter of private enterprise and expansion, partaking partly of the Scottish way, by individual actions, and partly the English, in being opposed all the way. The Normans' initial difficulty, of course, as in the Scottish Highlands, was in imposing themselves on a largely pastoral country, much of which was unfitted to support their lifestyle. Unlike England there was no central Welsh power which could be suborned and conquered, and unlike Scotland there was no king who could introduce the new Norman lords by invitation, and so in a more or less ordered way. Indeed, the Normans were resisted by almost every Welsh king who was affected by them. The Norman adventurers who penetrated into Wales did so independently, but with what in England would have been recognized as typical Norman violence. And Wales, of course, was much divided, providing multiple points of entry for the invaders – yet at the same time this meant there were multiple points of resistance, particularly in the more mountainous areas.

The result was a chaotic process of advances and reverses. It soon became clear that local stability could only be achieved by the integration of Normans into the Welsh system, intermarriage, the elimination of competitors and the usual Norman brutality – and some of the victims were Welsh kings. Politically, the result was an even greater fragmentation of authority than had been the case under the Welsh rulers, as the invaders established themselves as lords, sometimes in small territories. The traditional Welsh regions continued to underlie all the changes – commotes and cantrefs were often the bases of the new Norman lordships. In all the areas of Wales where individual Norman lords established themselves, they did so in these small principalities, perhaps taking over the former Welsh local divisions or simply controlling the land around their castle. This invasion was not organized by any English authority, though kings occasionally intervened to assist or impede. It was not clear for some time how far the Normans in Wales remained answerable to the English king, especially those Normans who had no estates in England, and eventually their individual powers tended towards an independence of royal authority.

The penetration of Norman power into Wales began almost as soon as the first Marcher Earls – at Chester, Shrewsbury and Hereford – had been put in place by William I. Their original emplacement was primarily as a defensive system, to block any Welsh exploitation of the chaos into which England fell during his conquest. The Norman adventurers moved into Wales along the obvious routes, along the north coast, the valley of the upper Severn and the south coast, but these early forays generally failed, largely because of the over-confidence of the invaders, their shortage of manpower and their geographical over-extension. Initial resistance centred on the king of Deheubarth in South Wales, Rhys ap Tewdwr, and when he was killed in 1093 there followed a widespread Welsh rising which drove the Normans out of Gwynedd, Ceredigion and parts of South Wales. Several previous

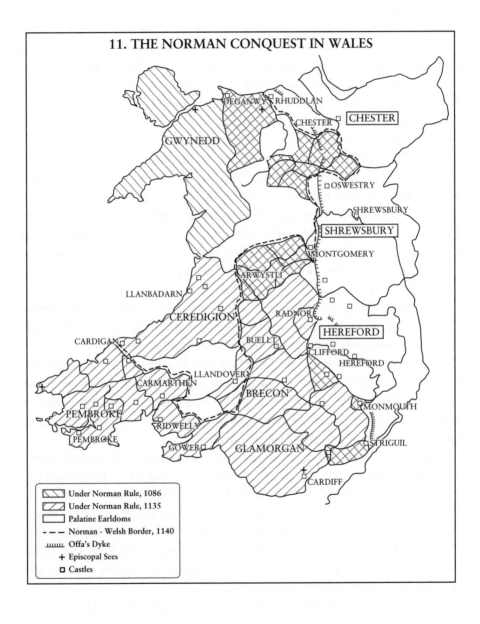

11. THE NORMAN CONQUEST IN WALES

CHESTER

DEGANWY RHUDDLAN

CHESTER

GWYNEDD

OSWESTRY

SHREWSBURY

SHREWSBURY

MONTGOMERY

ARWYSTLI

LLANBADARN

CEREDIGION

RADNOR

HEREFORD

CARDIGAN

BUELLT

CLIFFORD

HEREFORD

LLANDOVERY

CARMARTHEN

BRECON

MONMOUTH

PEMBROKE

KIDWELLY

PEMBROKE

GOWER

GLAMORGAN

STRIGUIL

CARDIFF

Under Norman Rule, 1086
Under Norman Rule, 1135
Palatine Earldoms
– – – Norman - Welsh Border, 1140
ⅢⅢⅢ Offa's Dyke
  + Episcopal Sees
  □ Castles

long-range conquests had to be abandoned; the following method relied on small advances, and it took a long time.

As a result, the main Welsh kingdoms survived. The Normans who campaigned through South Wales slowly imposed themselves on the Welsh population. The kingdoms of Gwent and Morgannwg vanished, and Dyfed in the south-west was seized by Norman lords who broke it into smaller lordships, though they mainly respected the Welsh archbishopric of St David's, while characteristically allocating to it a particular territory. King Henry I (1100–35) campaigned to stop the Welsh recovery. He built a royal castle at Carmarthen to supervise the whole of South Wales, and this became the base for royal power in the south. The English dynastic war between 1135 and 1154 encouraged further Welsh resistance and recovery, and a grandson of Rhys ap Tewdwr, Rhys ap Gruffydd – called 'the Lord Rhys' – strongly resisted the subsequent campaign of recovery by Henry II in the 1150s, until Henry gave up and recognized Rhys as the local lord. This stabilised the south for their lifetime. In the north, the authority of the king of Gwynedd had been re-established, after early Norman advances, by Gryffudd ap Cynan. The kings had thus succeeded in their resistance to later Norman attacks.

The successes of the Normans were very varied, but after the initial fighting ended, Welsh geography could be seen to have asserted itself. Norman penetration had overrun much of the more fertile parts of the south, along the Bristol Channel coast, and had largely failed in the mountainous areas of the centre and north. Early Norman settlement therefore largely replicated that of the Romans a thousand years before. The other lines of penetration, along the north coast and the upper Severn Valley, had been much more easily blocked by Welsh resistance.

And yet, despite Welsh resistance successes, substantial areas of Wales remained in Norman control. Along the line of Offa's Dyke, a complex series of small Norman lordships encroached over the border into traditionally Welsh territory, but then expanded as fragments of Welsh land were seized and converted into larger Norman lordships. The major Welsh kingdoms of Gwynedd, Powys and Deheubarth (the former Seisyllwg and Istrad Tywi) all survived, somewhat depleted in territory in several cases, but also strengthened by the need to fight the Normans.

The Normans built castles to hold what they had gained. The Norman advance was in large part a process of advances secured by castle-building. There were Rhuddlan and Deganwy on the north coast aimed at Gwynedd, Oswestry threatened north Powys, Montgomery was the base for advances along the upper Severn, Wigmore, then Knighton and Radnor were bases for campaigning towards Buellt, Clifford threatened Brycheiniog, Monmouth was a base from which to attack Gwent, and Striguil, Cardiff and Caerleon took Norman power into Glamorgan. Then, from the advance along the upper Severn, the Earl of Shrewsbury lunged into the south-west, and had planted his brother, Arnulf of Montgomery, in Pembroke, another castle.

The success of the Welsh resistance left only a few castles and lordships to the Normans; on the other hand, Gwent, Brycheiniog and Buellt were retained by their Norman lords, as were many of the lordships along the line of Offa's Dyke. That is, the process of conquest was erratic and slow and involved much fighting. After well over a century, most of Wales was still 'free', and Gwynedd, Powys and Deheubarth still had Welsh kings. Henry II, like Henry I, brought his royal power to bear, with no more success than many of the Marcher Lords; but the death of the more powerful Welsh rulers usually derailed the Welsh resistance. This had been the case at the death of Rhys ap Tewdwr in 1093, and it happened again at the death of his grandson in 1197.

The Welsh were as divided amongst themselves as the Normans, whose advances along different geographical routes isolated the invaders from other Norman campaigns. Also, the three Welsh kingdoms had occasionally allied with each other, though they faced different enemies, and were fully capable of including one of their fellow Welsh kings in their enmity. A decisive event came in 1160 when the king of Powys, Madog ap Maredudd, died, and his kingdom was then divided into four parts amongst his heirs, who were three of his sons and a nephew. It was never to be united again. When the Lord Rhys died in 1197, Deheubarth was also divided: two of his sons and two grandsons inherited parts of his kingdom. These divisions inevitably weakened their resistance decisively. So the Welsh system of inheritance, which had long prevented any permanent unification among the kingdoms, operated to undermine the effectiveness of Welsh resistance to its most dangerous opponent. By contrast, Gwynedd remained whole, a circumstance which shifted the base of the Welsh resistance to the north.

The net result in Wales was that the disunion of the country was made even more extreme. Particularly in the south, between the River Wye and Saint David's, the land was now divided between over a dozen minor Norman lordships, together with half a dozen under Welsh rule after the divisions, and there were more of both along the line of Offa's Dyke. Further, the Norman lords had their first loyalty directed towards the English king, at least in theory, and so they constituted an authentic 'fifth column' which would provide any conquering king with free entry into the country. The Norman assault had been slow and piecemeal. It was perhaps not yet menacing enough to threaten the independence of all Wales, and there had been plenty of distractions to direct the attention of English kings all through the twelfth century: complex disputes in England, English imperialism in France and the Norman invasion of Ireland. Wales after 1200 had a certain respite, but the condition of the country from an English king's viewpoint was obviously now interesting. All it needed was military power and a determination, and the 'Welsh problem' could be 'solved'.

The Further Norman Effect: Ireland

Ireland had been unaffected before 1100 by the Norman Conquest in England, and yet 'modern' influences were flying across the Irish Sea; above all, it was through the Church that they first began to arrive, thereby reversing the effect in Scotland. The Church throughout Europe was beginning to feel the effects of the reforms instituted by the imperialist Papacy during the later eleventh century, and by those involved in the regulation and reformation of monasteries and the expansion of new versions of the Benedictine rule. More than one Archbishop of Canterbury made a bid to bring the Irish bishops under his control, without any real success; he did succeed in Wales. The Archbishop of York tried the same in Scotland, but failed. This was also, of course, in a sense a manifestation of Norman power, and for Ireland it was a warning of approaching Norman interest in the island. The earliest trace of Norman influence appears to have been as much architectural as anything else – at the ancient ecclesiastical and political centre of Cashel, the year 1100 was marked by the inauguration of a new church, Cormac's Chapel, built on architectural principles imported from Europe. It stands next to one of those traditional cylindrical towers which dot the Irish landscape, and are marks of the pre-Norman ecclesiastical and political system. The new chapel was a harbinger of much change to come in Ireland in the coming century.

The Church's influence expanded. In 1142, the new monastery at Mellifont was founded with a small contingent of French Cistercian monks dispatched from Clairvaux on the instigation of Malachy of Down and Bernard of Clairvaux. The aim was for the French monks to instruct the Irish volunteers, just as fifty years before the Benedictine canons of Canterbury founded Queen Margaret's monastery at Dunfermline.

The scheme did not work out at Mellifont, and the French and the Irish soon quarrelled; the French left. No doubt the Irish understood quickly enough the imperialist impulse behind their arrival. It took over a decade to set up and build the basic Mellifont house, but even while it was being built, daughter houses were established, sometimes anew and sometimes by 'reforming' existing Irish monasteries. So the Cistercian 'family' spread throughout the island (except Ulster), and at the same time it took over a couple of earlier houses of the Savigny persuasion, founded earlier, but which had been struggling. There were seven daughter houses of Mellifont in existence before the building at Mellifont was finished in 1157, and another thirteen were founded before 1200. The effect of this campaign was powerful, and helped prepare Irish minds for the later invasion by the 'French'.

And it was the 'French' – specifically Norman French warriors from South Wales – who were the next, and rather more violent, invaders. They arrived by invitation of Diarmait Mac Murchada, the king of Leinster, who had struggled to maintain himself against a variety of enemies for thirty years. He had recently been driven out of Ireland by the High King Rory O'Connor, and now he returned with a Norman army to restore his kingdom. MacMurchada had earlier lent a fleet of his ships to Henry II, and Henry now repaid the debt. He gave Diarmait leave to recruit knights in South Wales, where many were idle thanks to the power of the Lord Rhys, who had stopped their depredations.

Diarmait eventually persuaded Richard de Clare, Earl of Striguil, also known as 'Strongbow', who had the name and influence to recruit a useful force. A series of expeditions crossed to Ireland in 1169 and 1170 and campaigned through Leinster, capturing three of the Viking towns – Wexford, Dublin and Waterford – and reinstalling Diarmait as king. They were too successful for Henry II's comfort, and he soon came to Ireland himself in 1171 to assert his sovereignty. This was decisive. Had he left the matter alone, the Irish might have gathered themselves together and driven the Normans out, but Henry's intervention firmly established the Normans. He conferred various grants and titles – Strongbow became Earl of Leinster, Diarmait having died in the meantime – and secured the submission of several of the Irish kings. But Ireland as a whole was not conquered by any means, and many of the Norman campaigns were only too clearly in the Irish mode, raids not conquest. When Henry left, therefore, he knew well enough that the work would keep the Norman invaders busy for many a year.

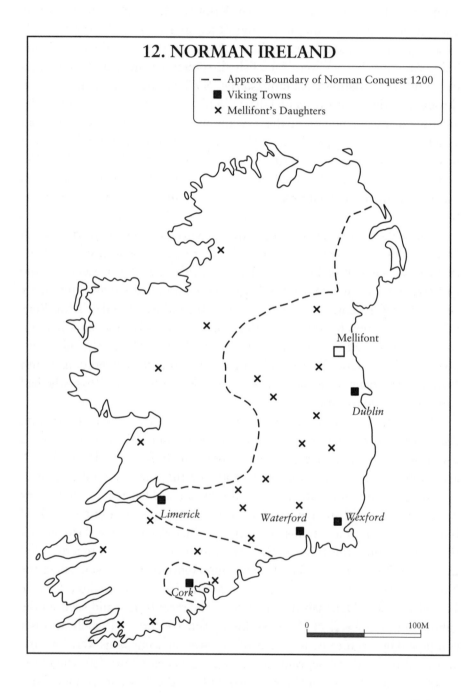

The High King Rory O'Connor, Diarmait's mortal enemy, had succeeded, when he drove Diarmait into exile, in establishing himself as the strongest High King for centuries. The Norman invasion, as Diarmait had intended, disrupted that position, and this resulted in new, or perhaps continuing, divisions in Ireland. The various Irish kings recovered from O'Connor's power, while the new Norman lords carved out lordships for themselves, increasing Irish divisions. It also introduced the ethnic enmity of Irish and Normans (which had been prefigured at Mellifont thirty years before).

The arrival of Norman power was surely not a surprise to any Irishman who could look overseas. Since the building of Cormac's Chapel at Cashel (where Henry II accepted the submission of the Irish kings and bishops during his brief visit), and the spread of the Cistercian monasteries from Mellifont, it should have been clear that a political and military invasion could well arrive at almost any time, especially after submitting to King Henry. Henry had persuaded the Pope as early as 1155 to sign off on a proposed royal expedition, and he had then taken the title 'Lord of Ireland'.

The only possible Irish reply would be to unify and organize for defence. Rory O'Connor might have had the strength to combat the invasion, but he was not in a firm position of power. Real unity was too extreme a solution for most of the Irish, and without unity there was little they could do. It was typical of Irish affairs that Diarmait MacMurchada put his own affairs before that of Ireland as a whole, and that Rory O'Connor was more concerned to bring Diarmait to subordination rather than to fight the Normans.

Conclusion.

The Norman presence in the British archipelago had a different effect in each of the four countries. It clamped decisively upon England a powerful governing system and a permanent political unity. In Wales it produced a condition of endemic warfare, and furthered the divisions which the Welsh polities had maintained since their origins. Even after a century of Norman attacks, their presence had not been enough to bring the Welsh to unification, though it was surely obvious that this was required. In 1170, these conditions were extended into Ireland by a new Norman invasion. This was in fact a relatively weak invasion, and its power had been stabilized in part by the English king (just as an earlier intervention in Wales had done the same). Henry II had enough problems elsewhere without spending years in Ireland.

In Scotland the effect of the Normans was different again, the reverse of the effect in Ireland, and without the violence and destruction in England. Their introduction reinforced the unification tendencies of King Malcolm Canmore and his successors, but without importing enough power to bring that unification about. So in three of the countries the Norman interventions had been disruptive in different ways, but inconclusive.

Bibliography:

See also earlier lists for Chapters 3 and 4.

Britain:

Carpenter, David, *The Struggle for Mastery, the Penguin History of Britain 1066–1284* (London: 2003).

Davies, R.R., *The First English Empire, Power and Identities in the British Isles, 1093–1343* (Oxford: 2000).

Frame, Robin, *The Political Development of the British Islands 1100–1400* (Oxford: 1990).

England:

Brown, R. Allen, *The Normans and the Norman Conquest*, 2nd ed. (Woodbridge: 1985).

Douglas, David C., *William the Conqueror, the Norman Impact upon England* (London: 1964).

Higham, N.J., *The Death of Anglo-Saxon England* (Stroud: 1997).

Holt, J.C., *Colonial England, 1066–1215* (London: 1997).

Kapelle, William E., *The Norman Conquest of the North, the Region and its Transformation, 1000–1135* (London: 1979).

Loyn, H.R., *The Norman Conquest*, 3rd ed. (London: 1982).

Mason, Emma, *The House of Godwin, the History of a Dynasty* (London: 2004).

Thomas, Hugh M., *The English and the Normans, Ethnic Hostility, Assimilation, and Identity, 1066–c.1220* (Oxford: 2003).

Scotland:

Barrow, G.W.S., *Kingship and Unity, Scotland 1000–1306* (London: 1981).

Ferguson, William, *Scotland's Relations with England, a Survey to 1707* (Edinburgh: 1977).

McDonald, R. Andrew, *Outlaws of Mediaeval Scotland, Challenges to the Canmore Kings, 1058–1266* (East Linton: 2003).

McDonald, R. Andrew, *The Kingdom of the Isles, Scotland's Western seaboard, c.1100–c.1336* (East Linton: 1997).

Oram, Richard, *David I, the King who made Scotland* (Stroud: 2008).

Oram, Richard, *The Lordship of Galloway* (Edinburgh: 2000).

Wales:

Davies, R.R., *The Age of Conquest, Wales 1063–1415* (Oxford: 1987).

Ireland:

Dolley, Michael, *Anglo-Norman Ireland* (Dublin: 1972).

Flanagan, Marie Therese, *The Transformation of the Irish Church in the Twelfth Century* (Woodbridge: 2010).

O Corrain, Donnchadh, *The Irish Church, its Reform, and the English Invasion* (Dublin: 2017).

O Croinin, Daibhi, *Early Mediaeval Ireland 400–1200* (Harlow: 1995).

PART II

ATTEMPTS TO UNIFY THE BRITISH ISLES

The existence of one powerful state among an array of much weaker brethren from 1066 put onto the international agenda the possibility that those weaker states could be enveloped by the greater into a single state. As it happened, the main interest of the kings of England from the Norman Conquest onwards turned to France, where large provinces could be acquired by inheritance. The 'Angevin Empire' faded away during the incompetent reign of King John, and later, under Edward I, expansion in the archipelago resumed, with only partial success – for Edward and his family also turned back to conduct warfare in France. When this failed, it took almost a century for the country to recover. But from about 1530 onwards a new campaign of expansion resumed under Henry VIII, based partly on inheritance and partly on conquest, and this time with some success, though it took over a century-and-a-half (1536–1691) to forge a united British state.

Chapter 6

Edward I's Wars

The English Dilemma

Henry II spent seven months in Ireland in 1171–72 and never returned there; he campaigned several times in Wales before reaching an agreement with the Lord Rhys in 1154; and he had to attend several times during his reign to Scottish invasions or problems. On the whole, however, these were clearly marginal to his main concerns, which were to maintain his grip on England and to service and preserve his vast domains in France. He was not helped by such intervening problems as the murder of Thomas Becket, Archbishop of Canterbury, and repeated rebellions by his sons; attending to Irish, Welsh or Scottish affairs was well down the list of priorities.

For his successors these problems were replaced by others, equally engrossing, the overall effect of which was to bring every king from Henry I to Henry III to a standstill: their international policies were overwhelmingly defensive and aimed at holding on, or shoring up, the lands they had inherited; as a result none could make any serious attempt to expand English power within the archipelago. Much of France was lost to the king of France by King John, but even then much English effort was directed into generally futile and expensive attempts to recover the lost lands, an issue which continued into the sixteenth century.

By campaigning from Ireland to Scotland and Normandy to Aquitaine, it was clear that the king of England was a powerful monarch. But having to do such extensive work strained that power to the utmost. It also aroused his enemies to unite. In such circumstances it proved to be very difficult for Henry II, for example, to think seriously and long-term about relations with the other lands of Britain. His attendances in Ireland and South Wales, and on the Scottish Borders, were directed mainly to restraining conflicts and securing peaceful local settlements which would last for a time and allow him to attend elsewhere, hence the agreement with the Lord Rhys and the carefully diplomatic visit to Ireland. An example of the possible linkages between his several problems came in 1178–79 when an internal rebellion by his son, Geoffrey, was exploited by both the Scots and the French. Thus there came into existence one of the enduring international relationships of the Middle Ages: the Scots' intermittent alliance with France. This was for the Scots a lifeline, and for the French it was a useful distraction when attacked or even threatened by the English. The advantage was almost always to the French; the costs were paid by the Scots.

There was, therefore, in all the contacts in the period after the conquest, no obvious intention on the part of any of the twelfth- or thirteenth-century kings to expand English power into any other part of the British Isles until the time of Edward I (1272–1307). Henry II reacted to events in Ireland, Wales and Scotland rather than shaping them, though it was clearly within English power to expand in the rest of Britain if king chose to. After all, it was a small Norman expedition which managed to secure a major foothold in south-east Ireland. Serious conquests in Wales would be quite possible – every expedition against Rhys ap Tewdwr had been an English victory, though he had restarted the fighting as soon as Henry withdrew. Relations with the Scottish kings might be generally peaceful, but they were sufficiently awkward that an excuse to attempt conquest could have been found without difficulty. Yet Henry II, who was the king who had the greatest opportunity to indulge in such a process of expansion between the reigns of William the Conqueror and Edward I, contented himself with requiring the king of the Scots to render homage, allowed the Welsh and Normans to balance each other in Wales and only went to Ireland to establish control over an adventurous South Wales vassal.

The conclusion must be made that the task of further English conquests was perceived by Henry II as being far too onerous for his resources. He might have been the lord of half of France, but this was hardly a source of strength in Britain, and it would be very difficult to bring French knights to Britain to indulge in conquest, though it was certainly possible to use English warriors in France. Henry II was thus fully conscious that he was over-extended, and any serious involvement in a war of conquest, which would certainly require the full resources of his kingdom, would immediately attract the predatory attentions of his other enemies. Maintaining his existing power and territory was taking all his strength; like the Roman Empire in its province of Britannia, the task of expanding his power into the rest of Britain was beyond him.

It was obvious that the English kingdom was the most powerful state in the islands. It was the only one which could successfully intervene in any or all of the others. The Irish and Welsh kingdoms did not, indeed could not, attack England with any hope of achieving anything but a hostile reply. Scotland could, and it is significant that this was the only other part of Britain which had made progress in unification. Had the English not been distracted by continental affairs, the rest of the islands could possibly have been conquered soon after the Norman conquest of England. The loss of much of the French lands in King John's reign might have therefore permitted that conquest to take place. Two things for the moment prevented it. One was the new king who followed John, his son, Henry III, who was a child at his accession and grew into an uncharacteristically pacific king. The other was that some French territories still remained to the English king, and so did the constant temptation to attempt to recover the lost lands. The result of this diversion of attention from England's neighbours was a long period of minimal English interference in them, and they could promote their own affairs. This meant the slow extension of royal power in Scotland, but a continuation of divisions in Wales and Ireland.

The Community of the British Isles: the Church's Influence

Another development was, however, also operating to make the possibility of political unity within the British Isles more likely. The expansion of Norman lordships into Scotland, Wales and Ireland had the effect of drawing those peripheral parts of the British Isles (peripheral from the English viewpoint, of course) into much closer relations with England than had existed before 1066. Furthermore, accompanying the arrival of Norman lords at the end of the eleventh century were monasteries founded to observe the procedures of the new Western reformed monasteries – Cluniacs, Benedictines, Carthusians, Cistercians and others. This process of reform in the Church had already been used by the Anglo-Saxon kings in the tenth century to boost their authority (and reduce that of the aristocracy, whose earlier control had extended to their 'own' monasteries, and of course the monastic lands). The reformed and reforming Papacy was in part behind this development, seeing these monasteries as useful shock troops in the Popes' aim to extend their power and authority throughout Christendom; another aspect of this was the establishment of bishops independent of the power of the kings, and therefore their rivals. There was quite enough in all this to keep every politician in Europe busy, but in many areas, including Britain, it was usually regarded through local political eyes.

The Scottish Church had been adjudged by a Council in 1072 to be part of the province of the Archbishop of York, though it seems unlikely that anybody in Scotland knew about this. (It was also the year of the Treaty of Aberfeldy, when William I marched an army into the heart of Scotland and imposed a subordinate treaty on King Malcolm III; a Council at York in that year was hardly likely to be on the side of the independence of the Scottish Church, or to be much noticed among these greater events.) The Council's decisions were ignored.

Queen Margaret, the wife of that same King Malcolm, began the process of importing Western European monasticism into Scotland by founding her own abbey at Dunfermline, basing the rule on the Benedictines of Canterbury. Her sons, Scottish kings ruling from 1097–1153, particularly David (1124–53), enthusiastically promoted their own foundations, while at the same time fending off any attempts by the Archbishop of York to establish his authority in the North (except in Galloway, whose bishops at Whithorn accepted York's supremacy until 1355).

The result was a gradual spread of the new monasticism throughout southern and eastern Scotland more or less in parallel with the importation of Normans as lords – indeed it was often Norman lords who founded the new monasteries – yet at the same time the churchmen and the kings always disputed any attempt by English kings and bishops to establish their authority in or over the Scottish Church. The number of bishops in Scotland slowly became localized at particular places on the usual European pattern – they eventually numbered twelve. Yet it was never possible for many centuries to secure the agreement of the Papacy to one of these bishops being raised to the status of archbishop. The claims of York were regularly put forward to prevent this; St Andrews was finally raised to an archdiocese in 1472 and Glasgow in 1495. So the Scottish Church remained different, a province without a head, for a long time, and yet still largely independent of English authority. The English influence in promoting reform and the foundation of new monasteries was thus acknowledged, but was strictly limited.

In Wales, at first, these new monasteries were not particularly liked because they tended to be promoted by Norman lords and bishops, who had their own political agendas in the matter. However, it did not take long before Welsh princes were founding their own versions, fully appreciating the increased prestige and power such actions provided to them. The Cistercians were particularly popular with the Welsh lords, and a string of Cistercian houses spread as far as the north coast. They began with Whitland in the south, founded in 1140 when the territory close to Carmarthen had been recovered from Norman rule by the Welsh during the English Civil War of the 1140s – a clear case of the political dimension of the process. On the other hand, these monasteries may have been founded by Welsh rulers, but there was no getting away from the fact that they were not originally Welsh, and that the Welsh tradition of monasticism faded away in the face of the more aggressive European types. In 1188, the Archbishop of Canterbury, Baldwin, made a preaching tour around Wales, and many of his stopping places were monasteries of this new and intrusive sort. His expedition was also a mark of the supremacy of his archdiocese over the Welsh bishoprics, and intended to reinforce that authority. These two developments in the Church in Wales were an indication that the country was being slowly drawn into closer association with the English.

Thus the difference between Wales and Scotland lay in the greater ability of the Scottish kings to resist English encroachments compared with the princes in Wales. This also applied in the bishoprics, where the Scots successfully resisted the pretensions of the archbishops of York, yet the four Welsh bishoprics were gradually subjected to Canterbury's authority in the first half of the twelfth century. Given the greater power and extent of the Scottish kingdom, and the extreme division of Wales, this is not surprising. The Scots could, with the support of the king, successfully dispute the attempts by York to control the Scottish Church; the lack of such a ruler in Wales meant that the English Church was able to establish its lordship over the four Welsh bishoprics without much difficulty. On the other hand, in both countries the spread of the Western European type of monasticism had its effect in bringing them both into some sort of ecclesiastical harmony with the rest of Europe, mainly England.

Ireland was different. There had been bishops in Ireland since St Patrick, and there never seems to have been any question that the country was an autonomous ecclesiastical province. No less than four Irish archbishops were recognized, with Armagh in the north as the primate, and Dublin, Tuam and Cashel in the east, west and south respectively; this was regularized at a Council in 1152. Like in Wales and Scotland, there had been a long local tradition of monastic devotion, but in 1127 the first of the new Western European type of monasteries became established at Erenagh in County Down (later removed to Inch), and then in Dublin, both of the Savigniac order. Mellifont was founded by Archbishop Malachy of Armagh in 1142 and daughter houses were then founded from the borders of Ulster as far south as Munster. By the end of the twelfth century there were twenty-one Cistercian monasteries in Ireland, all of them descended from the Mellifont original. The influence of Western Europe therefore began to pervade the country through the Church, its bishops, its monasteries and its architecture.

At the same time, the Irish Church had demonstrated that, while it was open to overseas innovation, it was also fully capable of organizing itself.

The extension of the authority of the Church in such ways was the intention of the reformed Papacy, but its instruments had to be local. So in Scotland and Wales the new monasteries were Norman and English in spirit, and were seen as embodying English influence; in Wales they went further, as the bishops were all appointed from Canterbury and consecrated at Westminster. In Ireland the impulse was French. Influences from England and the continent therefore flowed over Scotland, Wales and Ireland in various ways, particularly through the Church.

In Ireland the original invasion by Strongbow was followed by a widespread series of campaigns and conquests which resulted in Norman lords acquiring territory throughout much of the southern half of the island. At the same time, the ability of the Irish political and social system to absorb these outside intruders and make them their own – shown in the reaction to the earlier Viking attacks – was once again demonstrated, as the Norman intruders followed in the wake of the Vikings in becoming essentially Irish. As in Wales, they accommodated themselves quickly to the local conditions.

This ecclesiastical activity mirrored that of the Norman lords, indeed the two were often carried out by the same man. The effect was to link the four countries much more closely, both in Church affairs and in political matters. But the links were always between England and the other countries; there were few links between the several Celtic lands, apart from the original Welsh-Irish connection through Strongbow.

These Norman and Church linkages now for the first time brought the four neighbours into the approximation of a true community of states, the preliminary stage in the formation of a possible four-country union. Other links were less clear – for example, English and French (and Latin) were the only languages used in all four countries, but Welsh, Gaelic and Erse were the languages of the majority of the peoples in the periphery. Similarly, it is difficult to find other aspects of the community linkages, though commercial contacts were intensifying all the time. The net effect of Norman activity was thus to begin the construction of a community of British states.

Scotland: Expansion

In Scotland the successors of King David I gradually extended royal authority towards and into the territories which they claimed but did not directly control. Galloway in the south-west, Orkney in the north and the Isles in

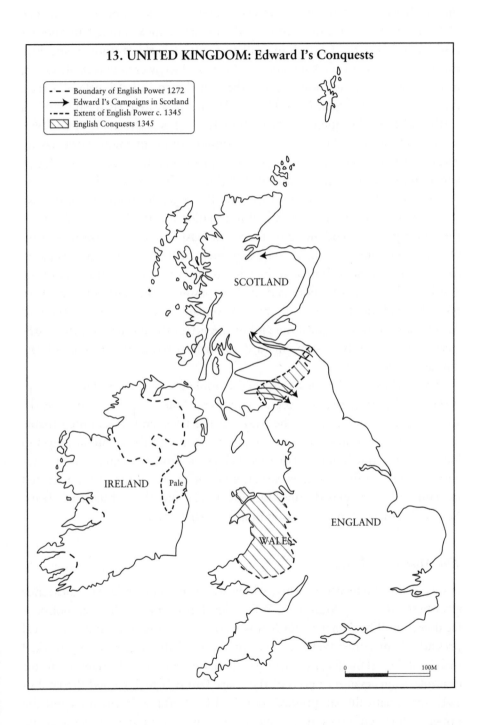

13. UNITED KINGDOM: Edward I's Conquests

- – – Boundary of English Power 1272
- ⟶ Edward I's Campaigns in Scotland
- ·–·– Extent of English Power c. 1345
- ▨ English Conquests 1345

SCOTLAND

IRELAND   Pale

WALES

ENGLAND

0   100M

the north-west were the main targets of their activities. The independence of Galloway was certainly suppressed, though it took more than another century to bring the Church of Galloway out of York's authority and into the Scottish system. Orkney and the Isles, in fact, were subject, distantly, to the Norwegian king until 1266, when, at the so-called Battle of Largs, the invading Norwegian King Haakon IV was 'defeated' (it wasn't really a battle). In the subsequent treaty he transferred his authority over the Isles to the Scottish King Alexander III, a curious example of a non-battle having great consequences. It was these consequences which led to the Largs encounter's reputation, not the non-fighting involved; it is as though no one could believe that a minor skirmish could have such important results, so the battle was invented. Legally and internationally, the Western Isles were thereafter part of Scotland and subject, at least in theory, to royal control. On the other hand, it proved to be extremely difficult for the Scottish king to exert any of that authority in the Isles in the face of the local power of the Lords of the Isles, who emerged in their power in the fourteenth century but who had predecessors in the Norwegian time. The lords exercised autonomous authority until the end of the fifteenth century. But the Largs treaty was certainly a step forward towards further integration for the kingdom as a whole.

The earldom of Orkney remained completely out of the king's grasp; it remained part of the Norwegian kingdom, though governed by its earls, who were as autonomous as the Lords of the Isles, and were quite capable of independent action. Disputes with pretenders to the Scottish kingship located in the north and north-west helped to limit the extension of royal authority in that direction, as earlier, while at the same time they attracted intermittent royal expeditions. Despite Largs and the subsequent treaty, Scotland remained in a condition of only partial unity.

The March of Wales

It was in the thirteenth century, which was a period of relative quiescence elsewhere, that the March of Wales developed into a distinct politico-legal region. The Norman lordships were not at this time under any real pressure from either Welsh princes or the English king, and they worked to consolidate their local control. In the large lordship of Glamorgan, for example, a succession of earls of the Clare family, which gained the land in 1217, systematically suppressed local Welsh chieftains in the hills and the upper valleys, either by disposing of them by conquest or by converting them into facsimile English. They enforced a strict jurisdiction over their Norman and English vassals, in the process creating a minor state. Other Marcher lords were doing much the same in their own lands. At the same time, pressures of depossession and inheritance were consolidating many lands under the control of a very restricted set of greater lords – the Clare, Mortimer and Braoze families in particular.

One result of this consolidation was the development in the March of the lords' near-independence of royal authority in matters of law. They could argue their need to be constantly armed and alert, given their frontier situation, and they developed a system of law which put them outside the scope of the English and Welsh legal systems. Marcher law had large elements of Welsh legal practice in it, including the right to wage 'private war' in a dispute with a neighbour. This harked back to privileges granted by earlier kings, which may or may not have been intended for the purposes they acquired, but which were accepted by long use. In the thirteenth century, the use of this law became normal in the March, and was, at times reluctantly, accepted by the kings. Its political effect was to detach the Norman lordships of the March into near independence of the king, and bring the Marcher lords closer to the independence of the Welsh kingdoms. Wales, in other words, both Welsh and Norman, remained almost entirely outside the reach of the English kingdom, even though many of the lords regarded themselves as subjects of the English kings. The kings were not pleased at this development, but when any of them attempted to suppress this 'private war', they generally failed.

The Partial Unification of Wales: the Princes of Gwynedd

It could not be said that English relations with Wales were peaceful in the thirteenth century, other than intermittently. The period was punctuated by frequent wars which eventually led to a series of campaigns of conquest. Each war was succeeded by a treaty which sooner or later broke down into another war. (It may be that these Welsh troubles were a major reason why Scottish relations were so peaceable during that century; England had room for only one serious neighbourly quarrel at any one time – a mark, once again, of the limits of English power, especially under an unmilitary king.)

The source of instability in Wales was the rise to dominance of the principality of Gwynedd. Its Welsh rivals, Deheubarth and Powys, had both broken down during disputes over inheritance. The consequent weakness of both these fragmented kingdoms opened the way for conquest

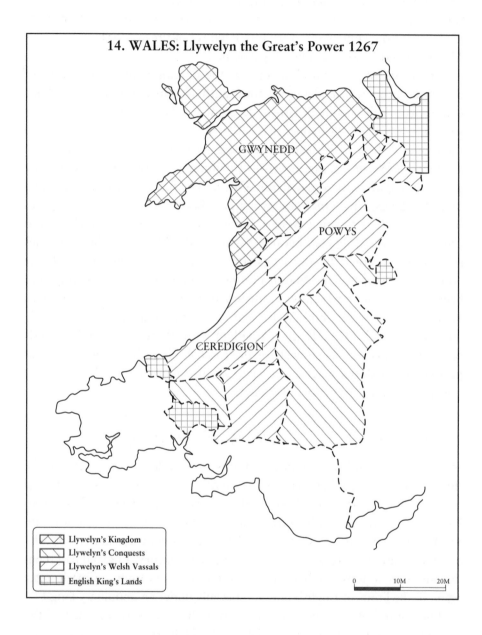

14. WALES: Llywelyn the Great's Power 1267

GWYNEDD

POWYS

CEREDIGION

Llywelyn's Kingdom
Llywelyn's Conquests
Llywelyn's Welsh Vassals
English King's Lands

0   10M   20M

by Welsh and English rulers. Gwynedd, on the other hand, was inherited whole through five generations of the family of Gruffydd ap Cynan (1081–1137); it also felt the heavy rule of Llywelyn ap Iorwerth (1194–1240), who disposed of his competitor relatives, uncles and cousins by murder and exile, and was thereby enabled to exert his power over the other Welsh kingdoms – it was he who presided over the partition of Deheubarth, for example, a perfect opportunity to acquire grateful allies. Naturally, he took advantage of the long internal crisis in England under King John, who gave him an illegitimate daughter, Joan, as his second wife to keep him quiet. Like the Scottish kings, Llywelyn involved himself in John's troubles, and eventually joined the baronial side as being the more likely to weaken the monarchy. (It was one of the Marcher lords, William Marshal, Earl of Pembroke, who emerged as the dominant political force during Henry III's minority.) Llywelyn also exerted himself to solve the internal disputes in the rival Welsh states – again collecting grateful allies – and took the opportunity to campaign vigorously against the Norman lordships, particularly in the south-west. At a Council of the Welsh princes held at Aberdyfi in 1216 (when Deheubarth was partitioned), Llywelyn was acknowledged openly as the overlord of the other Welsh rulers, and he began to use the title Prince of Wales, though not consistently. This was not an internationally recognized title; that is, it was not recognized by the English, which was the only recognition which would count. Recognition would have amounted to acceptance of the independence of Gwynedd, but no English king could do that.

Once a stable regime had become established in England, however, as was inevitable sooner or later, English power was exerted to recover what had been lost. King John had attempted to do this but had been distracted by his troubles at home, and it is noticeable that the Council at Aberdyfi in 1216 had coincided with war in England. Llywelyn's achievement was, in fact, the long-delayed effect of the pressure exerted on Wales since the arrival of the Normans in England in 1066, but it was made possible by the English preoccupations, and was also due to the partitions of Llywelyn's Welsh rivals. It had become all too obvious that divisions in Wales permitted the extension of Norman power throughout the south and along the Marches, and continued divisions amongst the Welsh princes had permitted the English to advance further. Llywelyn therefore argued successfully for a preliminary stage of unity amongst the Welsh princes, with himself as paramount prince, and he made it his policy to insist that internal Welsh disputes be settled peacefully, usually by him, in accordance with Welsh law, while at the same time he made strenuous efforts to substitute primogeniture for partible inheritance. It was the beginning of the development of a stage of partial unity.

To a degree Llywelyn was successful. When he died in 1240, his whole principality passed to his son, Dafydd (who was thus the grandson of King John). His daughters were married to several of the Marcher lords, and another to John, Earl of Huntingdon and Chester, a member of the Scottish royal house. Yet Dafydd did not have the force of personality of his father, or his longevity, and it became clear that the English had become very suspicious. A war between 1244 and 1247, during which Dafydd died, resulted in the partial collapse of Llywelyn's principality. In the Treaty of Woodstock in 1247, several Welsh territories were annexed to the English crown, including the considerable territory of Is-Conwy in the north, taken from Gwynedd, whose loss pushed the Gwynedd boundary back to the River Conwy. In central Wales, Buellt was recovered by the king; Carmarthen and Cardigan castles were also recovered, and Llanbadarn in Ceredigion was acquired. The defeat of Gwynedd also destroyed the overlordship and putative unity which Llywelyn had established over the other Welsh principalities.

A combination of factors soon reversed this Welsh defeat. Financial troubles in England forced a distinct weakening of royal power there, while at the same time the achievements of Llywelyn were inspirational in Wales; his nephew, another Llywelyn (ap Gruffydd), seized the moment to recreate the unity which had been destroyed in 1247. In the event, several years after the treaty, it proved to be very easy to do this, suggesting strongly that general opinion in Wales favoured the new unity that was now being re-established, and that the loyalty to the local states had been significantly weakened. The area of Is-Conwy in the north was recovered by negotiation, which returned the boundary of Gwynedd to the Dee estuary. Llywelyn was able to campaign without interruption to recover suzerainty over Ceredigion, remove the royal estate at Llanbadarn and seize Buellt, which had also become a Crown land by the treaty. Suzerainty was then established over the princes in the Tywi area in Deheubarth and in northern Powys, and enforced on southern Powys. At another Council, in 1258, where just about all the Welsh rulers were present, Llywelyn was accorded the definitive title of Prince of Wales, implying that the other rulers accepted their subordination to him.

England descended into another civil war during Llywelyn's advance, and its continued disruption provided him with an opportunity to secure a new treaty, the Treaty of Montgomery, in 1267. Llywelyn's gains since the earlier treaty were accepted, and he had therefore re-established the unity of the Welsh territories, more positively than before, and had also succeeded in conquering, and so eliminating, several of the Marcher lordships. His direct power stretched from the North Wales coast to within a few miles of the Bristol Channel.

However, the unity of Wales was still only partial and fragile. It had, as before, been achieved at English expense at a moment of extreme English distraction and weakness, which would not continue, while it was also the case that not all the Welsh princes were pleased to be subordinated to the man from Gwynedd; Gruffydd ap Gwenwynwyn of southern Powys, for example, did not submit for several years after being driven out of his principality. Most Welsh princes retained their territories, and their subordination to Llywelyn was thus only conditional on his continued success and activity. The conquered, and in some cases dispossessed, Marcher lords became a vocal centre of complaint in England, while some of Llywelyn's territorial gains had also been at the expense of the king's lands.

Nobody seriously expected the situation brought about by Llywelyn's victories to last, but the denouement was delayed by the need for England to recover, by the absence of the king's son, Prince Edward, on crusade in Palestine from 1270–74, and by the death of Henry III in 1272. But once Edward returned from the East in 1274 and assumed the kingship, he would necessarily have to turn his attention to the matter of Wales.

The Partial Unification of Wales: Edward I

Llywelyn I and II had brought about a partial unification of Wales, comparable to the condition of England and Scotland in the ninth and tenth centuries. He controlled his own kingdom and his conquests, and dominated the other Welsh states, but most of the Marcher lords in South Wales remained out of his reach, as did several in the south-east and along Offa's Dyke. Territorially, Llywelyn controlled only about half of Wales, and he clearly realized the limited nature of his achievement. He made various moves to enlarge his territories, presumably assuming that the weakness of the English government which had allowed his earlier expansion would continue. In particular he got into a continuous low-level dispute with Earl Gilbert in Glamorgan, whose Clare lands were now the largest of the Marcher lordships. When Edward I issued the usual summons to go to London to do homage, Llywelyn failed to obey; after argument, he effectively refused.

This brought the matter to a decision by Edward. In essence, Llywelyn was stating his independence.

This was, of course, not the only issue, and a series of moves by Llywelyn, each of which was fairly unimportant, but which cumulatively proved to be thoroughly annoying to Edward, were eventually perceived as a challenge to Edward's royal authority. Edward's reply was inevitably military. He conducted a major series of invasions along the traditional invasion routes. The main one was along the North Wales coast aimed at the heart of the Gwynedd principality, and a second, subordinate campaign went into central Wales along the upper Severn into the Marcher lands and royal lands which Llywelyn had recently taken. A third invasion went into Deheubarth from the south, based on the royal castle of Carmarthen, aimed at detaching the princes of Deheubarth from Llywelyn and recovering Llanbadarn. A further minor force marched along the upper Wye towards Brecon. Edward was assisted by the rapid defection of those Welsh princes in Powys and Deheubarth who only ten years before had accepted Llywelyn's suzerainty. It was thus seen that, at least at the royal level, no real sentiment for Welsh unity existed.

Nevertheless, Edward found that the campaign was slow, difficult and expensive, and he was quite willing to settle for Llywelyn's defeat rather than his removal. The subsequent Treaty of Aberconwy resulted in a great increase in the royal position in Wales, largely at the expense of Llywelyn's expanded principality, though Llywelyn still ruled Gwynedd. Welsh princes still ruled in much of Deheubarth and the two parts of Powys. Llywelyn's brother, Dafydd, with whom he was at odds, was given a large part of Is-Conwy. The crown's territories expanded strongly around Carmarthen, gained Buellt and the northern half of Deheubarth around Llanbadarn, and the king took control of the coastal route along the north coast as far as Deganwy and the River Conwy crossing. Deprived Marcher lords recovered their losses.

This was no more than a temporary suspension of hostilities. Edward's settlement attempted to further divide the Welsh by creating the small principality for Llywelyn's brother, but this only whetted Dafydd's appetite and when he began fighting to acquire more territory Llywelyn supported him. This seems to have persuaded Edward that Wales must be conquered completely. The new war came in 1282, only five years after the Aberconwy treaty.

The campaign was not particularly difficult, for the strategy was obvious, and had been practiced already in the first war. Llywelyn began

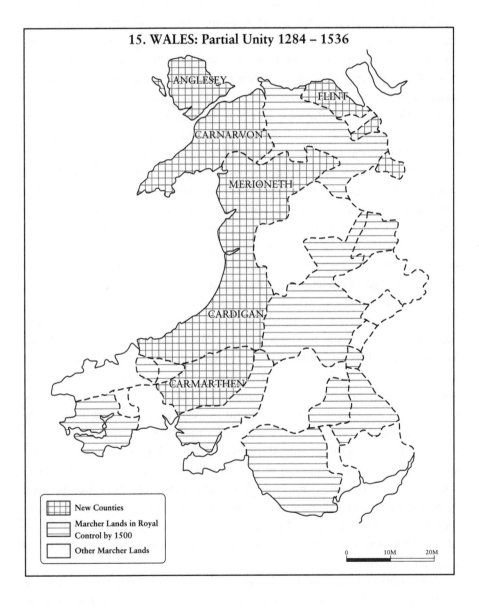

15. WALES: Partial Unity 1284 – 1536

ANGLESEY

FLINT

CARNARVON

MERIONETH

CARDIGAN

CARMARTHEN

New Counties

Marcher Lands in Royal Control by 1500

Other Marcher Lands

0   10M   20M

by launching a major offensive south from Gwynedd, designed to recover control over the Welsh territories he had dominated earlier, clearly expecting local Welsh support; Edward's strategy was a major North Wales campaign directed at the Gwynedd heartland, and subsidiary campaigns into central and South Wales mounted from Montgomery and Carmarthen. Edward had started building castles to hold his territories during the first war, and had continued building more in his new territories after the Treaty of Aberconwy. Llywelyn had done the same, confronting Montgomery, for example, with a castle at Dolforwyn, which became the first target of the English campaign. One of the causes of the new war was Llywelyn's imitation of Edward's policy by beginning the construction of that very castle. Castle building was extended by Edward, in order to hold all Wales in its stony grip.

Welsh successes were rapidly reversed and led to the definitive English conquest. By attacking Gwynedd with his main force, Edward compelled Llywelyn to return from his southern expedition to defend his own kingdom. He blocked the English advance, but then returned to mid-Wales in December 1282, where he was killed in battle. Dafydd assumed the leadership of Gwynedd, but by this time the English, buoyed by the death of the Welsh leader, were able to defeat and capture him.

This ended the war, which the English king regarded as a rebellion – Dafydd was executed as a traitor. Edward's success was so complete that the decision was made to suppress most Welsh princes and to reorganize Wales along English lines. The castles were multiplied and dotted around, particularly in the north of the country. Conwy and Caernarvon were especially notable constructions, displaying strength and size in an obvious aim to suggest permanence and power, and to be intimidatory. The territories of the princes in Deheubarth were taken over, and along with Gwynedd were organized into shires on the English pattern. Six new shires were created, four of them out of the territories of the Gwynedd dynasty – Anglesey, Caernarvon, Flint and Merioneth. Gwynedd was thus divided, in part in order to weaken local loyalties, but also for ease of administration. Two more shires were created from Deheubarth, centred on the royal castles of Cardigan and Carmarthen. These shires were therefore annexed to the English kingdom.

The southern part of Powys remained with its Welsh ruler, the old enemy of Llywelyn, who had taken the English side in the war. The Marcher Lords had held to Edward's alliance, so he could hardly annex them; they remained intact and their privileges were confirmed. The result was that Wales was still divided, this time between the many Marcher lordships along the Midlands border and in the south, and the group of royal shires in the north and west.

This period, in which Llywelyn II and Edward I fought their wars over the future of Wales, was in fact the second part of the preliminary unification of the country. The two Llywelyns, and principally Llywelyn II, achieved that often enough to show that a united Wales could be a viable state if the English had left it alone – though it was the English threat which was most persuasive towards unity. The English conquest in effect took over the extended principality of Gwynedd and united the Welsh part of the country, but left the rest of Wales alone. Edward's conquest was therefore as limited as was the Llywelyns' principality. Everybody in Wales was now a subject of the king of England, but Wales was still treated as a separate country, and was in part subject to a military occupation. From many points of view this was unsatisfactory, and Wales was to be the scene of a major rebellion in 1294–95, and then a century later Owain Glyndwr succeeded in more or less uniting Wales, shires and Marcher lordships together, for a brief period before going down to defeat in the face of the usual overwhelming English power. (His success, as usual, coincided with a period of English weakness and confusion.)

It is noticeable that the preliminary moves towards unification in Wales had come from the princes of Gwynedd, whose campaigns had destroyed the previous geopolitical arrangement, by reducing the rival Welsh rulers to subjection, and by evicting many of the Marcher lords. This development was quickly seen by the English as a threat, and lead to the repeated warfare between 1216 and 1295, as a result of which the process of unification was in effect taken out of Welsh hands and imposed on Wales by the English kings. Edward I, therefore, played the part in Welsh history which Edward the Elder played in English. This was not yet the full unification which the Normans had imposed on England: the divided legal system, the mixture of royal counties and Marcher lordships, not to mention the two languages, continued a new sort of division. It was instead only the first unification stage, partial unification. Full unification would not come for well over two more centuries.

The Matter of Scotland

It was, of course, coincidental that a major succession crisis in Scotland followed on almost at once from Edward I's conquest of Wales, and yet the latter experience, and its success, clearly had an influence on the king's approach to the Scottish problem. The death of King Alexander III in 1286 had been preceded by the deaths of all three of his children, with the result that his heir was his infant grand-daughter, Margaret, the daughter of the marriage of King Eric II of Norway and Alexander's daughter. The child was brought across the North Sea to Scotland but died in 1290. The direct line which descended from David I had therefore died out. By this time all the competing descendants of earlier kings, the MacWilliams and others, who had been rebelling regularly for two centuries, had also ended.

Inheritance by primogeniture had become the practice in Scotland since the time of David I, though there was no definition of this in legal terms. A careful examination of David's other descendants showed that Margaret's nearest heir was John Balliol, who was lord of Barnard Castle in Yorkshire and Lord of Galloway through his wife. He held extensive estates in England, as well as the family's ancestral estate at Bailleul in Ponthieu in France. This conclusion was contested by Robert Bruce, lord of Annandale. These were the two main contenders, 'the Competitors' they were called, though there were plenty of others, eleven in all, with Henry Hastings and the Count of Holland also in with plausible claims. Balliol and Bruce, however, were clearly recognized as having the best credentials. The main problem was, of course, that there was no legal definition of the right of succession. But by accepting that the infant Margaret should become queen, the Scots had also accepted that descent through the female line was acceptable; all claimants based themselves exactly on this point. It is noticeable that the claimants were all Normans, which might be considered another aspect of the disruption the Normans had brought, if it was not that the Scots had inflicted the succession problem on themselves. We might alternatively see it as the triumph of the Normans, whose competence and judicious marriages had brought so many of them to such eminence.

There was clearly a real danger of civil war over the issue, for it seemed impossible to decide the matter within the kingdom. A civil war might well have been the best solution; it might be brief and decisive, with one single clear and obvious winner, who would then found a new dynasty (and in fact a particularly nasty civil war did in the end occur). However, first, there was also Edward I.

Edward had a number of interests in the Scottish situation. First, he regarded himself as the overlord of Scotland, a position which kings of England had repeatedly managed to enforce since William I and Malcolm III at Aberfeldy in 1072 (or even by Athelstan in 937). This was, however, an assertion which the Scottish kings had rarely accepted more than briefly. Edward was able to collect a certain number of historical records to demonstrate it, though the Scots would never be convinced by them. Several of the Scottish kings had, in various ways and on varying terms and with various degrees of sincerity, performed homage, but this was not necessarily conclusive for everyone, and enforcing the suzerainty had rarely gone further than Scottish kings fighting in France briefly on the English king's side. They had also been allies of France at times, and more frequently at war with the English kings. Edward's claim to overlordship remained to be proved; it was an assertion, no more.

Edward was also concerned as Scotland's immediate neighbour, a neighbour with whom the Scots had been frequently at war. Who ruled there was clearly of material concern to him. He had, when Queen Margaret was alive, suggested that she be betrothed to his own son, Edward (later Edward II), who had been born in 1284 and was immediately made Prince of Wales. The aim was clearly to put the younger Edward in as king of Scotland, while the elder Edward would act as the regent and guardian of the Scottish kingdom. It may indeed have been this which was the origin of Edward's eventual policy which was aimed at uniting the two kingdoms, as he had England and Wales.

Once it became clear that the Scots could not solve the succession issue themselves, Edward was the obvious arbitrator, and his offer to do this coincided with a request by the Bishop of St Andrews. Inevitably he used his position to attempt to develop his claim to be the overlord and so the investigator of the claims. For the Scots it seemed to be a useful legal fiction by which to avoid a civil war – or having to decide the matter themselves. But merely by asking Edward to intervene, the Scots were in a way accepting his pretensions to suzerainty. He tried to get his own interpretation accepted collectively, but had to be content with individual submissions by many of the Scottish lords; this ensured that the decision reached on the kingship would be accepted. A conference followed to discuss the process and the powers of all involved, and in the end Edward's position, somewhat modified to reduce the incidence of his power in Scotland, was accepted as an arbitrator by all the contenders.

Edward spent July 1291 touring eastern Scotland as far north as Perth. The actual decision about the succession was made in a conference at Berwick attended by forty men nominated by Bruce and forty by Balliol, with twenty-four nominated by Edward. After much discussion, the decision was that John Balliol was to be recognized as king. This would have been sufficient to solve the issue, except that Edward now stated his price. He made Balliol perform homage, proclaimed his own rights as overlord to set aside any judgments made in Scots courts and demanded that Balliol perform military service in his coming campaigns in France. The first of these was perhaps expected, and such homage had been performed by earlier Scots kings, without restricting their power. The third demand had also happened before, and Alexander III, King John's predecessor, had campaigned in France with the English army with no ill effects in Scotland. The second demand, however, was a direct interference by the English king in Scottish internal affairs, and would easily develop into a powerful restriction on the sovereignty of both the king and the country. Edward chose an awkward case in order to exercise that power, and deliberately reversed the Scottish legal decision. It became clear to the Scots that King John Balliol was not capable of combating this assault on their independence – he was, of course, in a very difficult personal position, and clearly did not feel he could simply repudiate the agreement, since this might invalidate his occupation of the throne.

Yet it was neither the homage King John proffered, nor the insulting demand to oversee the Scottish legal decisions, which finally brought on the crisis, but Edward's demand for military service in France, for he demanded it not simply from the king, but from Scottish knights individually and by name. This was not what had happened before, for then the Scottish king had gone to war accompanied by a group of knights who were his own men and who had travelled because they were in his service. Edward was now directly demanding military service from Scottish knights without going through King John or even asking his permission, doing so as overlord of the kingdom. It was a demand which went too far for the Scots, and a group of lords took the decision out of King John's hands. He was set aside – though not deposed – by these Scottish lords in 1295. They took over the government of the kingdom, and made an alliance with King Philip of France, with whom Edward was now actively at war.

Edward had pushed to an extreme the subordination which he had compelled the Scottish king to accept, without seriously considering the reaction it might cause. He clearly understood, however, the position into which he had put King John, which paralyzed him between his word to Edward and his duty to the Scots, and this was presumably deliberate. It may be noted that it was the issue of homage and its implications which had finally brought on the war in Wales; all these rulers clearly took the matter very seriously, and felt it was crucial to their authority and reputation.

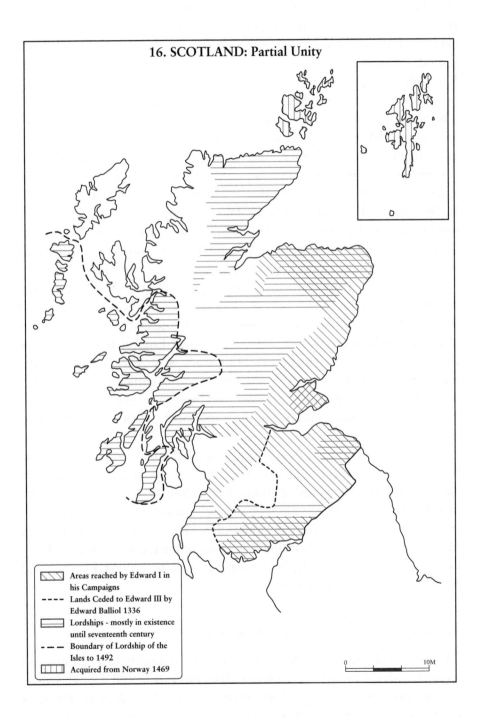

16. SCOTLAND: Partial Unity

Areas reached by Edward I in his Campaigns

Lands Ceded to Edward III by Edward Balliol 1336

Lordships - mostly in existence until seventeenth century

Boundary of Lordship of the Isles to 1492

Acquired from Norway 1469

0   10M

But the wider situation with regard to Scotland was very different from that for Wales – in particular, Wales was defeated more than once and had been militarily conquered and occupied, whereas Scotland had only been visited – and no Welsh Prince of Wales had existed to be intimidated as King John was. Edward was attempting in Scotland to reach his final Welsh position without having to go through the awkward stages of conquest. The Scots' sidelining of King John brought Edward to the military stage, and he reacted by launching an invasion. Moreover, since the Scots had allied themselves with France, with which he was already at war, he had a reasonable *casus belli*. His aim was to reduce the Scots lords to obedience, and in a long campaign as far north as the Moray Firth he largely succeeded. In the process he compelled King John to abdicate, and then sent him to imprisonment in England. This was not accepted by the Scots, who continued to regard him as their king for several more years. King John was then transferred to the Pope's custody, who gave him to the French.

Apart from a brief fight at Dunbar, Edward's march was generally unopposed, and he could assume that he had succeeded in subduing the country. But as soon as he went back to England a rising began in reaction, Sir William Wallace defeating a small English force at Stirling Bridge. This was sufficient to both bring many Scots back to aim for their independence and to enrage Edward, but it was not sufficient to secure that independence. The English 'conquest' had been so superficial that it could be undone by a minor setback, but the minor Scots victory was insufficient to guarantee success.

This was not what Edward had intended, and certainly not what he wished to happen, but he took what he now saw as an opportunity to eliminate the Scottish kingship and so bring Scotland to the same condition of subordination as Wales. He was, that is, moving on from imposing his suzerainty on the Scots through a subordinate king to subduing the country in total, and, like Wales, remaking it as a part of his English kingdom. From establishing his dominance, he was moving on to uniting England and Scotland into a single kingdom.

The Independence of Scotland Regained

The war which followed lasted, with truces, for a quarter of a century, and its aftermath continued for many decades longer. It is well enough known so that only the most important points need to be made here. (It is, of course, much better known in Scotland than in England, though not in detail even there, and often inaccurately; only the Scottish victories are accepted as worth relating.) For ten years, the Scots were without a king.

Edward campaigned almost every year in various parts of the country, but without reaching a final victory; and, of course, the more he attacked and sacked and burnt, the less likely it was he would ever do so. He faced the perennial English problem of a war in France and one in Scotland simultaneously, and he also had to survive a major financial crisis. Like other commanders who controlled England, his wars were stretching his resources to breaking point – Agricola would have sympathized.

Nevertheless, Edward was steadily making progress. It was above all necessary to control the Scottish lords, and this meant bringing them to obedience, defeating them if they were in arms, persuading them that English suzerainty or union was advantageous, or if they were recalcitrant carrying them off to English prisons. By 1304, much of this had been accomplished. The key to persuasion appeared to be the Comyn family, while in military terms control of Stirling Castle was crucial. In 1303–04, the castle was taken by siege, and John Comyn of Badenoch organized a large-scale Scottish submission in 1304. Next year, the leader of the military opposition, Sir William Wallace, was captured, tried for treason to King Edward and executed. In 1305, Edward attempted to organize Scotland as a part of England, with a governor ('warden'), but with strategic military positions garrisoned by English troops. Scots law was to be subject to amendment and there would be no king of Scotland; it was a similar conclusion to that imposed in Wales.

This marked the high point of Edward's policy in Scotland, but also the point at which the Scots' willingness to accept that he was offering a reasonable and moderate solution ended. Most Scots still took King John to be their king, but it was clear that he would never return. The next in line for the succession, Robert Bruce (the son of the original claimant), also realized that Edward's intentions would deny him the throne. He met John Comyn, the head of the family who had been working, somewhat reluctantly, with Edward, but they could not agree that Bruce should replace King John. Bruce sacrilegiously murdered Comyn, and was then illegally crowned at Scone by a group of his followers.

Robert Bruce clearly timed his meeting, his *coup d'etat* and his declaration of himself as king with English exhaustion in mind, together with the fact that Edward, by 1306, was clearly dying. When he did die the next year, the campaign he had begun against Bruce failed. Bruce had little support in Scotland at first and fought a guerrilla war for several years, mainly in the north. During this time he slowly gathered support, and eliminated opponents, assisted by English devastation tactics. He was eventually able to face the English army in the field at Bannockburn, and defeat it, in 1314. The war then spilled over into Ireland, where Bruce's brother, Edward, campaigned for three years, aiming to secure an Irish kingdom for himself, at the expense of both the English in Ireland and the Irish themselves. He used the English devastation methods to advance his cause, with as little success as Edward had in Scotland. King Robert took the war into northern England as far south as York, though this was essentially a series of intimidatory raids, not an attempt at conquest.

Long before the war was brought to an end (in 1328) it was clear that the attempt Edward I had made to unite England with Scotland, however tentatively, had failed. It was in fact clear enough at the time of the financial crisis in 1297, and had Edward accepted the implications of that, much misery might have been avoided. A revival of the Balliol claim in the person of John's son, Edward, in the 1330s was just as unsuccessful as that of his father, but it also highlighted the weakness of the Bruce kingship – Robert I had never had the full support of all the Scots, his murder of Comyn of Badenoch was always held against him, and he had seized power illegally and enforced it by a civil war. In that war, many Scots lords had been driven into exile or killed, and their lands seized and given to Bruce partisans. Only his eventual success in the war against England excused him.

These wars therefore caused major changes in the lordships in Scotland, as supporters of the Bruce kingship replaced his opponents. In other words, the war in Scotland was also a type of civil war, a result of the methods used by Bruce to seize the throne and to fight to keep it. But the process did result in his supporters succeeding. This was indicated in 1320 when they put their names to an appeal for the Pope to assist in the ending of the wars. The 'Declaration of Arbroath' was a claim to national independence, but it was not, so far as can be seen, acknowledged by the Pope, still less by the king of England. Its importance has been much exaggerated by Scots.

Robert I died in 1329. His successor was a child, David II, who was soon captured and imprisoned by the English. Edward Balliol, John's son, seized the throne briefly, then had to be supported by English forces. Edward III (1327–77) – who also seized the throne by a *coup d'etat*, which involved the murder of his father – organized the Scottish borderlands as a series of English shires, just as his grandfather had done in Wales. The rest of the country was divided for a time between supporters of Edward Balliol and David II. Balliol's position gradually faded, and when David returned to

Scotland in 1341, he fairly quickly gained control. Edward III held onto some Border towns, as a forward defence against a repetition of the deeply unpleasant raids which had so damaged northern England under Robert I, at a time when he was embarking on a new war in France. But it was also a recognition that his grandfather's and father's attempts to unite England and Scotland had failed.

This had perhaps been in Edward I's mind since the attempt to organize the betrothal of his son and the infant Queen Margaret, but until 1296 he was aiming to support King John. It was very like his Welsh policy, taking account of the differing circumstances. In both cases Edward had begun with a quarrel and had kept pushing until he brought the country to submission, clearly hoping that the submission of the king or prince would be sufficient, but it never was. The Welsh fought three wars in fifteen years before they were subdued; the Scots fought twice as long, and in the end only just escaped, due in large part to Edward III's involvement in war in France. Both countries suffered extensive damage, damage which also extended over much of the North of England and into a large part of Ireland. This was the cost of the attempts to unite Wales and Scotland with England; it was clearly a policy in which force would not easily bring success.

Decline in Ireland

Ireland had not been at the forefront of English royal concerns since the time of King John (of England), who was made Lord of Ireland by his father, and made some progress in developing an effective royal administration. The policy of granting estates to individual Anglo-Norman lords, and then expecting them to conquer the lands awarded, was successful in the central area of the island, but it did mean that the process of conquest was patchy. In some areas Irish resistance was strong enough to block any Norman advances, in others the Norman lord was unwilling to persist in the face of difficulties, or preferred to stay on his estates in England.

The method of conquest used was the usual Norman system of war. Using a relatively small force of mixed infantry and armed knights, a territory was conquered and then a castle was built to hold it. This was therefore a different form of war from the usual Irish methods, which had been raids and devastations followed by withdrawal with booty and slaves. The Normans, by contrast, occupied and held their conquests. The early castles, as in England and Scotland, were mottes (or motes), mounds of earth crowned by a stout wooden fort. Some were later replaced by stone castles, and these two sets of buildings map out the Norman progress. Stone castles in particular attracted people to form a market town next to them, and as the Norman efforts were spread the urbanization of Ireland advanced from the coastal towns which had been founded by the Vikings into the Midlands and the south.

The Anglo-Norman assault, which is how the Irish see it, had therefore succeeded in securing some sort of control by the Norman lords over much of the southern half of the island, and by 1300 shires had been organized in much of that area, though their effectiveness varied. Several of the families which dominated much of Irish history – Butler, Burke, Fitzgerald and so on – owed their origins to royal grants in these early years. Other areas were set aside as 'liberties' – Ulster under John de Courcy was the most successful one. This mixture of advances and castle building meant that the area under Anglo-Norman control became very similar in its mixture of direct royal rule and semi-independent lordships to that of the Welsh March before Edward I's wars. The island was in theory governed by sheriffs and English lords, but the lords, like the Welsh Marcher lords, had a strong tendency to independence. Parts of Ireland in the west and north, notably in Ulster west of the River Bann and in much of Connacht, were unsubdued.

Such a policy might have succeeded in the end in bringing all Ireland under English occupation, though it would have taken a long time and considerable reinforcements from England. Periodic campaigns by English kings would have helped, but English kings after John devoted themselves to warfare elsewhere. Further progress came to an abrupt halt with the Scottish invasion led by Edward Bruce in 1315. Bruce's actions demonstrated that events in any one of the four countries of the British Isles could have repercussions in the others. His campaign of devastation was directed at the English position in Ireland, but it affected the Irish even more.

Even before this, the Norman wars had been conducted by Norman knights (speaking French), archers who had been largely recruited in Wales and infantry recruited in Flanders or England. The Scots invasion thus was hardly a surprise, though it was extremely unpleasant. Between 1315 and 1318, Edward Bruce made a serious attempt to remove English power from Ireland and replace it with his own, which would make him king of Ireland – he was actually proclaimed High King in 1316. A preliminary agreement had been made with a group of Irish lords so that his campaigns were deliberately directed against Norman power. Edward won several victories, and devastated any Norman lord's lands which he could reach. The result was widespread misery – this was also a time when the whole of Europe was suffering famine. Bruce was finally defeated and killed in 1318, but his campaigns had been so destructive to the Norman lordships that they gravely weakened the whole Norman presence in Ireland.

The Scottish war occupied English attention for about forty years, followed by French wars launched by Edward III. All this prevented any further serious English involvement with Ireland, although by directing English aggressiveness towards France, it now spared Scotland. Gradually the extent of English authority in Ireland shrank, and many Irish chieftains and Norman lords withdrew their allegiance. Irish resistance had already been hardening before Bruce's invasion, and the weakening of the Anglo-Norman position made that resistance all the more effective. Some Irish lords who had submitted ignored the royal administration; the number of shires where that administration operated effectively declined, largely because people simply ignored their existence. By the end of the fourteenth century, English authority was restricted to the area around Dublin which became called, from the fence they built to keep out the Irish, the Pale.

Success and Failure

If it can be assumed that Edward I was making a serious attempt to unite the British Isles – which he certainly seems to have aimed for when he deposed his own choice as Scottish king in 1296 and appointed a guardian of the kingdom in 1305 – he had clearly failed. He had conquered Wales, but left it in a state of only partial unification, though joined to England. He had clearly failed to bring Scotland into his kingdom, at the cost of a long and devastating war. He had not even attempted to do anything in Ireland, and the spillover from the Scottish war which was Bruce's invasion had effectively ended the earlier gradual advances of the Anglo-Norman lords.

His original political assumptions were probably that he would become the overlord of a set of local rulers – the Prince of Wales, the king of Scotland, perhaps the Irish kings – just as he was the overlord of English earls and dukes and the Marcher lords. Thus the Balliol kings were reduced to the equivalent of an English earl. In Wales, where the same thing was attempted with the Welsh princes of Gwynedd, they failed to meet his obligations and were progressively removed and replaced by the English shire system; surviving Welsh rulers, in Powys and elsewhere, were assimilated into the Marcher system. He then attempted the same in Scotland, an attempt continued by his grandson in the 1330s.

The shires were the master institution of local government which King Alfred and his son had developed as a means of enforcing royal control in the Midlands and the Danelaw. It was applied in Wales, in parts of Ireland and in southern Scotland, but only in Wales did it endure without interruption. It probably would have worked in Ireland had there been a systematic conquest, and a proper, constructive and consistent attention paid to government there, but the Scots would have none of it and the only serious attempt to impose an English-type shire system, in southern Scotland under Edward III, vanished almost as quickly as it was imposed. The Scots preferred their own system, which was 'Sheriffdoms', a local adaptation of the English system.

On the other hand, the question has to be asked whether Edward was really trying to unite the several countries into one. He clearly did not expect the Scots to do without a king, at least until his attempted settlement in 1305, and for a long time he clearly also expected that the Welsh would be ruled by their princes, just as in the March of Wales the Marcher lords ruled their little principalities – if only Llywelyn had offered homage. In Ireland, if he ever really thought about it, the country was always a mosaic of lordships, Norman and Irish, most of which were technically under his distant authority as 'Lord of Ireland'. In that sense it could be claimed that Edward's aim was to create an English empire of subordinate kingdoms, principalities and lordships. A good parallel would be contemporary France, or Germany under the emperors.

The problem with such a system is that these lords and kings, formally subordinate though they might be, were quite likely to strike off in independent directions given half a chance, just as the Marcher lords in Wales were quite capable of waging 'private war', and ignoring any royal commands to desist, or the Irish lords ignored both royal commands and the royal administration when it suited them. Edward surely did not expect that any king of Scots would knuckle under in every minor matter which came to Edward's attention, and in at least one case King John did his best to evade or prevent a judgment in a Scottish case brought before the English king. The Welsh princes had shown an equal recalcitrance, and the Norman lords in the Marches were notoriously independent – more so than Edward expected the king of Scotland to be. Wales was only half subdued; there were plenty of areas of society where the Welsh – Marcher and Welsh alike – retained their independence of action. Similarly in Scotland, where Edward's attention was directed to control the south and the east; he paid as little attention to the Highlands and the Isles as he did to Ireland.

Edward's political assumptions – which he shared with his subjects and with those whom he tried to make his subjects – therefore got in the way of any serious attempt to create a unified British kingdom. Insofar as he aimed to unify Wales and Scotland with England it would have been only a partial version, which is what he achieved in Wales. It would take a lot more of an effort to subdue Scotland than he and his successors were prepared to undertake. Quite possibly this was a lesson from his Welsh experience. It had taken two major wars and a nasty rebellion before Wales was brought to a condition where it might be considered to be conquered, but it was quite clear that further rebellions might well take place, especially if some sort of support from outside might be available. It must be concluded that Edward did not seriously aim to unite the British islands into a single kingdom, because his political assumptions concerning suzerainty and lordships did not permit him to think in those terms. The main reason, however, is that it was well beyond English strength, and he must have known it early in the campaigns. But if nothing else, in the whole series of crises and wars which from 1277–1330 involved every part of the British Isles, Edward I had demonstrated that all parts of the archipelago were involved with each other. The issue of the unification of the islands had been brought to the table in a serious way for the first time since the time of the Roman Empire, and once in view, it would not go away. The archipelago was in the state of being a community of states; Edward's career had brought it close to a condition of partial unity, but he had failed.

Bibliography

See the books by Barrow, Carpenter, Davies and Frame noted in the last chapter.

Britain:

Brown, Michael, *Disunited Kingdoms, Peoples and Politics in the British Isles, 1280–1460* (Harlow: 2013).

Davies, R.R., *The First English Empire, Power and Identities in the British Isles, 1093–1343* (Oxford: 2000).

England:

Prestwich, Michael, *Edward I* (London: 1988).

Prestwich, Michael, *The Three Edwards, War and State in England, 1272–1377* (London: 1980).

Tuck, Anthony, *Crown and Nobility, 1272–1461* (London: 1985).

Scotland:

Barrow, G.W.S., *Robert Bruce and the Community of the Realm in Scotland* (Edinburgh: 1976).

Duncan, A.A.M., *The Nation of Scots and the Declaration of Arbroath*, Historical Association pamphlet (London: 1970).

Ferguson, William, *Scotland's Relations with England, a Survey to 1707* (Edinburgh: 1977).

Stones, E.L.G. (ed), *Anglo-Scottish Relations, 1174–1328, Some Selected Documents* (London: 1965).

Ireland:

Cosgrove, Art, *A New History of Ireland, vol. II, Mediaeval Ireland, 1169–1534* (Oxford: 1993).

Frame, Robin, *Ireland and Britain 1170–1450* (London: 1998).

Lydon, J.F., *The Lordship of Ireland in the Middle Ages* (Dublin: 1972).

Wales:

Davies, R.R., *The Age of Conquest, Wales 1063–1415* (Oxford: 1987).

Taylor, A.J., *The King's Works in Wales, 1277–1330* (London: 1974).

Williams, Glanmor, *Renewal and Reformation, Wales c.1415–1642* (Oxford: 1987).

Chapter 7

The Tudor Groundwork for Unity

After the reign of Edward I, the kingdoms of the British Isles could not be said to have 'settled down' to any sort of peaceable existence, either internally or together. The English position in Ireland had been weakened to such an extent that it slowly shrank to the 'Pale' around Dublin, and even a visit by King Richard II had little effect. Wales was conquered, but was hardly acquiescent and broke out into the great rebellion led by Owain Glyndwr, a descendant of the kings of Deheubarth, which lasted for fifteen years from 1400. Scotland, under a series of weak and unfortunate rulers, was constantly racked by internal rebellions, disputes, royal minorities and assassinations, and other complications for two centuries from the time of Robert I's death.

Wars in France and elsewhere, launched by Edward III (1327–77), exhausting to both sides, were followed by problems of the English royal succession. These bedevilled England throughout the fifteenth century. Once one English king had been overthrown and replaced by another, as Richard II was usurped by Henry IV, it became possible for other claimants to do the same, especially as Edward III had sired many sons. The old English custom of royal *coups d'état* therefore revived. Henry VI inherited the throne as a baby and grew to be an insipid and possibly insane king; he was twice displaced by Edward IV. Edward V was murdered by Richard III, and Richard III was killed in battle by Henry VII. These dynastic civil wars, the Wars of the Roses, left little room for foreign adventures. One of the elements feeding into England's internal problems was the steady loss of the continental dominions, until by 1453 only Calais was left; it was not a coincidence that the dynastic civil war began the next year. The English holdings in southern Scotland shrank to the fortified city of Berwick and no more, in Ireland they were reduced to the Pale and in France to Calais.

In such circumstances it was difficult for any progress to be made towards further unification, either in the several countries, or within the archipelago as a whole. From the end of the fifteenth century, matters became less fraught and the civil warfare in the various countries died away, and in the sixteenth century decisive advances were made in all three of the still disunited kingdoms, and finally in their mutual relations.

Scotland

In Scotland, the country's problem was centred on the difficulties of the royal succession and the weakness of royal power, matters closely connected. Robert I, by his success in maintaining Scottish independence, had established himself and his son firmly enough on the throne to see off both the Balliols and the English. But – and this became the besetting problem of the Scottish kingdom – his heir, David II, was a child, and that child had no sons of his own, so the descent went through the female line to the Stewart family.

The Stewart dynasty, however, was to be excessively accident-prone. The early years of David II (1329–71), Robert I's son, were disrupted by the near successful intervention of Edward Balliol (1332–34), and as soon as he became adult he was captured by the English and kept a prisoner for eleven years; in his reign of forty-two years, he actually ruled in Scotland for only about half that. Once released and returned to Scotland, he had the major task of reviving and enforcing his royal authority, which had inevitably decayed in his absence, and this took some years to achieve.

David II had no direct successor, and his nephew, Robert Stewart – King Robert II – therefore inherited. He suffered from ill-health for most of his reign (1371–90), and a sick man was a weak king. His successor, Robert III (1390–1406), sired a son, James I, but James was captured by English pirates before his accession and held a prisoner for a decade and more. When he came into his kingdom in 1424, he had to spend several years gaining control, just as had David II; then he was murdered, in part because he was becoming successful. This pattern of absences, minorities and untimely royal deaths beset the Scottish kingship for most of the fifteenth and sixteenth centuries.

One result was a continuing delay in the assertion of royal authority within the kingdom. Any royal absence or minority was a time of baronial conflict, a situation which eventually became endemic. The contenders aimed to secure the person of the king and therefore the regency of the kingdom, a position which allowed them to pursue their own enemies and enrich themselves, either from the confiscated lands of those enemies or by helping themselves to parts of the royal estates. When the kings reached their majority, these ex-regents usually fell from power almost at once and were compelled to surrender their gains. This could involve a civil war. James II (1437–60), for example, came to his majority in 1449, and in the next years he destroyed the power of the Livingstons, who had been his regent, and the Black Douglases, who had gathered together large territories in southern Scotland, so much so that they were powerful enough to challenge royal power. The civil warfare lasted until 1455, and was then followed by an English war in which the king was killed when a gun he was firing exploded.

James III (1460–88) was only 9 when he succeeded as king, so the process of regency, conflict, recovery and the reassertion of royal power had to be repeated. This time the regency was held by Lord Boyd, who had captured the king and kept him prisoner. Upon his majority, James executed a swift *coup d'état* and drove out Boyd and his family. This minority had lasted for ten years, and in reasserting his power the king made enemies, including his own brother, Alexander, Duke of Albany, and the Hume family. These disputes produced two civil wars, and eventually the murder of the king himself. Another minority followed, though this time the new king, James IV (1488–1513) was 15 when he inherited, so his minority was short. He was also one of the more able of the Stewart kings.

Repeated deaths of kings by violence, and a total of forty-two years of minorities in the fifteenth century, meant that it was only for brief periods that Scotland could be said to be a united country. Repeated minorities meant repeated civil wars, with the royal power reduced and having to be reasserted in every reign, which amounted to a continual division of the kingdom. The lords in their estates could act with independence, and often had to be compelled to submit by violence. The English occupation of varying sections of southern Scotland and the quasi-independence of the Lordship of the Isles continued, so that progress in the unification of the country was nil. This was a continuation of the conditions which had existed from the time of David I and his father, exacerbated by the repeated collapse of the kingdom in the succession problems from 1292 onwards.

James III and his son, however, were able to make some progress towards unification, beating down much of the baronial opposition, though feuds between baronial families lead to not infrequent private warfare (as in the Welsh Marches). In the Border country, fighting was frequent, especially when on the English side the land was similarly disturbed. Yet solutions were reached in two external issues. In 1468, James III married Princess Margaret of Denmark, but King Christian's promise of a large cash dowry for his daughter could not be paid, so he pledged Orkney as security. James was able to insert his own men into the islands' government, and since the cash to redeem the islands for Denmark was never available, the islands were fully forfeited to Scotland in 1496.

The Lordship of the Isles had grown during the fifteenth century, largely by marriages and inheritance. Angus Og held Islay and Jura in 1300; the Western Isles and parts of the western mainland were added by later lords. Continual conflict within the kingdom helped the lords maintain their independence. The marriage of Donald II, Lord of the Isles (1387–1423), with the Countess of Ross, however, led to his son, Alexander II, inheriting both lordships, so that he held both the Isles and Ross, his power thereby stretched right across from Skye to Inverness, and from Islay to Harris. James III reacted by compelling John II (1449–93) to forfeit both territories in 1475, though the Isles (but not Ross) were restored to him next year; then in 1493, James IV, in one of his earliest major acts, compelled John to forfeit his territories in full. This was a complex business, but by the end of the fifteenth century, the Lordship of the Isles had in theory been wholly annexed, but then the separate parts were granted out to local notables, heads of clan families and so on. The lordship may have been dismantled, but the kings found it impossible to impose their own control: the basic disunity of the western part of the kingdom continued.

All this amounted to major advances in the cause of bringing the fragments of peripheral Scotland into the united kingdom, though the unity was not yet definitive. The acquisition of Orkney scarcely disturbed the power of the local Sinclair earls. The disunity was thus obscured by these annexations, but it nevertheless remained real. It was emphasized further by the language division. Orkney people spoke Norse ('Norn'), as did most of the inhabitants of Caithness (of which the Sinclairs were earls as well as of Orkney). The rest of Scotland was divided between English- and Gaelic-speakers, with the former slowly advancing at the expense of the latter. Yet in 1500, when the country was theoretically fully united, the whole of the Highlands and Islands were still Gaelic-speaking, as was much of Galloway. The boundary between the two languages lay just north of Dumbarton and Stirling, and it was only during the previous century that Fife had become a land of English speech. This was to be a major source of division within Scotland for the future. The two languages also implied two different societies, particularly as Gaelic became confined to the pastoral Highlands, with English in the more arable south and east. The acquisition of Orkney and the Isles, and the reduction of baronial power, were thus advances in unity, but even in 1500, Scotland was still in a state of only partial unity.

James IV was the most capable and successful Scottish king since Robert I until he challenged Henry VIII and was killed, along with a large proportion of the Scottish nobility, in battle at Flodden (1513). His successor, James V, was, of course, a child. His minority lasted until 1528, and only ended when he escaped from Edinburgh, collected a large squad of lords and summoned a Parliament, through which he re-established his position and removed the incumbent regent; the over-powerful Douglases were also removed.

Even then the king had to fight to destroy the power of the regent Angus, and meanwhile the English border was continually turbulent, and always liable to provoke a war with England. This was the heyday of the border raids, the reivers and the border ballads – romantic in retrospect, murderous at the time. It was one of the problems of Scotland which required detailed, constant, long-term royal attention, which the long series of royal murders and minorities had rendered impossible. There were thus other ways for a kingdom to be disunited than simply the geographical; Scotland throughout the early Stewart centuries – 1329–1560 – cannot be described as a united kingdom. James V had to redo much of the work which had been repeatedly done by his predecessors. After a decade and a half, however, he was killed, like his father, in battle against the English, at Solway Moss (1542); this time his heir was a week-old baby girl.

Henry VIII

In England, the royal succession problems of the Wars of the Roses were in the end resolved, at least for a time, by the quick succession of royal deaths of the Yorkist kings – Edward IV, Edward V and Richard III – all within two years, and the success of Henry VII in thus overthrowing that dynasty. Henry was further successful in holding onto the kingship for two decades (1485–1509). Henry was followed as king by his adult son, Henry VIII (1509–47), one of those extraordinary kings who turn up every now and again in every dynasty, who was able, flamboyant and exceedingly ambitious. Part of his work was to push forward the unification of the British Isles in decisive directions, and therefore return the issue squarely to a central part of the political agenda.

It scarcely needed to be explained to any king of England that one of the major issues he had to solve was that he must have an adult male successor. The contemporary example of Scotland was quite sufficient in this regard, even if the English troubles of the fifteenth century did not drive home the lesson. But after twenty years as king, Henry still had no male heir, only a daughter, Mary, and it was not clear that female succession was possible or acceptable in England. The memory of the civil wars weighed on all. This issue was one of the springs of the policies Henry pursued in the latter half of his reign, but it was hardly the only one, despite the continued fascination it has attracted. Henry had succeeded in a war against James IV, but his wars against France were failures. This was due more than anything to the old problem of the lack of resources available to the English royal government. Then there was the issue of religion, where the new sects of Protestants had succeeded in defying the Pope and governments in many parts of Europe, and whose criticisms of the Catholic Church struck home to many in England.

All these issues combined in the 1530s to propel Henry and his minister, Thomas Cromwell, into a major reorganization of English society, a change amounting in many ways to a revolution directed from the top, and which encountered much resistance from below. A break with the Pope rendered the Church in England vulnerable to an assault by the government on its resources. Henry claimed he was a good Catholic, and that he was carrying through his own reform of the Church in England, something he believed that the Pope would never do in the larger Church. This amounted to the sequential closing down of all the monasteries and the confiscation of their lands and wealth, first the most corrupt, then the smallest, then the rest. Some of the confiscated resources were used to endow new bishoprics, a long-felt need, but the rest remained in the king's own control, and he used this windfall to boost his own resources and buy support for his policies. Opposition came in the form of a large rebellion in the north of England (the 'Pilgrimage of Grace'), which was costly to suppress. Other internal opposition was disposed of by the distribution of the confiscated Church lands – that is, by bribery – but it also compelled Henry to bring on the introduction of further measures aimed at tightening up and extending the royal administration.

Quarrels with Scotland had become steadily more serious since the 1480s. Partly this was due to the unsettled and disturbed nature of the border, partly to the bellicosity of both Scottish and English kings. The deaths in battle against Henry's armies of both James IV and James V (Henry's brother-in-law and nephew) reduced Scotland yet again to regencies for infant kings – or in the case of the second, the infant Queen Mary, another romantic figure whose character and work fails to impress on close inspection.

Henry VIII's solution to the Scottish problem was to propose a betrothal between his son, Edward (born in 1537), and his first cousin, Queen Mary – the policy advanced by Edward I two-and-a-half centuries before. Henry also suggested that he should act as supervisor during the queen's minority, as part of the potential marriage agreement. He hoped to get the Scots to agree first to the marriage, which would make his son King of Scots, and then, if the queen died young (a strong possibility in that time), that he or his son would become ruling king. He had captured a good collection of Scottish lords at Solway Moss and released them in exchange for bonds by which they agreed to act as an English party in Scotland.

The scheme went awry, and Henry fumbled the case. He ended up with another Scottish war, called by the Scots 'the Rough Wooing', which lasted from 1544–50. Since Henry died in the middle of the war, it is hardly surprising that the English attacks, though devastating large areas of south-east Scotland, were in the end unsuccessful.

The pointlessness of the war was emphasized by the fact that Mary had been quickly evacuated to France to be raised there. It was clearly far too dangerous for an infant queen to be raised in Scotland – not just because of the war with England, with English armies repeatedly coming close to Edinburgh, but also because of the deeply unpleasant politics of aristocratic affairs at home. The competition for the regency, with the queen out of the way, could now be even more open and brutal than usual.

During the queen's childhood and absence, the old problem of a disorderly, ambitious, not to say greedy, disloyal and murderous aristocracy set about feathering their nests and pursuing their feuds. Their behaviour made it all too clear why a vigorous and adult king was required. During her absence, a new problem also emerged which a royal presence might have prevented, or at least, as in England, harnessed: the Scots went through their own religious reformation to become a largely Protestant country. Meanwhile, Queen Mary was being brought up as a Catholic.

Henry VIII's attempt (which was continued by the English Lord Protector, the Duke of Somerset, after his death) to promote a union with Scotland based on a marriage between the two royal children failed, but one reason he had promoted the idea was that his sister, Margaret, had been married to James IV and was therefore the mother of James V (and thus the grandmother of Mary). So the two royal families were already closely related, and the marriage of cousins was a fairly common royal practice. The inheritance of several crowns by one king was also a common enough event at the time – this was the era of the Emperor Charles V, whose collection of kingdoms and duchies and other lands spanned Europe; of the union of Poland and Lithuania; and of a Scandinavian kingdom which spread from Iceland to Finland, all constructed on royal marriages. A union of England and Scotland by inheritance was a better way than conquest. Henry's scheme may have failed for the moment, but succeeded in the long-term. Meanwhile, his schemes in Wales and Ireland were much more immediately productive.

Welsh Unification and Union with England

The Tudor dynasty could claim a Welsh origin, and Henry VII was born in Wales. The Welsh Marcher lords, better armed than most English lords, had intervened more than once in the English succession problems under the Yorkist kings. One result of the Wars of the Roses had been the confiscation of huge areas of the Marcher lordships to the Crown, so that well over half of the Marcher territories became Crown land. When Henry VII landed in Wales in his expedition to claim the throne from Richard III, he was able to collect substantial support, not only among the surviving Marcher lords and from the Crown lands, but also from among the Welsh. He marched across Wales, entering England by way of the route along the upper Severn, thus in the opposite direction to the original Norman invaders, or those sent by Edward I. His victory at the decisive Battle of Bosworth in August 1485 could be seen in a sense as a Welsh *coup d'état*.

Necessarily, however, any king of England, wherever he came from, had to be based in London and had to respond most of all to English matters. Henry VII became a thoroughly English king despite his Welsh origins, and Henry VIII showed no particular interest in Wales other than a suspicion of the possible hostility of the some of the Marcher lords – and given their behaviour in the last century, and their intervention in the English civil wars, such a suspicion was probably well justified. Closing down the Welsh monasteries was a thoroughly unpopular action, perhaps more so in Wales than even in the north of England. Henry VIII thus forfeited much of the goodwill amongst the Welsh collected by his father.

For the king, the issue was essentially that the Marcher lords had inherited a legal regime which set them outside direct royal control. Marcher law had evolved into an independent legal system which no king was able to control, other than by military action. Further, the Marcher lordships were volatile, both in ownership and in politics. Neighbours had tended to choose different sides in the various civil wars of the fifteenth century, based on

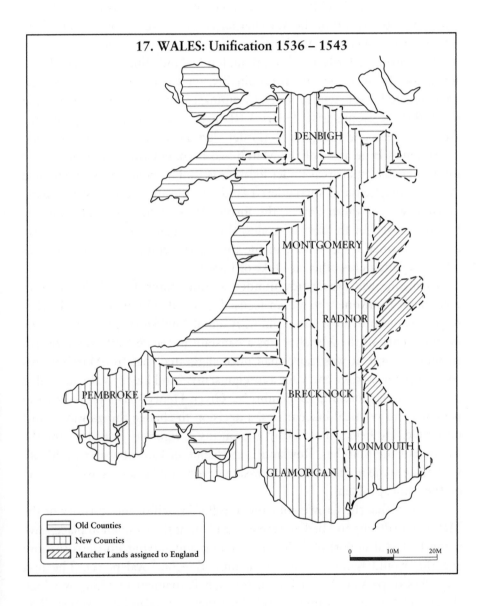

17. WALES: Unification 1536 – 1543

their local feuds and enmities. This had led to repeated confiscations by the winners in the wars. No king had ever been strong enough, or concerned enough, to attend to the issue of the effective independence of the March.

From Edward IV (1461–83), however, the king increasingly regarded the internal behaviour of the Marcher lords themselves as close to criminal. Edward established a Council of the Marches of Wales, whose main aim was to control the lords' conduct, though it had only limited success. It did act to coordinate responses to criminality, for English and Marcher legal systems side-by-side tended to allow criminals to jump from one jurisdiction to another to escape trial. Henry VIII in particular found that both the Welsh Marches and the Scottish Border were a constant source of disorder.

Although large areas of the March had become Crown lordships, there were still substantial areas under local lords, and Marcher law still operated in the confiscated and surrendered lands. Ironically, the largest surviving lordship was southern Powys, the former Welsh kingdom, still under its Welsh dynasty. In the rest of Wales, the principality consisted of the six counties formed by Edward I in the thirteenth century; some other areas fell to the king in his office as Duke of Lancaster.

To anyone who was a tidy-minded administrator, the whole situation was a mess: to anyone who was an accused criminal in England, the Marcher regions could provide a haven out of reach of English law; to the king, the independence of the Marches was a constant nuisance, and even a threat. In times of war, it was more than once suggested that the Marcher area could provide an easy entry for a foreign army – and Henry VII had landed in the Marcher lordship of Pembroke. Given Henry VIII's problems and personal and political insecurities, a decision to change things was almost inevitable. He began in 1534 by appointing a vigorous President for the Council of the Marches, Rowland Lee, Bishop of Coventry and Lichfield, who made some progress in suppressing crime, and became a useful expert on the whole problem.

The fact that the Crown controlled well over half of the territory of the Marcher lordships and had an active President of the Council in place, gave it the first real opportunity for intervening and tidying up the situation; and this would remove an awkward limitation on royal power. The first stage was to pass an Act of Union through Parliament in 1536, by which Wales and England became a single kingdom – 'England and Wales'. The next stage used the traditional instrument of extending royal authority used by Henry II and John in Ireland, by Edward I in Wales and by Edward III in Scotland: the shire system. The Marcher lands were organized into seven new shires – Pembroke, Glamorgan, Monmouth, Radnor, Brecknock, Montgomery and Denbigh – to go along with the six created by Edward I (some lordships were enfolded into neighbouring English shires). Marcher law was in effect abolished, and everyone in the former March of Wales became subject to English law and the English king. An assize circuit system was instituted. This all took time to organize, and required another Act of Parliament so that the process was only completed in 1542.

In effect, these Acts accomplished two basic political changes. One was the union of England and Wales into one kingdom, as the 1536 Act stated. The other was the definitive unification of Wales into a single country, to replace the partial unification achieved by Edward I. Since it was accompanied by the union of Wales with England, however, the whole package was an outcome not necessarily to be welcomed by the Welsh.

The stages of Welsh unification had, nevertheless, been accomplished. From the community of Welsh states which had existed from the end of the Roman province until the thirteenth century, the unification had come in two, or perhaps three stages. First was the evident aim of the two princes Llywelyn of Gwynedd to unite the Welsh principalities – Gwynedd, Powys and Deheubarth – into one state, and their less stated one of 'recovering' the Marcher lands for Wales. Their campaigns had progressively reduced the authority of the other princes, and had successfully expelled some of the Marcher lords, in effect beginning the destruction of the Welsh political system. But the result was enmity and understandable suspicion from the English kings, who had no wish to see a strong independent Wales on their western frontier. The strength of this reaction was shown by the fact that it extended even to the pacific Henry III. The other reason for its failure was the constant, if at times intermittent, opposition of the non-Gwynedd princes, who had no wish to be subordinated to, or removed by, Gwynedd. Nevertheless, the work of Llywelyn I and II had begun the initial unification of Wales in a more decisive way than had been achieved by the earlier kings who had gathered several of the Welsh kingdoms together briefly.

The extension of Gwynedd's power was the preliminary to the English conquest. Edward I's reaction to the threat from Wales was military conquest, once he found that political subordination failed. This conquest saw the completion of the partial unification of the country – the principality and the Marcher lordships. Both areas were technically under English rule, but their separate administrations meant that Wales remained disunited. Henry VIII's measures therefore performed the final act of unification by converting the Marcher lands into shires, abolishing the difference between the two areas. The fact that this came along with the unification of Wales and England was partly the result of geography and partly the Welsh inheritance of the king himself, but it was perhaps mainly inadvertent, a necessary result of the abolition of the Marcher lords and their law.

Ireland

In the year after the Act of Union with Wales was passed, it was noted that the English hold in Ireland had been reduced to its smallest since the invasion of Richard Strongbow in the twelfth century. The territory of the English Pale around Dublin stretched north along the coast as far as Drogheda, and inland for little more than a day's journey from the city of Dublin. It was a region little larger than the territory of Dublin as a Viking town in the tenth century. In the rest of the island, political authority lay very largely with the greater families, partly descended from the Irish kings of the past, or from the Norman invaders. Their men were independent of the English royal administration. The reach of that administration was by this time extremely limited and was generally incapable of dealing effectively with any of the greater lords who chose to defy it. In some areas indeed the royal authority had never operated at all, particularly in Ulster, where a preliminary attempt in the thirteenth century at a Norman incursion had failed; any surviving lords in the area had been eliminated by the Scottish campaign of Edward Bruce.

The situation from the English king's point of view was problematic. Ireland – that is, Dublin – had been used during the dynastic civil wars of the previous century on more than one occasion as a base from which to attack or invade England. It had been a Yorkist base against the Lancastrian Henry VI (at the time of Henry VII's invasion of Wales, most of the Irish lords who had bothered to take sides had supported his opponent) and it had been the base for the Yorkist adventures of Perkin Warbeck and Lambert Simnel in the 1490s. For Henry VIII, facing rebellions in England, contentious reforms in Wales and disputes with Scotland, it was clearly dangerous not to have some control in Ireland. The trigger for the new assertion of royal control was the rebellion of 'Silken Thomas', Earl of Kildare, in 1534; until then the earls of Kildare had been one of the main royal supporters.

A new policy was devised, called 'surrender and re-grant'. (This new policy was worked out at much the same time as the new policy for Wales was produced, and as the dissolution of the English monasteries began.)

In return for accepting the authority of the king and a legal title to their territories, lords could be created earls or barons. A considerable number accepted this, for it seemed to increase their legal security. It did not much extend royal power, since the effect was to use these earls to control the country in the name of the king, and the king could exercise little control over the earls. It was, that is, very similar to the original policy of Henry II in the Norman Conquest period, and might have resulted in an Irish version of the Marcher lords of Wales. Nevertheless, this did amount to a considerable expansion of royal influence. Henry himself acquired the new title of King of Ireland to replace the mediaeval 'Lord of Ireland'. This latter had been a grant from the Pope, so once Henry had broken with papal authority, a change was clearly required. The title of king was in fact in form a grant by the Irish Parliament, a technique he had been using in England to carry through the reforms in the Church and elsewhere (including Wales).

After the Kildare rebellion, the Kildare lands were confiscated, which amounted to a threatening alternative to the surrender and re-grant policy. Henry also used the Irish Parliament to take power over the Irish Church, as he did in England and Wales, and identified the monasteries as an element in need of reform, a conclusion which was widely accepted in Ireland. During the next fifty years, many of the Irish monasteries were closed down; the process was also resisted, as it had been in England and Wales, but with greater effect, since royal power was absent from much of the country. Irish opposition to royal power coincided with opposition to the Protestant Reformation which the English were pushing forward.

After Henry's death, there were rebellions by O'Connor of Offaly and O'More of Leix against the aggressively Protestant government of Edward VI. Their lands were confiscated after their defeat, and the opportunity was later taken to settle families from England in the confiscated territories; these were formed into two new counties, King's and Queen's. This finally took place in 1556, so the king and queen being referred to were Mary I and her husband, Philip of Spain. It was clear that the newly aggressive royal policies did not change with the religious policies of the kings or queens.

The result in Ireland was a new activity in the royal administration, and a new assertiveness in royal policy, but it had not yet extended very far. Many monasteries still existed, the new shires were by no means guaranteed to continue (others had vanished before) and converting Irish lords into earls had extended royal influence somewhat, but not much. The effective parts of Henry's policy, therefore, were his ability to confiscate the Kildare lands – a standing threat to other obstreperous lords – and the prospective expansion of royal counties by the settlement of English colonists.

The Effects of Protestantism

All four of the countries of the British Isles went through a Protestant Reformation, but each arrived at a different destination at the end of the process. In England, Henry VIII might have begun the change but he always claimed to be a loyal Catholic; his attitude to Protestants was distinctly hostile. All he claimed to have done was to break with the authority of the Pope while maintaining the English Church as a truly Catholic organization – a condition which certain Anglicans claim to be the case to this day. Considerable numbers of Protestants already existed in England during Henry's reign, so it was possible for the regents for Edward VI to push through a true Protestant Reformation with considerable public support. This was reversed by Mary I, but then changed again in the first years of Elizabeth I's reign. This was an extremely untidy process which left different groups of Christians demonstrating loyalty in different directions, often making themselves vulnerable to any change in the political winds. It is clear that large numbers of members of the Church of England continued to consider themselves to be Catholic, and welcomed the arrival and ministrations of papal loyalist Catholic priests for many years after Elizabeth's enactments at the beginning of her reign. At the same time, there were Protestants who felt that the condition of the Church had been left mainly unreformed by the Elizabethan compromise and wished to push the process much further, while there were also Catholics who regarded with suspicion the attempts by foreign powers – who included the Pope – to meddle in English affairs.

The Scots were much more rigorous in the application of their own Reformation. The absence of the queen in France assisted the process, so that it was eventually carried through by a Scottish Parliament without the serial reversals seen in England. The process began under the queen's first regent, the Earl of Arran, who had permitted the publication and circulation of translations of the Bible into English – thereby hoping to replicate the policy of Henry VIII. Parliament enacted the necessary legislation to shift the Church in a Protestant direction. Abolition of monasteries was a necessary action, which largely benefited the aristocracy – again as in England.

By the time that Queen Mary returned from France in 1560, aged 18, already a widow and demonstrably a loyal Catholic, the country she arrived in was under Protestant control. As in England, there were remnant Catholics – 'recusants' – while the strength of feeling that the Protestant Reformation had not yet gone far enough was very much stronger than in England. In Scotland, Mary did little to reverse the process of the Protestant Reformation – unlike the English Mary – but then she wasn't queen for very long or very effectively, and only became a voluble Catholic when it became politically useful during her imprisonment in England, after her deposition as queen in Scotland.

Wales suffered severely from the suppression of the monasteries, for this eliminated almost all the educational provision in the country, and a good deal of the commercial opportunities. One of the ironies of the situation is that a translation of the Bible into Welsh was commissioned by Elizabeth's government as a means of extending the Protestant cause in Wales, and this assisted in the continuation of the use of that language, which in turn helped very much in continuing the distinctiveness of Welshness. The expansion of English at the expense of Welsh nevertheless continued; perhaps without the Welsh Bible that expansion could well have been all the greater. The Church as a whole tended to use English, once Latin was abandoned, so it was hardly a focus of Welsh loyalty. The schools that were now founded were organized on the principles of the English grammar schools and also used English. They were mainly patronized by the middle classes, who were already English-speaking. The result was that Welsh national feeling, which had been growing particularly in the fifteenth century, in the face of annexation to the English crown, was encouraged by the continued use of Welsh, while the Church became identified with Englishness. This also meant that the loyalty of the Welsh towards the English Church steadily reduced, and alternative versions of Christianity took hold, in part as a reflection of the Welsh repudiation of English authority.

The Reformation made some initial progress in Ireland, particularly where English was spoken, and the suppression of the monasteries took place slowly during the reigns of Henry VIII and Elizabeth I, but met with decreasing success. It was an untidy process which was much resisted locally. Orders could be given from Dublin for religious houses to be dissolved, and this could be reported to have happened, and yet the houses continued to exist with local support. In other areas, religious houses were protected by local lords. Yet Protestantism did begin to make inroads into Irish opinion, particularly in the towns, where the authority of the English government was strong enough to enforce the new rules, and its ability to push forward the reformed religion was clear.

The Effects of Henry VIII

The results of the work of Henry VIII in promoting the unity of the British Isles was thus mixed; this had probably never been his explicit aim. Such advances in the cause of unity as had occurred, as with the unification of Wales and its simultaneous unification with England, had come about largely as a by-product of the problems which the king faced in governing England. Any advance which is discernible in Ireland came about similarly as a result of the king's perceived need to gain greater control in that island, partly to deter intervention from any Yorkist or European enemies. This was a factor which also featured in the suppression of the Marcher regime in Wales. His policy towards Scotland can only be described as disastrous, not only in promoting wars in which two Scottish kings were killed, but in the 'Rough Wooing' war between 1544 and 1550, and yet the two royal families were now closely related. It was easy for kings to resort to force when thwarted by a weaker state, but the net result was always to intensify the enmity felt by the weaker party for the bullying stronger. To some extent this also operated in Wales and Ireland.

Nevertheless, despite the inadvertent results of his policies, the expansion of Protestantism in England, Wales and Scotland did promote a common feeling in religious matters, as against foreign hostility and interference, and suggested that the three countries might be considered fellow sufferers in the Protestant cause. In all three countries, the result was also an increase in governmental authority and power. In England, the Act of Uniformity gradually convinced the majority to accept the dispensation of an Anglican Church, and pushed the extreme Protestants and the recusant Catholics to the margins.

Between 1534 and 1544, therefore, Henry VIII's policies had forwarded the increase in royal power in all three of his kingdoms, and had promoted the cause of the unification of the British Isles. That issue was now clearly once more on the table: England and Wales were politically united, Ireland was being slowly brought under greater royal – that is, English – control and Henry had made himself king there, presaging a further extension of his royal powers. In another inadvertent result of Henry's policies, the Scottish royal family, at last failing after its long catalogue of incompetence and disaster, had become strongly linked with the Anglo-Welsh Tudors, through the marriage of Margaret Tudor with James IV. After James' death in battle (against Henry's army), she remarried, to Archibald Douglas, Earl of Angus. By her two marriages, Margaret was the grandmother of both Mary Queen of Scots and her first Scottish husband, the ineffable, murdered Lord Darnley. Their son, who became James VI when Mary fled her ungovernable kingdom, inherited, by this ancestry, the kingship of Scotland, and a strong claim to the English throne, a claim which became steadily stronger as it became clear that Henry's daughter, Elizabeth I, was not going to marry. Amongst many other elements in his bizarre life and reign, Henry VIII was one of the main founders of the united British state.

The Partial Unification of Ireland

In Ireland, Queen Elizabeth continued the policy of her sister, her brother's regents and her father in making a reasonably sustained effort to subdue the island. This had become all the more important given the fact that the Irish proved to be stubbornly recalcitrant towards adopting Protestantism, and as the great international conflict between Catholics and Protestants developed, this became crucial to her policy. The wars which England fought against Spain in the late sixteenth century were in part religious wars, and that meant that Catholic Ireland was a major weakness in the English defences. This was not, however, the only issue involved.

The practice of planting groups of English families in parts of Ireland provoked much opposition, not surprisingly. It was often the cause for further confiscations of land and more plantations of Protestants – always at the expense of Catholics and their land. Ireland had never been a particularly peaceful place, but the renewed English intrusions, combined with the new religious conflict, caused fighting to spread throughout the island. The fighting was confused and was essentially warfare on the Irish model, with raids, devastations, looting and seizures of food and cattle. This was done by both the English forces and the Irish, and was largely inconclusive. But it did stoke much resentment amongst the Irish, both lords and commons. Add in religious differences and personal ambitions, and an explosive mixture resulted.

A series of English expeditions only added to the devastation, and in the 1590s the various conflicts coalesced into a full-scale war, called in Ireland the Nine Years' War, which was led by members of the Catholic aristocracy and was aimed at driving out the English presence. It began with the spread of rebellion, as the English called it, through Ulster. The leaders made contact with King Philip of Spain, thereby initiating the English strategic nightmare which was the basic reason for them seizing and conquering the island. This was a reason which applied in every European war from

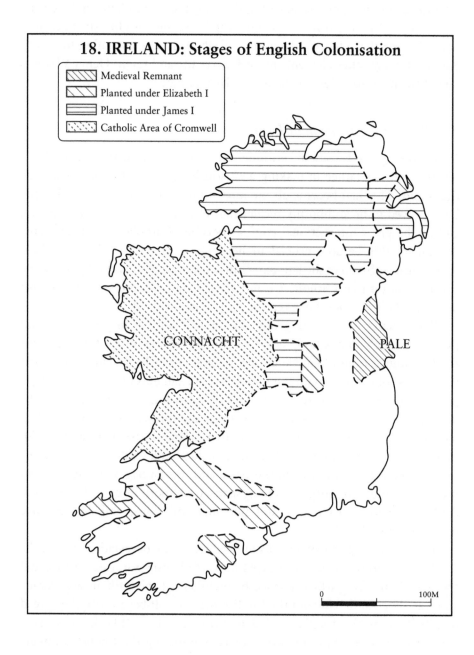

18. IRELAND: Stages of English Colonisation

Medieval Remnant
Planted under Elizabeth I
Planted under James I
Catholic Area of Cromwell

CONNACHT

PALE

0   100M

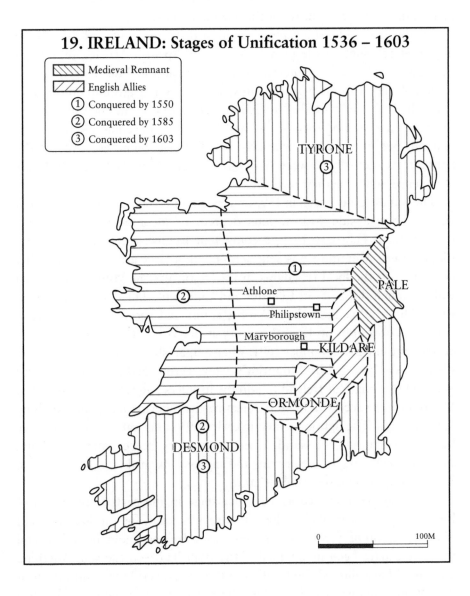

19. IRELAND: Stages of Unification 1536 – 1603

Medieval Remnant
English Allies
① Conquered by 1550
② Conquered by 1585
③ Conquered by 1603

TYRONE
③

PALE

①

② Athlone
Philipstown
Maryborough
KILDARE

ORMONDE

② DESMOND
③

0   100M

then until the twentieth century – the fear that Ireland could be used as a hostile base for an invasion of the bigger island. It was, of course, the same fear which a Franco-Scottish alliance produced, and which had been one of the underlying reasons for Edward I's conquest of Wales and Henry VIII's determination to gain control of the Marcher lands.

On the Irish side, the war was more a drive for independence than a matter of religion. In the great crisis of the Spanish Armada in 1588, a quintessential Catholic-Protestant conflict, Ireland had not moved. When several of the returning Spanish ships, *in extremis*, ran aground on the Irish coast, the Irish vied with the English soldiers in murdering the shipwrecked Spaniards and looting their ships. Irish rebellions were never solely about religion, but were almost invariably anti-English. Some elements of the fighting were actually between Irish lords or groups, using the general state of violence to pursue their own ends.

The war officially began in 1593 and lasted until 1603, and was conducted on the English side with various degrees of incompetence and waste. Eventually, in February 1600, a competent English commander, Charles Blount, Lord Mountjoy, was sent across with a large army. Systematically he dealt with the local rebellions in the south, first in Munster, and then without much difficulty in Leinster and Connacht. The defence of Ulster, which Hugh O'Neill, Earl of Tyrone, conducted successfully for several years, was broken by an English victory at the Moyry Pass. The final crisis of the war came in September 1601, when a Spanish force landed at Kinsale, where it was besieged by Mountjoy's army. Tyrone gathered his allies and marched the length of Ireland to join the invaders and relieve the siege, but Mountjoy was successful in both defeating the relieving force and expelling the Spaniards. The fighting ended in early 1603. This war was the definitive English conquest of Ireland, a major military achievement outdoing anything the Vikings, the Normans and anybody else had ever done. English rule was imposed on the whole island.

This may be described as a further stage in the partial unification of Ireland. Again, as in Wales, the initiative was local, for the logical result of the rebellion of Tyrone would be to unite Ireland under Irish rule, and this would have been maintained if the Irish had won the war. Anything less would have allowed the English to return, especially if a contingent of local Protestants had survived. The alternative had become either English conquest or agreement among the Irish. Tyrone would have been the obvious man to rule, but, given that he had independent allies amongst his supporters who were rivals and covert enemies, it seems likely that any unified Irish state would be, at least, fractious: it would need a powerful and continuing threat from England to compel unity.

The sequel to the English victory was the collapse of Irish resistance, followed by a first 'flight of the earls', when the leaders of Irish society deserted their fellow countrymen, followed by several thousands of the people. This left the island to the English, who soon resumed the policy of 'planting' – that is, colonization – which had already put colonies of English in Ulster, Munster and the Irish Midlands. Large areas remained in Irish occupation, to become bases for later rebellions, and the plantations were slow to become established. The country was still divided, between English and Irish, between Catholics and Protestants, and between Irish and Irish. The English might govern, but with constant uneasiness; Ireland was hardly fully united.

Conclusion

The English conquest was, in effect, the culmination of Henry VIII's policy. He had achieved the final unification of Wales and joined it with England: his daughter had achieved the painful, partial unification of Ireland. He had beaten down a major rebellion in the north of England (one which had revived with Elizabeth, with similar results). In his family marriage policy he had prepared the next step in the formation of a united British island, when his great-grandnephew, the King of Scots, would inherit the English throne in the year in which the conquest of Ireland was completed. Henry's brother-in-law, James IV, had himself secured the final unification, if only loosely, of Scotland with the annexation of the Isles and Orkney.

The period from 1490 (the year of Margaret Tudor's marriage to James IV) to 1603 had therefore seen clear advances in the unification of Scotland, Wales and Ireland, and towards the union of the three countries. It could now be said that the British Isles consisted of three united kingdoms – England-plus-Wales, Scotland – which now included the islands to the north and west – and the kingdom of Ireland. The variety of methods used to achieve these conditions was instructive. The original conquest of Wales had been violent, and had left a good deal of work still to be done. But then, after more than two centuries of English rule, it had proved to be possible to complete the unification by Acts of Parliament. The same sort of process had had similar results in Scotland, where a reduction in disorder within the main kingdom had permitted James III and James IV to advance their programme of uniting that kingdom with the outlying territories, which the kings of

Scotland had been attempting to bring into their kingdom for the past several centuries. Both of these unifications were therefore accomplished effectively by negotiation and persuasion.

It is all too obvious that this had not been the method attempted in Ireland. For a short time after the introduction of Protestantism, it seemed possible that many Irish might be persuaded to accept that version of Christianity, but the Catholic Church was able to dispatch mission priests not only to England, where they tended to be found and executed fairly quickly, but also to Ireland, where they succeeded in combating English-cum-Protestant persuasions. In this, of course, they were assisted by Irish memories of resentment at foreign invasion and by English behaviour when faced by Irish recalcitrance. From an English point of view, the existence of a united and independent Catholic Ireland on its westward flank could not be accepted. The conquest of all Ireland had therefore become a strategic necessity for the English, and this, as it happened, also required the unification of the island.

Bibliography

See also the works of Ferguson and Williams in earlier chapters.

Britain:

Bradshaw, Brendan and Morrill, John (eds), *The British Problem c.1534–1707, State Formation in the Atlantic Archipelago* (London: 1996).

Brown, Michael, *Disunited Kingdoms, Peoples and Politics in the British Isles, 1280–1460* (Harlow, Essex: 2013).

Ellis, Stephen G. and Barber, Sarah (eds), *Conquest and Union, Fashioning a British state, 1485–1725* (Harlow, Essex: 1995).

Hirst, Derek, *Dominion, England and its Island Neighbours, 1500–1707* (Oxford: 2012).

England:

Bindoff, S.T., *Tudor England* (Harmondsworth: 1950).

Cross, Clare, *Church and People, 1450–1660* (London: 1976).

Fissel, Mark Charles, *English Warfare, 1511–1642* (London: 2001).

Gillingham, John, *The Wars of the Roses, Peace and Conflict in 15th Century England* (London: 1981).

Ives, H.W., *Faction in Tudor England*, Historical Association pamphlet (London: 1979).

Lander, J.R., *Conflict and Stability in Fifteenth-Century England* (London: 1969).

Loades, D.M., *Politics and the Nation, 1450–1660, Obedience, Resistance and Public Order* (London: 1974).
McFarlane, K.B., *England in the Fifteenth Century, Collected Essays* (London: 1981).
Scarisbrick, J.J., *Henry VIII* (Harmondsworth: 1968).
Youings, Joyce, *Sixteenth-Century England* (Harmondsworth: 1984).

Scotland:

Bingham, Caroline, *The Stewart Kingdom of Scotland 1371–1603* (London: 1974).
Donaldson, Gordon, *Scotland, James V – James VII* (Edinburgh: 1965).
Downie, Fiona, *She is but a Woman, Queenship in Scotland, 1424–1463* (Edinburgh: 2006).
Fraser, G. MacDonald, *The Steel Bonnets* (London: 1971).
Grant, A., *Independence and Nationhood* (London: 1985).
McDougall, Norman, *James IV* (Edinburgh: 1989).
Marshall, Rosalind K., *John Knox* (Edinburgh: 2008).
Patterson, Raymond Campbell, *My Wound is Deep, a History of the Later Anglo-Scots Wars 1380–1560* (Edinburgh: 1997).
Phillips, Gervase, *The Anglo-Scots Wars, 1513–1550* (Woodbridge: 1999).
Ryrie, Alec, *The Origins of the Scottish Reformation* (Manchester: 2006).

Ireland:

Ellis, S.G., *Ireland in the Age of the Tudors* (London: 1998).
Ellis, S.G., *Tudor Ireland, Crown, Community, and Conflict of Cultures, 1470–1603* (London: 1985).
Falls, Cyril, *Elizabeth's Irish Wars* (London: 1950).
Lydon, James, *Ireland in the Later Middle Ages* (Dublin: 1973).
McCurtain, Margaret, *Tudor and Stuart Ireland* (Dublin: 1972).
Moody, T.W., Martin, F.X. and Byrne, F.J. (eds), *A New History of Ireland, vol. III, Early Modern Ireland 1534–1691* (Oxford: 1987).
Silke, John J., *Kinsale, the Spanish Intervention in Ireland at the end of the Elizabeth Wars* (Liverpool: 1970).

Wales:

Jones, J.G., *Early Modern Wales, 1525–1640* (London: 1994).
Skell, C.A.J., *The Council of the Marches of Wales* (London: 1903).
Thomas, W.S.K., *Tudor Wales* (Llandysul: 1983).

Chapter 8

The Union of Crowns

For a thousand years, various sections of the British Isles had been moving erratically towards their separate unifications. How far any of this was deliberate, with that specific aim in view, is difficult to estimate, but it seems clear that by the fifteenth century at least the unifying intention was clear in Scotland, as progress was made to capture Orkney and the Western Isles. The unification of England in the tenth century, which had been accomplished by Alfred and his son, Edward, had clearly been achieved, though whether it was thought of in such terms is not known; it had certainly resulted from the reaction of the English to the threat of Danish attacks. The later brutal completion of this process by William the Conqueror was mainly a by-product of his need to simultaneously remove the over-mighty territorial earls and to break down popular opposition, so 'unification' as such was not his aim, only the result of the earls' defensiveness.

It must have been clear to at least some politicians and rulers in Wales and Ireland at the time of the Norman invasions of these countries that the best defence against these attacks would be the unification of the several principalities. In Wales the princes of Gwynedd in the thirteenth century did make serious efforts to achieve that, though they faced much resistance from other parts of Wales, and opposition from the English. In Ireland, the intervention of the Bruce invasion and the campaign he directed at English power so weakened the English position and reduced the pressure they were exerting that the Irish could argue – as perhaps they had in response to the Viking attacks, at least afterwards – that they could continue in disunity in the belief that the danger was over. When it was resumed, Henry VIII's policy of 'surrender-and-re-grant' meant that the authority of the English king as King of Ireland was widely acknowledged. With the programme of plantations of Henry VIII and his children from the 1540s, the intrusion did not seem more than narrowly territorial, threatening at the local level only. When the serious attempt at total conquest finally came in the 1590s, it was too late; this again was a by-product of events elsewhere, an English defensive reaction to the threat of Spain.

Two conclusions seem evident. First, the impulse towards union usually came from the need to counter some sustained threat – the Vikings, the Danes, the great earls, potential Welsh power – surmounting which compelled the defeated elements to surrender their power, end their threat and so they were thus united with the enemy. The second point is that at some stage it was borne in on the political classes, and perhaps on the wider audience, that political unity was an aim which it was necessary to pursue in itself. The two elements were needed, because only with the appreciation that unification was the solution to the political problem, usually a foreign threat, would the required resolve develop. It would be very easy to stop halfway. For example, the English, having survived Haestan's campaigns in the 890s, could have then sat back and relaxed, leaving the Danish conquests within England alone. This is exactly what the Irish did, after the end of Edward Bruce's campaigns, even though it was surely clear that the English pressure was very dangerous.

A third point may be made, but this is not prescriptive: there was no case where a voluntary process of unification, without outside pressure, took place. The English and Scots were threatened by Danish or Viking violence and conquest, the Welsh by the English, the English by the Normans, the Normans by the English rebellions; in no case did any of the resulting unifications come into place voluntarily. In Scotland, the continuing threat of English attack in the generation after 1292 was not enough to cement the kingdom's unity – and indeed one result of Robert I's reign was to exacerbate internal Scottish differences, and the partial unity of the kingdom was worse after him than in the century before his reign.

The defensive reactions, however, only produced a minimal, or as I have termed it, a 'partial' unification. It is at that point that it is possible that an internal mechanism may develop to push the unification onward, as particularly was the case in Scotland in the later fifteenth century, where it became a long-term royal aim to complete the unification of the original kingdom by including the peripheral regions of the Western and Northern Isles and Galloway, a process somewhat derailed by the deaths of James IV and James V, so that this resulted in no more than a partial unification. The final push into full unity, such as had been achieved by William the Conqueror in England, was still needed. In the two cases where this forced unification had already taken place, in Wales and England, it was ominous that it was violent pressure from outside, by William I, Edward I and Henry VIII, which brought it about. In Wales, the unification remained only partial in the face of the divisions between the royal counties and the

Marcher lords' territories, only to be completed by the equally overbearing Henry VIII.

Henry VIII, however, for all his bluff heartiness and propensity to cut off heads, had actually brought about his unification of Wales by peaceful means, an Act of Parliament. In his Irish policy, the most significant item had been the essentially peaceful and widespread 'surrender-and-re-grant'. For Scotland, he had adopted, probably unknowingly, the original suggestion of Edward I that marriage between the heirs to both kingdoms could unite them, a policy which had operated widely in Europe.

So the seventeenth century was the period when this process of unification moved into a new dimension, and into a less violent phase. The old impulses had not died, and there was plenty of fighting still to come, but the issue now was the unification of the whole archipelago.

Preparations

The union of England with Wales, which was achieved by the two Acts of the English Parliament promoted by Henry VIII in 1536 and 1542, proved to be the legal means by which later unifications took place, and this became the preferred method of further unifications. Yet for Scotland and Ireland it could not simply be a matter of the English Parliament's action, but would require the agreement of the parliaments in those two countries. The Acts of Union passed by the English Parliament could only be considered to be the consent awarded by the English.

Before the stage of unification was eventually reached, however, there was a long and tortuous journey to be covered. Meanwhile each country pursued its own course, not only remaining separate states, but in religious terms moving further apart. In 1560, Queen Elizabeth's parliament passed the Acts of Uniformity and of Supremacy. By these acts, all the English became members of the Church of England; the queen, and later kings, was designated to be the Supreme Governor of that Church. It followed that the power of the monarch was much enhanced, becoming in one manifestation an English Pope. The Church of which Elizabeth was the head remained a facsimile of the Roman, with archbishops, bishops, priests, laws, powers of persecution and all. Elizabeth followed fairly closely in her father's path, therefore, avoiding as much change to the Church's positions and practices as possible. Yet there were those who could not accept this: a minority of Catholics refused any changes; a minority of Puritans agitated for more. Both of these hovered at the religious fringes, while the majority accepted the 'Elizabethan Settlement'.

In the same year as this English settlement was enacted, the Scots reorganized their own Church into a Church of Scotland. This eventually became fully Presbyterian, eliminating bishops altogether and putting authority at the local level. This tended not to be accepted by the monarchs, who made repeated attempts to return bishops to power and influence. Queen Mary remained a Catholic, ruling, at least theoretically, over a Presbyterian Church; James VI was an Episcopalian. From the viewpoint of this study, the Scottish change meant that the Scots could not be dragooned into the Church of England, though a minority Episcopalian Church of Scotland did continue to exist, favoured, when he became adult, by James VI, as did a considerable population of Catholics. In Ireland, the Protestant Reformation, though it made some progress in the early years of Elizabeth's reign, ultimately failed to convince the Irish, in part because it involved the acceptance of English political supremacy and was promulgated by the English administration. The majority of the Irish kept well clear of the (Anglican) Church of Ireland, and insisted on the practice of the Catholic Church, even when, or especially because, it suffered English persecution. As a contrast, and presumably because the country was part of England, the Welsh were provided with a series of translations of Gospels, prayer books, epistles and eventually (in 1588) the whole Bible into Welsh. As a result, for the whole of the seventeenth century Wales became a staunchly Anglican country. The function of the Church in the Middle Ages had been unifying; in the wake of the Protestant Reformation it became divisive.

King James's Inheritance

The first stage in the union of the four (now three) countries of the British islands came by genetic intention. Hardly surprisingly after the marital experiences of Henry VIII, and wholly unwilling to give up her royal power, as would happen if she took a husband, Queen Elizabeth refused to marry, while using the possibility that she might do so eventually as a useful lure for impressionable men, a classification which seems to have included almost the whole of the male English population and considerable numbers of those in Europe for several decades.

This circumstance thrust the succession outside England. For a time the English establishment was frightened that the Catholic Queen Mary of Scotland, Elizabeth's nearest relative, would survive long enough to inherit from her cousin, even though she was imprisoned in various castles in

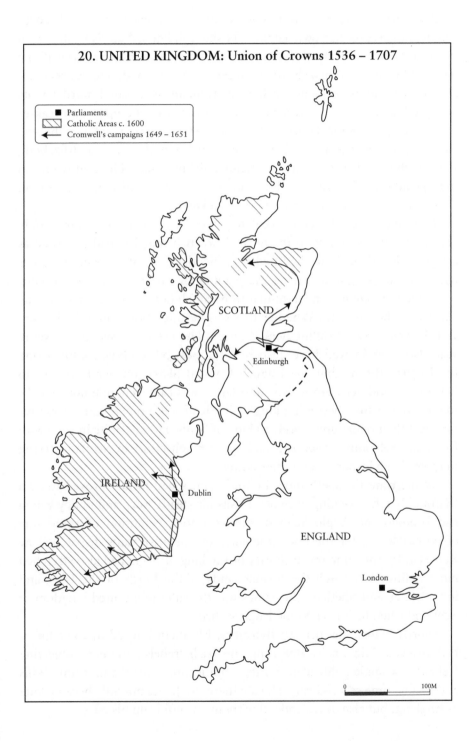

20. UNITED KINGDOM: Union of Crowns 1536 – 1707

■ Parliaments
Catholic Areas c. 1600
← Cromwell's campaigns 1649 – 1651

SCOTLAND

Edinburgh

IRELAND

Dublin

ENGLAND

London

0   100M

England from 1567; this was, of course, another means by which Elizabeth was able to control her own agenda. As she well knew, Mary's Catholicism made it highly unlikely that she would ever actually inherit, even if she outlived Elizabeth. When she finally accepted that Mary should be executed, after overwhelming evidence of her involvement in repeated murder plots was produced, her fears were at once realized with the open outbreak of war with Spain. King James in Scotland, Mary's son, acted as if he was annoyed, but he was as good at feigning such emotions as was Elizabeth; the possibility of a war with Scotland quickly faded. The apprehension in England that Mary might inherit says more about English instability than about Mary's abilities, never more than feckless.

The inheritance therefore went to James VI of Scotland, Mary's only child, who, in keeping with the normal Scottish practice, had inherited as a 1-year-old infant. Mary had fled from Scotland in 1567, abandoning her child and her kingdom, having exasperated all parties there. Her absence was widely welcomed and assumed to be an abdication – especially as she had left an heir behind. Whether that was her intention cannot be known, and she never ceased calling herself queen. Her eventual execution, twenty years later, might well have destroyed the possibility of James inheriting the English throne, but the English Council played on her treachery to her hostess and her Catholicism, and James was canny enough not to make too much of a fuss; becoming king of England was a much more attractive prospect than remaining merely as king of Scots. He was quite in tune with England's religious settlement, and spent much effort in Scotland trying to re-establish bishops – and their power.

By the time Elizabeth died, in 1603, James had in fact proved to be a thoroughly effective king of Scots. It was his steady work and policy which had brought the Anglo-Scottish border into a condition of some sort of peaceableness for the first time since the Scottish raids dispatched by Robert I. By this time the authority of the king of Scots had also stretched more definitely through the former lands of the Lords of the Isles, and into Orkney and Shetland. So James was the ruler of a united kingdom of Scotland when he inherited the English throne.

Shortly before she died, furthermore, Elizabeth learned that her forces had succeeded in finally defeating the Irish 'rebels', thereby subjecting Ireland to a single political authority – unification – for the first time. This at the same time secured English rule there. So James not only became king of England, but also of Ireland; all without any effort on his part.

The Union of the Crowns

King James arrived in London in the summer of 1603 full of enthusiasm for making into a reality the union which had fortuitously taken place of England-with-Wales, Scotland and Ireland. James was thus king of three countries. However, in aiming to strengthen and deepen the unity of his joint kingdoms, he came up against powerful opposition, which was enough to prevent his realizing his aim. He wished to be known as the king of Great Britain, but had to be content with England, Scotland and Ireland as separate kingdoms. He wished the union to become a union of countries with a single government and administration – an incorporating union, in the language of the time – and not just a union of crowns. Neither the Scots nor the English liked the idea – and nobody thought it worthwhile asking the conquered Irish. Scots were disliked in England, Englishmen were despised in Scotland and both despised the Irish. The union of two or three of the kingdoms would take more than the whim of a king who had inherited both kingdoms by accident of birth for it to become a reality.

James' attempts to integrate his kingdoms did not succeed, though he was successful in conciliating the English and in maintaining contact with and the loyalty of the Scots. At least James succeeded in being followed on his several thrones by an adult son, the first time a Stuart king had done so for more than two centuries. But Charles I turned into a disaster as king. He certainly made a further effort towards creating a more integrated set of kingdoms, but by choosing religion as his vehicle he simply enhanced their divisions. His devotion to the Anglican Church, and his appointment of William Laud as Archbishop of Canterbury, promoted the idea of that Church as a British institution rather than simply an English one. This had little effect in Ireland, whose problem was different, but in England, religious opinion was tending to shift towards the Puritan end of the spectrum in response to Laud's hectoring. In Scotland, the promotion of an Episcopalian Church and prayer book – James had not insisted too strongly on this, fully understanding Scottish sensitivities – brought about the revolution of the Covenant in 1637, and the categorical rejection by perhaps a clear majority of the Scottish population of the royal policies. This proved to be the point at which King Charles' regime came to the point of collapse.

The defiance of the Scots compelled the king to reply, and he chose to try to use force, recruiting troops and ships in England and Ireland. An elaborate invasion plan, intended to land forces at several points from Argyll round to Aberdeen, failed in every respect, and failed twice, in 1639 and then again in 1640. The fighting had hardly been serious or prolonged, and it might have been possible to patch things up, but in effect Scotland had resumed its independence, and had resigned from the regal union.

Both England and Ireland took advantage of the king's discomfiture to put forward their own complaints. The English demand took the form of Parliament refusing to cooperate in suppressing the Scots, and then by extending its demands towards a restriction of the royal powers in favour of those of Parliament. This may well not have gone anywhere, and the Scottish issue might well have been settled if the king had acted more in the conciliatory spirit of his father, but in Ireland the opportune paralysis of royal power was seized on for a full-scale Catholic rebellion, and this reacted further on the conditions in both England and Scotland.

So the final push into widespread civil warfare came from Ireland. Charles' policies in Ireland had been less religious than dictatorial, through the medium of the harsh government of Sir Thomas Wentworth, later Earl of Strafford – he called it 'thorough' – who shared the king's autocratic bent. In a sense, therefore, Ireland had been governed in a different way to either England or Scotland, which only emphasized the continuing differences between the three kingdoms. The growth of resentment at Charles' and Wentworth's policies and methods was shared by most of the Irish population, with only the English – and only the English Episcopalians – seriously accepting the royal policy as implemented. Resistance built up a serious head of steam as a result. So when the king, the English and the Scots were distracted by their increasingly acrimonious quarrels – and the royal army's defeats in the Bishops' Wars – Catholics in Ireland who were especially aggrieved broke out into a huge rebellion. The question was then how to suppress that rebellion. Both king and Parliament were serious about raising an army with which to do so, but they could not agree to the other appointing a commander over that army. Trust had faded to such a degree that even a common enemy could not bring any sort of agreement.

These disputes amounted to the dissolution of the union of the crowns. King Charles could not pretend to be governing any of his kingdoms from 1641/42 onwards. All of them were divided, and most of their territories were under governments which were independent of royal authority, having withdrawn allegiance. This condition continued while all three of the kingdoms pursued their own civil wars, which were in many ways conducted more or less independently of each other, though with a tendency to interfere where advantage was possible.

In England, the dispute was between Royalists and Parliamentarians, with the advantage gradually shifting towards Parliament. Wales was largely Royalist. In Scotland, the initial advantage lay with the king's enemies, but a spectacular set of campaigns by the Marquis of Montrose briefly recovered large areas for the king; the Highlands had a tendency towards the king. In Ireland, the dispute was religious at base, though also a matter of land. The Catholics formed a confederacy, and the Protestants divided between Royalists and Parliamentarians, though only hanging on in some coastal areas. The irony was that the Catholic Irish had finally instituted a unified state, but it was to be subjected to a devastating English attack.

The end for all became clear when, in England, the Parliament organized a disciplined army, the New Model, which was in effect a professional force, and put it under the command and direction of several highly competent commanders. The New Model Army was, as it turned out, also a highly politicized force, and no more obedient to the Parliament that created it than Parliament had been to the king.

So from 1641 onwards, for a decade, the composite kingdom of the three kingdoms had ceased to exist, replaced by an army dictatorship which for the first time unified the whole archipelago.

An English Military Unification

The series of civil wars between 1642 and 1648 were superficially distinct, but were in fact closely interconnected. Irish forces were recruited to fight in England, English armies were sent to preoccupy the Irish Catholic Confederacy, and Scottish armies repeatedly intervened in the English quarrels. It was a curious demonstration of the partial political unity of the three kingdoms which had been achieved by James I, where each kingdom had its own civil war, but all of them intervened in the others' quarrels. At the same time such connections provoked real unease and enmity. The use of Catholic Irish soldiers in the English war by the king provoked outrage not only from a vociferous Parliament, which was noisy about it largely for propaganda purposes, but also by men on his own side. The behaviour of the Scots, who were technically Parliament's allies when they campaigned in England, was regarded as disgraceful, and only increased Anglo–Scots mutual dislike. The Scots were also liable to go home abruptly when their own civil war turned awkward. Catholic Irish were fighting essentially with the object of expelling all the English from Ireland, and the Scots too. When the time came, Parliament's soldiers campaigning in Ireland and

Scotland eagerly took revenge for these earlier slights and humiliations. Overall casualties have been reckoned to be 10 per cent of the population, a hideous rate.

In the end, even after losing two English civil wars, Charles I continually refused to acknowledge the fact that he had been comprehensively defeated, or alternatively, even if he had been, it made no difference to his position or his divinely appointed powers. This uncompromising attitude – fully in character, of course – finally provoked the English Parliament into having him executed, though going through a form of trial first. The Scots now professed themselves outraged that someone else had killed their king. Despite the obvious conclusion the trial was heading for, they professed surprise as well as anger, though it is quite likely that they would have done the job themselves had they had the chance; and one wonders what an Irish Catholic government would have done to an English Protestant king if he had come into their hands.

The union of crowns system had clearly failed, but in the process the agony of the civil wars had confirmed the unifications of the four countries. The Irish Confederacy for several years ruled most of Ireland. In Scotland, the Presbyterian party was able to co-opt patriotic feeling against an oppressive king, though it still had considerable internal opposition. Wales was largely united in its support of the Royalists, while in England, there was no question of any permanent division, no matter that the two sides each controlled part of the country for years – one would eventually control all.

The partial union of the four, however, had clearly failed. The main reason was that the king had failed to govern the several parts intelligently, sequentially angering the people of each of his kingdoms to the point of rebellion, and because two of the three kingdoms involved rejected rule by the third. The alternative might have been the renewed separation of the three kingdoms into independence, though it is unlikely that the English would have surrendered control of Ireland. They might have been willing to let Scotland go, but the execution of the king had set every monarchy in Europe vociferously against the new Republic – the Commonwealth – and this was certainly directed at the Scots also. The most active early opposition came in fact not from the Catholic monarchies, who proclaimed the divine right of kings, but from the Calvinist republican Dutch: when even these were shown to be hostile, the English Republic had no friends anywhere. For the time being, immediately after the execution of the king, the Commonwealth government was very much on edge at the general hostility.

In theory Parliament was allied with the Scots, so for a time any hostility from the north was deferred. The main problem on land was therefore Ireland, the proximate cause of the fighting in England. An independent Catholic Ireland now raised once more the strategic problem which had been one of the main reasons for its conquest by Queen Elizabeth: it would be a useful base for a hostile Catholic power to use if it decided that the Protestant regicide Republic should be extinguished. Therefore, with commendable speed, Ireland became the first object of Parliament's and the army's attention.

There were in the island a variety of factions – Catholics in the Irish Confederation, an alliance of Catholic Irish and Catholic 'old English' – but these had differing objects. The arrival of the papal nuncio, Archbishop Rinuccini, widened the division between these groups. An emphasis on Catholicism by Rinuccini precluded any sort of compromise which the 'old English', who were principally Royalist, were prepared to consider. There were also the Presbyterians in Ulster – who were regularly assisted by support from Scotland – other Royalists and supporters of Parliament. These groups had fought each other intermittently since 1641, occasionally forming alliances with each other and breaking them. The fighting was regularly interrupted by truces, and this had gone on without any sign of reaching a result for the past eight years. The main power in theory was the Confederacy, which controlled most of the country, but its troops were short of weapons, militarily badly organized and poorly led and commanded.

The Catholics had also gathered to themselves an extremely unfortunate reputation. The original Catholic insurrection in 1641 had certainly been accompanied by atrocities, which were vastly exaggerated by the Protestant propagandists, particularly those of Parliament's side, with the result that a substantial head of hatred had been generated amongst English Protestants; combined with Rinuccini's rigidity, this deterred any suggestion of compromise.

It may be pointed out that one of the results of this Irish Civil War had been the construction of the Irish Confederacy, the first united state formed by the Irish people. This was an alternative political construction to the unification which had been imposed on Ireland by Elizabeth's conquest, but at the same time it was incomplete (just as Tyrone's military alliance had been). Many parts of the island remained outside the Confederacy's control, including Dublin, parts of Ulster and Cork, while other areas fell in and out of its control as the fighting ebbed and flowed. In particular, since the Confederacy was an avowedly Catholic construction, and deliberately thereby excluded the considerable proportion of the Irish population which was Protestant, it faced the enmity of those Protestants as well as those who felt loyalty to the various factions in England, Royalist or Republican. But then all of them now faced the hostility of the victorious and well-armed English Parliamentary forces, whose soldiers had learnt their trade very well in the past few years. Parliament could see clearly that an independent Catholic Ireland would be a perfect base for an active enemy, and the Catholic kings in Europe were very likely to become active enemies in 1649 – there were hostilities with France and Portugal at an unofficial level in 1649–50, and the Dutch War soon after. The best way to deter such enmity was to prove that the Parliamentary army was perfectly capable of dealing both with the situation in Ireland and with any possible invaders.

The English Parliament therefore organized a military expedition to suppress the Catholic Confederacy in Ireland – and any other Irish opponents – using as its weapon the New Model Army and its strictest, most capable general, Oliver Cromwell. It was, given the animosities involved, an unsurprisingly vicious campaign. The tone for much of the conflict, and for the later reputation of Cromwell in Ireland, was set by the siege of Drogheda, where the Royalist defenders repeatedly evaded or refused the terms Cromwell offered, and therefore suffered the unpleasantness of being taken by assault, with consequent heavy casualties among the garrison and clergy. No doubt some of the inhabitants died also, and prisoners taken in arms were shipped off as slave labour to Barbados. It has been a perennial complaint ever since by those in Ireland who have been determined to maintain old enmities that a massacre took place, though this seems not to be so. Considerable casualties at Wexford came in similar circumstances, but from then on Cromwell had little difficulty in persuading a series of towns to consider surrender at summons – they now knew the alternative to evasion or refusal. In a campaign lasting just nine months (August 1649 to May 1650), Cromwell's army therefore conquered much of eastern and southern Ireland. After he had been summoned back to London, the campaign continued more slowly under other parliamentary commanders who had smaller forces at their disposal; but the whole of Ireland had been conquered by April 1652. This was yet another unification.

Ireland was then subjected to a new settlement dictated by the English. Much of the land was allocated to settle debts contracted by Parliament during the Civil War; more than half the island was assigned to the soldiers who had conquered it, with a quarter of the land, in Connacht in the west, reserved for the Irish. This was, in effect, yet another attempt by the English to establish control over the island – after those of Henry VIII, Elizabeth, James I and Charles I – and at each attempt the land taken by the English increased, so that the land under Irish ownership or control diminished. In no case could it be said that any real attempt had been made to conciliate the Irish population. The country was also subjected to a large-scale military occupation for the rest of the Commonwealth period, in which the occupiers had to be supported out of Irish resources, with the usual heavy taxation and immiseration.

Cromwell had been called back to London by Parliament because a crisis had developed with the Scots. Scottish annoyance at the execution of 'their' king by the English had emphasized to them that they were actually an independent state once more. In 1650, they welcomed the arrival of the heir to all three thrones, Charles II, as their own king. He had a very unhappy time at their hands, being subject to constant pressure and exhortation and the exposition of Presbyterian tenets by a number of dour preachers. He also found that Scotland was less than united internally and worked to revive the Royalist party, thereby justifying the suspicions which many Scots had entertained of him from the first. This restoration of the Stuart monarchy in one of the kingdoms brought a reply from the English in September 1650 in the form of an invasion of Scotland by the New Model Army, again under the command of Oliver Cromwell.

This campaign was considerably more difficult in a military sense than that in Ireland, since the Scots' forces were more competent than the Irish. It was also not marked by unpleasant sieges. The Scots' supervising ministers – commissars – had a tendency to purge their army of those who were less than religiously enthusiastic, or in their view orthodox, which tended to remove some of the more competent soldiers and also any men with independent opinions about anything. This so weakened the command of their army that the policy operated strongly in the English interest. A preliminary attack on Edinburgh by Cromwell's forces was deflected, and his retreat was followed up by the Scots until the two armies met in battle at Dunbar, where the Scots were defeated, thanks to a display of Cromwell's superior generalship. This, paradoxically, opened the way for Charles and the Royalists to develop their own control over the Scottish government, while at the same time a Western Association – a combination of four counties in the south-west – produced its own rival army; this last was quickly defeated by an English detachment, so contributing further to Scottish weakening and demoralization.

These Scottish divisions and defeats once again assisted the English advance, and another Scots defeat at the crossing of the Forth at Inverkeithing persuaded the king and his commanders, after these successive losses, that the best thing to do would be to invade England, on the assumption that large numbers of Englishmen were waiting for the chance to join a Royalist army led by the king. This didn't work either, partly because the king was untried, but mainly because it was a Scots army, and so to the English it was a foreign invasion. Cromwell's forces marched south in pursuit and, together with several other English military detachments converging from all parts of England, cornered the Scots at Worcester and destroyed them. Charles escaped in another romantic escapade whose retelling deflected attention from the general military incapacity displayed by both him and the Scots.

Cromwell now returned to London, leaving a part of the army in Scotland to continue and conclude the conquest. Further defeats of the Scots at Kilsyth and Stirling followed, and the English forces spread themselves throughout the kingdom, though very few penetrated far into the Highlands. Scottish casualties had been heavy, both those killed in battle and those taken prisoner; as with the Irish, the prisoners were ordered to be sent as slaves to Barbados, though many died before they could be shipped out. Few, if any, ever returned.

There was a certain degree of sympathy in England for the Scottish religious position, and the country was not treated anyway nearly as ruthlessly as Ireland. On the other hand, it was certainly subjected to a continuing military occupation by the English forces, and this was inevitably resented.

A Military Dictatorship

Cromwell's return to London eventually resulted in his *coup d'état* in 1653, dismissing the Parliament which, having been purged repeatedly, was no longer anywhere near representative. This was followed by his own installation as Lord Protector, in effect appointed by the army.

England had become a military dictatorship. This was partly disguised by Cromwell's repeated attempts to find an acceptable Parliament, though he impatiently dismissed each one. In the period 1649–53, the New Model Army had been installed as the military occupiers first of Ireland, then of Scotland, and had then turned to seize power in its home territory of England: at one point the local government was even placed under the supervision of a set of major-generals, whose very incompetence and personal social preferences were less than persuasive to the population. This was not what those who had fought against the king had ever envisaged happening, and at no point could the military regime under Cromwell be said to have enjoyed very much support. It survived by force and by suppressing the occasional risings in various parts of Scotland and England.

Successful resistance proved to be impossible. The army, though its rule was detested, was militarily extremely competent. Nevertheless, resentment was universal. For the Scots there was little alternative to submission. They had produced two armies to face the English invasion: one was captured almost entirely at Dunbar and the second had been rounded up and destroyed at Worcester; the prisoners were sent to the West Indies as slave labour. The result of these two defeats, on top of a dozen years of earlier fighting, was the almost literal decimation of a large part of the young adult male part of the Scottish population; the country suffered such a loss of its potential military manpower that it was effectively demilitarized while the English Commonwealth rule lasted. The Scots were exhausted, and they accepted English rule because they were no longer capable of resisting.

Wales had conspicuously supported the Royalist cause during the Civil War, but it was neither rich nor populous enough to do more than contribute some forces to the king's army. When that army in England had been defeated, it proved to be relatively easy to mop up the Royalist supporters in various parts of Wales, though the ubiquity of castles made the conquest fairly laborious. These Royalist supporters turned out to be mainly lords and gentry; the ordinary Welsh population were prepared to enlist in various armies but apparently had little serious wish to see the king victorious – he was an English (or Scottish) king, after all.

The treatment of the three subject regions varied. Ireland was treated differently from the other countries once the English Commonwealth could turn its full attention to the island. Scotland was under military occupation, and the occasional rebellion was put down, but it was exhausted, and there was a certain fellow feeling between the Puritan English army and the Presbyterians of Scotland. The same might be said of Wales, where a tendency towards Puritanism was given a substantial boost by a series of schools founded under the Act for the Propagation of the Gospel of 1650. These schools did not last beyond the period of the military dictatorship, being subsidised, but they had their effect while they lasted.

Ireland, however, was regarded, after its second conquest by the English, as a subject colony, and the people, largely Catholic, were not to be treated as anything other than an enemy, and its lands were regarded as being at the disposal of the victors. There were plenty of people in Ireland who had taken the 'wrong' side at some point during the various wars, and could be dispossessed. One of the requirements was a large-scale and reasonably accurate survey of the country in preparation for the distribution of lands, the first such survey to be undertaken.

Above all, the continuation of a large military establishment to hold Ireland and Scotland, and to suppress English opposition, was extremely expensive. Such expedients as the allocation of confiscated Irish land to the support of the soldiers could not really help, since the soldiers in the army still had to be paid and supported – and the army's pay was generally well in arrears, stimulating some military discontent. In addition to the existence of the army, the population had therefore to be heavily taxed to support it.

The New Model Army had, nevertheless, accomplished what Agricola, Severus, Edward I, Henry VIII and James I had all failed to do: it had united under a single government the whole of the British islands. It had, of course, conquered Ireland and Scotland only after those countries had been debilitated by their preceding decade of warfare, so that the conquests had been relatively straightforward. Yet it was a unification even so. But it was a unification which from the start was detested by virtually all the populations of all three countries, and so it was most unlikely to last. The one pillar which held it up was Oliver Cromwell himself.

For the New Model Army, of course, the assumption was that its military abilities and size were sufficient to ensure its continuation in power, but this was not actually enough. This became clear as soon as Cromwell died in September 1658. He was followed by the steady disintegration of the Commonwealth regime, first under his son, Richard, as the second Lord Protector, then under gradually reinstated and enlarged Parliaments which were eventually returned to a new version of the original Parliament elected in 1640. In two years the experience of 1640–53 had unreeled like a film run backwards. In May 1660, Charles II once again crossed the sea to become king of the three kingdoms, this time by English invitation. The toxic political memory of the military regime has helped to keep any military ambitions towards a new military dictatorship in Britain well in check ever since.

The Army had nevertheless demonstrated that English power and wealth, always predominant in the islands, was capable of enforcing a political union on the whole archipelago. This was, therefore, one type of the available forms of unification, to go along with a loose union of crowns of the type James I and Charles I had presided over. A third alternative was an 'incorporating union', which implied a voluntary surrender of local powers and sovereignty to a central authority. Given the necessarily voluntary nature of the union, this authority must be a Parliament. Between 1603 and 1660, therefore, all the countries of Britain had experienced the first two types of union, neither of which worked. The third was still to be attempted.

Restoration of the Union of the Crowns

Charles II returned to rule three separate kingdoms, the military union having vanished with the New Model Army. Each kingdom had its Parliament, each had its particular religious tradition and establishment, and each had its own varying and different problems. The new government began by wreaking revenge on the regicides of Charles's father, but then raised a large sum of tax money to pay off the Army. The king aspired to return to the pre-Civil War, pre-revolutionary situation, but of course this could not be. The English Parliament had tasted power, and no matter how Royalist its elected members might be after 1660 – and not all were – they were not prepared to surrender the real powers which their predecessors in the 1640s had gained before the king began the Civil War. Since Parliament controlled the money supply through taxation, Charles II had no option but to accept the situation.

Scotland's disturbed condition continued, which argued the existence of an extensive and difficult political problem, though the English tended to shrug the problem away. Ireland returned to English rule with scarcely a break from that of Cromwell – few of the beneficiaries of the English conquest were dispossessed, and none of the Irish were compensated. The English army of occupation might have theoretically gone, but the English landlords remained, and an English administration ruled from Dublin Castle.

Above all, the political relations between the three kingdoms were always strained. King Charles might be king of England, Ireland and Scotland, a triune kingship once again, but this meant that he had to cope with three separate Parliaments, none of which was at all interested in cooperating with the others, or in cooperating in any serious sense with the royal government. He had to appoint trusted – he hoped – viceroys for both countries, the Earl of Lauderdale for Scotland, then James Duke of York, and the Duke of Ormonde for Ireland. These men were, as royal agents, generally unpopular, and a little too reminiscent of Strafford in Ireland for comfort. It was an unstable situation, which was just as ripe for collapse as that which had existed before the civil wars, or that which had been constructed by the army in the 1650s. By mainly employing Scots in Scotland and Irishmen in Ireland, however, it was slowly dawning on the English that conciliation and cooperation was the best way to make the union work.

In England, the relations between king and Parliament were sufficiently strained to bring on political crises throughout the reign of Charles II, culminating in several plots against him, but he was adroit enough on the whole to avoid a disastrous confrontation for twenty years. Eventually, in 1681, he felt that Parliament has sufficiently put itself in the wrong to allow him to strike back – and he had acquired a substantial subsidy from the French King Louis XIV, which would render his policies independent of parliamentary taxation.

The disputatiousness in England was largely concentrated in political circles, above all in Parliament, and when Charles dispensed with Parliament from 1681 onwards, there were relatively few complaints. Wales was generally quiet, and in Ireland the exhaustion of the country after the military conquest and the rapacious military occupation in the 1650s had reduced activity – especially since part of the government's policy under Charles II was Catholic toleration.

Scotland, however, was turbulent. Twice, in 1666 and 1679, popular risings took place, originating in the south-west: the Pentland Rising and the Bothwell Brig rebellion. This was just the area where the Western Association had been formed and had fielded its own army during the English invasion of 1650. Both risings were essentially incoherent, originating in government attempts to coerce unwilling people into obedience to the Scottish Church, on which government had reimposed bishops, and to collect taxes in a relatively poor country. Both risings were fairly easily suppressed, but the insurgents' lack of clarity in their aims made it difficult to fully suppress them and made repetition very possible.

Revolution

The second collapse of the regime of the Union of Crowns came in the 1680s. King Charles succeeded in doing without Parliament in England from 1681. Several plots against him – real, invented or imagined – all failed; Parliament had proved unpleasantly gullible over these and Charles capitalized on the plots' failure. He was also particularly annoyed at Parliamentary attempts, by a devious manoeuvre, to exclude his Catholic brother James from the succession.

Meanwhile, the Irish Parliament, composed mainly of Protestant landlords, knew full well that it required the support of the government in England, of whatever ideological persuasion, if the English conquest regime was to continue, and was thus unassertive. The Scots Parliament was managed by a succession of Scots lords in King Charles' name, the last of whom was the king's brother, James Duke of York.

Charles set about purging the English local administration of political enemies, but even with that level of support he failed to call a new Parliament, though one was legally due, thereby demonstrating that a mere Act of Parliament was not sufficient to ensure that Parliament could oversee royal activities, and insist on the king obeying his own laws. A wider political participation was needed to compel him to do so. Charles was as determined an absolutist as his father, if rather more cautious in implementing such a policy. Charles' successor was this same brother whom Parliament had attempted to exclude. He came to the throne in 1685 as King James VII (of Scots) and II (of England). James succeeded in persuading the English Parliament, once its selection procedures had been adjusted to his satisfaction and its hand-picked members had met, in voting him sufficient money to live on and rule for the rest of his life and reign: in effect, the English Parliament was voting itself out of existence for the foreseeable future. James was Catholic, and this raised all the old fears of Popery and persecution amongst the English Protestants. As a result of these policies, he was faced with an invasion, summoned in the names of a group of lords who claimed to represent widespread political opinion. The invasion came from the Netherlands, under the command of the Dutch Protestant William III, who was the husband of James' Protestant daughter, Mary.

James had been openly bullish and partisan in his internal policies. In Ireland, he appointed Catholics exclusively to public office, and had recruited his army there mainly from Catholics, and had marginalized Protestants everywhere. In England, he encouraged Catholics by proclaiming toleration and encouraging conversions, but more ominously, he had also built up his English army, thereby adding the unpleasant memories of military autocracy to the perception of his Catholic absolutism. (In France, the Revocation of the Edict of Nantes in 1685 had led to a large exodus of French Protestants (Huguenots), many of whom came to England for refuge; the lesson for the English seemed clear.)

The concentration of threats to the Anglican Church, the existence of a large army – partly officered by Catholics – which had to be paid for out of heavier taxation, and the potential end of Parliament, was a set of conditions which were sufficiently alarming in England to bring about the revolution of 1688. The invasion from the Netherlands was successful, and James fled to France. This allowed the new Parliament which was soon called to claim that he had abdicated – while in Scotland, the more clear-headed Scots Parliament concluded that he had forfeited the throne – just as had Queen Mary over a century before.

This 'Glorious Revolution' could be explained away by James' Catholicism and the dangers of the international situation, where King Louis XIV of France was becoming all too menacingly powerful and ambitious. It could also be camouflaged by the fact that William was married to James' daughter, who was James' direct heir. Yet it was actually still another royal *coup d'etat*. It was carried through in England, which did not mean it was acceptable in Scotland and Ireland. This crisis eventually brought on, therefore, the next stage in the unification of the archipelago. However successful the revolution had been in the three countries separately, as a system for governing the three kingdoms as another union of crowns, it was to fail.

This was to be the fourth attempt to make the Union of Crowns work. That of James I collapsed under the pressure of Charles I's policies; that of the English Commonwealth military dictatorship collapsed without Cromwell in power; Charles II's system failed under the unpopularity of his and his brother's policies in the 1680s; and now here was another attempt. The prospects were not good. The alternatives were a closer union or complete political separation.

The effect of the revolution was at first to destabilize the union of crowns. This took some time to set up again, and was soon obviously even less acceptable than the earlier versions. The three countries had all reacted in different ways to the revolution. The English Parliament, having decided that James could be said to have abdicated because he had fled the country with his family, assumed that the throne was vacant and awarded it to William III and Mary II, James' nearest heirs, who were to occupy it jointly. Parliament also took the opportunity to enforce a variety of constitutional practices – regular Parliamentary elections, Parliamentary control of financing the army and of taxation, and so on – all of which had all been violated by Charles and James.

The Scots Estates, also meeting as a Convention Parliament, acted in a different way, claiming that James had actually forfeited the Crown by his desertion. The implication was that he was king because he had been accepted as such by the population, and that through his behaviour and policies he had broken that implied contract. The Estates then began a different task, dismantling the Episcopalian Church settlement which had been put in place by Charles II. This created much dismay and confusion in the Church. Ministers were expelled from their parishes and many others resigned; the effect was most notable in the south-west, the area of the former Pentland Rising and Bothwell Brig rebellion, though it affected all parts of the country. The change put the Presbyterian system back in control on a much firmer basis, and this probably had the support of most of the people.

There was, however, a substantial element of Episcopalians in the country, and the expelled ministers were mostly given refuge in other parishes or in the houses of great men who sympathized. Especially in the Highlands, there were blocks of Catholic clans. In part associated with these religious groups, there was also a strong element of loyalty to the Stuart dynasty, much more so than in England. When the Convention Parliament met in Edinburgh, it was unclear how its members would decide on the question of the monarchy. It received written submissions, manifestoes, from both candidates, and whereas William, a much more adroit politician than James, was polite, ambiguous, conciliatory and clearly Protestant, James was arrogant, Catholic and threatening. As a result, the decision was clearly for William as king of Scotland.

Not all members accepted that. James Graham, Viscount Dundee, left the Convention and raised a rebellion in favour of James. Basing himself on his own regiment, he marched off northwards, hoping to gather support among the Catholic clans of the Highlands and Stuart loyalists. He was the original Jacobite. He was pursued by a Williamite force, which he defeated at the pass of Killiecrankie, though Dundee was killed in the fighting. His army was then defeated at Dunkeld by a force of Cameronians, who had been recruited from the strongly Protestant south-west – the revenge, as it were, of the defeated Pentland and Bothwell Brig rebels. This decided the matter in Scotland in favour of William and Mary, and the Convention settled down to its own tasks, arranging the government of the Church and of the kingdom, in which Parliament, as in England, was now clearly supreme over the Crown.

Ireland behaved differently again. King James was able, by way of France, to return to Ireland and take up the reins of power there at once. He already had a governor present, the Earl of Tyrconnell, who had been overseeing the progressive Catholicization of the island's government and army during

James' reign. James' control of the government was therefore so complete that he was immediately able to issue writs summoning an Irish Parliament; these writs were accompanied by letters from Tyrconnell naming the persons he wished to see 'elected'. Having purged Protestants from the local councils, Tyrconnell's wishes were generally met; it was an Irish version of the method which James had used to secure his perpetual power and his tax resources in England. No members came from the Ulster towns or from three of the Ulster counties, where Protestants predominated, but James did collect a Parliament of 230 members out of the 300 who had been summoned, so it was quorate and could claim to be properly representative. It was overwhelmingly Catholic, only six members being reckoned to be Protestant, so it was more representative of the Irish population than the Parliament that succeeded it, which was summoned by William and was almost entirely Protestant.

James' Irish army was thus a threat to England, where King William had also convened a Convention Parliament. William collected an army, composed of a wide variety of contingents from all the Protestant countries of northern Europe, and with this invaded Ireland, landing at Carrickfergus in Ulster. The Catholic army's failure to capture Londonderry had already exposed its weakness, and the relief of the siege of that city by sea, and the landing at Carrickfergus, showed that the sea was William's. Other landings could therefore take place wherever he wished. The decisive defeat for the Catholic army at the River Boyne put James' forces in retreat, a campaign of another year or so resulted in James fleeing to France once more and the Protestant army triumphed. This was the third Protestant conquest of Ireland in a century.

Another punitive settlement was imposed. A new Irish Parliament was elected, almost entirely Protestant, and quite unrepresentative of the Irish population. Many Jacobite Catholic landowners were expelled, lost their lands or fled. This was the major change, since from then on the ownership of land in Ireland was even more overwhelmingly in Protestant hands, while their workers and tenants were mainly Catholic. This was the foundation of the 'Ascendancy', the name given to the Protestant system of political and social control which lasted for the next two centuries.

Another Revival of the Union of Crowns

The events of 1685–91 in the three kingdoms had exposed, yet again, the weaknesses of a union of countries which was based solely on allegiance to a single king, with no greater integration. The wilfulness of that single king was clearly potentially harmful to large numbers of his subjects. It also proved very easy for the three countries to go their own way, and all three had done so in the crisis of the Glorious Revolution. The result not only exposed those general weaknesses, but produced a new union of crowns which was even weaker in its links than before. Once the dust had settled for a time, it was still the king (and the queen) who were the only elements which showed that the union existed. All three countries had Parliaments of their own, and these were exclusively focused on their own affairs. All three had majority populations whose religious allegiance was directed more to their national Churches than to the king – the defence of the Church of England had been one of the English priorities in the revolution, while in Scotland the Parliament destroyed the Episcopalian superstructure imposed by Charles II and produced an exclusively Presbyterian system. In Ireland, between 1680 and 1690 the majority Catholic population had, for the first time in a century, an effectively national Catholic Church, and it set about persecuting or expelling Protestants; this was followed by a complete reversal, putting the Protestant Ascendancy in control. Each of the Parliaments had become active and assertive against the Crown during the time of the revolution, and they retained that assertiveness afterwards.

The royal prerogative, which had tended towards royal absolutism in the last years of Charles II and decisively so during James II's reign, was now much reduced in effectiveness. King William retained control over foreign policy, and command of the army and navy remained with the king, so these aspects stayed part of the royal power, but both were subject to parliamentary agreement and supervision through parliamentary provision of the necessary finance. These elements, together with the general suspicion of royal motives, meant that royal absolutism was no longer an option.

As a result, King William, and then Queen Anne, had to deal with three separate Parliaments, which could very well enact contradictory measures, or differentially refuse royal requests. The tenuousness of the links between the three countries meant that the revived Union of Crowns which emerged from the revolution could scarcely be considered a true political union any more. The fact that the Glorious Revolution was immediately followed by a French war in which one of the aims of the enemy was to put James back in power acted as a strong pressure to keep the three countries in line. But the return of peace would bring a much stronger test.

Bibliography

Britain:

Grainger, John D., *Cromwell against the Scots, the last Anglo-Scottish war, 1650–1652* (East Linton: 1997).

Hirst, Derek, *Dominion, England and its Island Neighbours, 1500–1707* (Oxford: 2012).

Kishlansky, Mark, *A Monarchy Transformed, Britain 1603–1714* (London: 1996).

Lenman, Bruce, *The Jacobite Risings in Britain 1689–1746* (London: 1980).

Russell, Conrad, *The Fall of the British Monarchies, 1637–1642* (Oxford: 1991).

Smyth, Jim, *The Making of the United Kingdom 1660–1800, State, Religion and Identity in Britain and Ireland* (Harlow, Essex: 2001).

Speck, W.A., *Reluctant Revolutionaries, Englishmen and the Revolution of 1688* (Oxford: 1989).

England:

Ashley, Maurice, *Charles II, the Man and the Statesman* (London: 1971).

Ashley, Maurice, *The Glorious Revolution of 1688* (London: 1966).

Hill, Christopher, *The Century of Revolution 1603–1714* (London: 1961).

Hutton, Ronald, *The Restoration, a Political and Religious History of England and Wales, 1658–1667* (Oxford: 1985).

Vallance, Edward, *The Glorious Revolution, 1688 – Britain's Fight for Liberty* (London: 2006).

Wheeler, James Scott, *The Making of a World Power, War and the Military Revolution in Seventeenth-Century England* (Stroud, Glos: 1999).

Woolrych, Austin, *Commonwealth to Protectorate* (Oxford: 1982).

Scotland:

Brown, Keith M., *Kingdom or Province? Scotland and the Regal Union, 1603–1715* (London: 1992).

Devine, T.M., *Exploring the Scottish Past, Themes in the History of Scottish Society* (East Linton: 1995).

Dow, F.R., *Cromwellian Scotland, 1651–1660* (Edinburgh: 1979).

Fraser, Antonia, *Mary Queen of Scots* (London: 1969).

Lane, Jane, *The Reign of King Covenant* (London: 1956).

Paterson, Raymond Campbell, *King Lauderdale, the Corruption of Power* (Edinburgh: 2003).

Stevenson, David, *King or Covenant? Voices from the Civil War* (East Linton: 1996).

Stevenson, David, *Revolution and Counterrevolution, 1640–51* (Edinburgh: 1977).

Stevenson, David, *The Scottish Revolution 1637–44, The Triumph of the Covenanters* (Newton Abbot, Devon: 1973).

Young, John R. (ed.), *Celtic Dimensions of the British Civil Wars* (Edinburgh: 1997).

Wales:

Gaunt, Peter, *A Nation under Siege, the Civil War in Wales, 1642–1648* (London: 1991).

Jenkins, Geraint H., *The Foundation of Modern Wales, 1642–1780* (Oxford: 1993).

Jones, J. Gwynfor, *Early Modern Wales, c.1525–1640* (London: 1994).

Ireland:

Barnard, T.C., *Cromwellian Ireland, English Government and Reform in Ireland 1649–1661* (Oxford: 1975).

Beckett, J.C., *The Making of Modern Ireland 1603–1923* (London: 1966).

Childs, John, *The Williamite Wars in Ireland, 1688–1691* (London: 2007).

Clarke, Aidan, *The Old English in Ireland, 1625–42* (Dublin: 2000).

Foster, R.F., *Modern Ireland 1600–1972* (London: 1988).

Hirst, Derek, *Dominion, England and its Island Neighbours, 1500–1707* (Oxford: 2012).

McKiever, Philip, *A New History of Cromwell's Irish Campaign* (Manchester: 2007).

Simms, J.G., *Jacobite Ireland, 1685–91* (Dublin: 2000).

Chapter 9

The Union of England and Scotland

S ince the Union of Crowns took place in 1603 it had, as a political
system, collapsed three times – in 1639, 1650 and 1688 – and had
been interrupted by the English Civil War, a military dictatorship
and a revolution. These last presented the traditional method of uniting
the countries involved, by military conquest, which, in effect, was a
throwback to the old mediaeval and Roman method. The several parts of
the union, the three constituents, were as alienated from each other and as
determinedly independent as they had been before the crowns had been
united. The war that was fought by William III between 1689 and 1697,
called the War of the League of Augsburg, or the Nine Years' War, was also
a War of British Succession, for one of Louis XIV's war aims was to restore
James II to his three thrones. The Glorious Revolution had been part of
that war, in fact had been at the root of it from the British viewpoint, and
so it was also a war in defence of that revolution. It was clear, however, even
during the war, that the Revolutionary Settlement of 1689 had not settled
the real geopolitical issue in Britain, which was the relations between the
three countries. This remained to be dealt with.

The Issue of Unification

By the 1690s, after the three generations of the Union of the Crowns, the
problems had become clear. England was the richest of the three countries,
the largest and the most populous, and was liable to treat Scotland as a
provincial appanage, just as it treated Ireland as a subject colony. None of
the kings since Charles I had been to Scotland (except Charles II in his ill-
fated visit in 1650). The Stuart monarchy had in effect become an English
monarchy, gravitating necessarily to the wealth of England. 'England' was
being used as a term for the whole three countries, Scotland being reduced
to an English component, to general Scots (and Welsh) annoyance ever
since. At the same time, the English Parliament was wont to enact measures
which excluded Scotland as a foreign state. The Navigation Act of the Rump

Parliament in 1651 had regulated commerce, by which time Scotland was, as a conquered country, united to England and part of the Commonwealth. Later, when Cromwell's Parliaments were elected, Scottish members were included, though they were only few, reflecting its much smaller population; the country's subjection was therefore followed by integration of a sort. But at the Restoration in 1660, that military-imposed unity was broken and the separate Parliaments revived. When the Parliament at Westminster re-enacted the Navigation Acts, it did so with reference to England alone, so that Scotland was treated as a foreign state (as was Ireland). The Acts also enclosed the colonies within the English system, so that Scottish settlers were not welcome in the American colonies – though some had already settled in such places as Jamaica and New Jersey – and, more important, Scottish trade and merchants were also excluded. It was not just royal policy and national preferences in religion which were operating to drive the countries apart.

The many divergences – religious, parliamentary, political, economic and others – highlighted the difficulties in moving from a union of the monarchies only, to something deeper and more integrated. The Commonwealth episode had hardly persuaded anyone to work for a closer relationship, and the army's *force majeure* methods were not possible afterwards, if only for lack of an army. The difficulties of any voluntary integration therefore looked formidable. Total separation would have been much easier to accomplish. On the other hand, the advantages to both England and Scotland of a thoroughgoing union were as evident to an unprejudiced view as the difficulties in accomplishing it were great. It is worth looking at exactly how such a union might, or might not, be carried out.

The Military Option

Three serious attempts at a military conquest of Scotland by an army based in England had taken place. Those by the Roman Governor Agricola and King Edward I had failed. That of Cromwell had succeeded, but the memory of it poisoned later relations between England and Scotland. In view of the resentment the occupation engendered in Scotland and Ireland, it would never have been possible to relax the military grip had it continued. The conquest failed partly because the Protectorate was unpopular, but also because it was a very expensive option, and the English refused to bear the cost.

It may be argued that a military conquest was in fact successful in uniting England with Wales, but the achievement of Edward I in conquering the

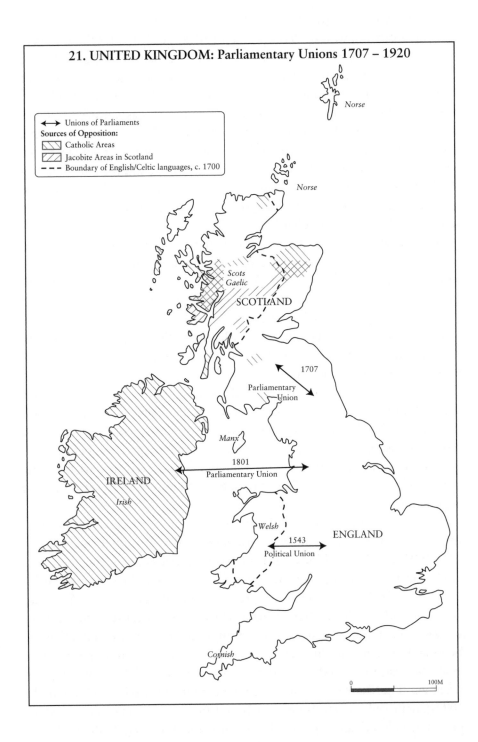

21. UNITED KINGDOM: Parliamentary Unions 1707 – 1920

Norse

◄───► Unions of Parliaments
Sources of Opposition:
▨ Catholic Areas
▨ Jacobite Areas in Scotland
- - - Boundary of English/Celtic languages, c. 1700

Norse

Scots Gaelic

SCOTLAND

1707
Parliamentary Union

Manx

1801
Parliamentary Union

IRELAND

Irish

Welsh

1543
Political Union

ENGLAND

Cornish

0   100M

Welsh principality of the dynasty of Gwynedd was actually only partial – only the north and west of Wales – and it had succeeded, after three wars in less than twenty years, mainly because of Welsh exhaustion. A good half of Wales had remained un-united, since the Marcher lordships retained their own legalities and customs, in which the English Crown was unwilling to interfere. The resentment in Wales at the conquest was sufficiently long-lived to give general support to the rebellion led by Owen Glyndwr a century after Edward I's conquest. The failure of this great rising may well have convinced many Welsh to accept their situation, and the emergence of the Tudor kings, which in one aspect was a self-consciously Welsh dynasty, may have persuaded their contemporaries in Wales that a Welshman had somehow taken over in England.

The actual unification of Wales and its unity with England was achieved by Henry VIII in 1536 and 1542 by Parliamentary enactment. This was successful, and even in the Civil War a century later there was no attempt to detach Wales from the union. The previous period of political union had already imposed English law, and now the Marcher people were subject to it also; Welsh members entered Parliament. This unification therefore was very largely only a matter of legislation, a relatively easy task once it had been decided to undertake it.

It follows that much more needed to be done to make a unification successful than mere military conquest. Even the relatively straightforward unification with Wales had required two Acts of Parliament – the second to put right mistakes in the first – and a considerable preparation beforehand. Any attempt to unite England and Scotland would need to start from the impossibility of conquest. The only options therefore were separation or negotiation.

It may be objected that military conquest had successfully brought Ireland into a sort of union with England, and that military occupation after 1603, and in the 1650s, held the island under control. But there was only a fairly minimal military presence after 1603, and the Commonwealth army in the 1650s was as disliked a presence in Ireland as it was in Scotland (and England, for that matter). Ireland was held less because of the military occupation and more because of the immigration of substantial numbers of Scots and English into the island, in particular into positions of government and administration, and as landlords, and because of the emigration of Irishmen. The 'flight of the earls', a phenomenon repeated in 1650 (and in the 1690s), deprived the remaining Irish population of the layer of society which provided political and military leadership, and rendered Irish rebellions, even that in the 1640s, largely incoherent. Ireland was controlled for much of the time between 1603 and 1688 by an installed English government, and by English and Scots ownership of much of the land.

The Familiarity of Neighbourliness

The most important element in promoting a political unification must be a mutual acceptance by both parties that such a unification is necessary; if it is not perceived as necessary, a true unification will not take place – and only if it became necessary would it happen. The Welsh acceptance of the Church of England after the Reformation was the basis of the country's later loyalty to the king (or kings). The Scots attachment to the Presbyterian Church was by contrast a major obstacle to unification. The political necessity would be best understood when it became clear that union would save both parties from their enemies. No unification in Britain in the past had happened without it being a matter of self-preservation – the Viking menace in Scotland, the Danish threat in England, the English threat in Wales which pushed the princes of Gwynedd to attempt a union, or in Ireland where the alliance under O'Neill in the face of the Elizabethan attack, and the Confederacy facing English attack in the 1640s, had come near to unification. The Norman campaign against internal enemies in England had been necessary for William I to save his conquest. In the 1690s, the main reason holding England and Scotland together after the Glorious Revolution was the French and Catholic menace, and Louis XIV's intention to return James VII and II to his thrones.

To this defensiveness may be added the fact of a long experience of both having lived in the same island. This experience had been in large part, at least until the reigns of Elizabeth and James I in the later sixteenth century, usually, if inevitably, hostile. But wars breed familiarity as well as dislike, and both Scots and English knew plenty about each other by the time they were yoked together into the Union of Crowns. This general familiarity might well be thought to be the basic necessity for any union; two peoples in states who knew nothing about each other are unlikely even to contemplate a union.

Neighbouring countries trade with each other, and this is another aspect of familiarity. England was inevitably one of Scotland's main trading partners, though a substantial amount of Scots trade was also done with the Baltic countries and the Netherlands. One problem here was that English and Scottish exports tended to be the same goods, though Scottish exports were less in manufacturing items than in mineral or agricultural goods. The Scots therefore found it difficult to export to England, since the English already produced the same goods and exported them themselves. Scots prices were lower, a matter resented as unfair competition by the English, and was one of the reasons behind the restored Navigational Laws. Those Navigation Acts created considerable difficulties for the Scots exporters to England. Unification into a single country would, for the Scots, solve that issue. On the other hand, the Scottish market was not large or rich enough to tempt English exports, so the attraction for them was minimal.

Institutional aspects also had some weight. After centuries of separate but neighbourly existence, the two countries not only had differing religious systems, but also differing Protestant systems. The Scottish Presbyterians evoked bad memories in England, since that had been an aspect of the Commonwealth Protectorate period, where the English had been somewhat less intolerant, though the Anglican Church of England had been persecuted. The two countries' parliamentary affairs were also organized differently – characterized by the different names for the Parliaments – the Estates in Scotland, Parliament in England – each with different powers and procedures. They also had varying legal systems, with the Scots law being based on a version of Roman law and the English based on common law. Linking these together would be almost as difficult as the merging of the religious establishments, which would probably be, after the events of the Glorious Revolution, impossible. All these matters were fully understood by all those who had thought about them; what they could not do, other than theoretically, was suggest solutions to the problems.

Increasing Anglo-Scots difficulties

The journey from the Glorious Revolution in 1688–89 to the Act of Union in 1707 was slow, difficult, winding, controversial and devious. But it was only the last action in a century-long process. It will not do to ignore the fact that the two countries had actually been in a political union – or perhaps a series of such unions – since James I's accession to England in 1603, and that the people of both were already familiar with the problems involved in a deeper integration. After all, James I had made such an attempt soon after reaching London. It is not sufficient, therefore, to consider only the events leading to the passing of the Act of Union, nor even those of the few years before that. The very least time period to be considered must be from the Revolution of 1688–89 onwards – and once the Acts of Union were passed, there was a period during which, as usual when a major political step is taken, a reaction developed against the change. The process of devising, enacting, enforcing and accepting the union set up animosities and annoyances which took half a century and more to sort out, until the hapless failure of the Jacobite expedition of Prince Charles Edward in 1745–46 (to be dealt with in Chapter 10).

The relations of England with its neighbours, Ireland and Scotland, were founded on two very different approaches, but there was one element common to both. Ireland had been conquered three times by English armies, or at least armies fighting on behalf of an English government, in the 1590s, 1640s and 1690s. The reason, at least in English eyes, was that, if it remained independent, Ireland's Catholicism, and its anti-English resentment, made it dangerous as a possible base for an enemy. This had been demonstrated three times in the previous century: in 1601, a Spanish force had landed at Kinsale to assist the Irish warriors in their war against Elizabeth's army; in 1689, French troops joined James II's attempt to recover his throne; and in the 1640s, a papal nuncio had helped to organize the Irish rebels into the Confederacy of Kilkenny. To the English, all this implied that, were the Irish successful in regaining their independence, they would very likely become a platform for any enemy with which the English found themselves at war; the answer to this was for England to maintain control over Ireland.

This was also an English fear, if a lesser one, with regard to Scotland. There was a long history of alliances between the Scots and France going back to the twelfth century. This 'Auld Alliance' had usually resulted in serious damage to the Scots without much assisting the French, and its attractiveness had certainly faded a good deal since the two countries diverged in terms of religion. Relations had soured even more since the Huguenots – Calvinists like the Scots – had been expelled or persecuted after the Revocation of the Edict of Nantes by Louis XIV in 1685, and the savage French military ravaging of the Protestant Palatinate in 1688. Nevertheless, the apprehension still existed in England that Scotland, like Ireland, might, if wholly separated, become a stepping stone for an enemy to invade England.

The other main aspect of the relationship with Scotland was the issue of trade, already noted. The second half of the seventeenth century saw England's wealth greatly increase. Its empire was growing and its overseas trade greatly expanding. None of this happened to Scotland, which remained a generally poor country whose trade was restricted mainly to nearby northern European countries, including England, and exporting products such as wool and timber. England therefore saw no advantage in being linked with Scotland commercially, or in any other way than by the Union of Crowns, which provided some sort of defensive shield, pre-empting the possible alliance of Scotland with a foreign enemy. Scotland, on the other hand, was keen to participate in the growth of England's wealth.

The English Navigation Acts were enforced increasingly rigorously, with the English Royal Navy acting to suppress Scotland's export trade with the English colonies, which was against the Navigation Laws, and was regarded in England as smuggling. One reaction in Scotland to this was to make still more persistent attempts to flout or evade the Navigation Laws. Scots merchants and shippers became adept at trading in English (and other) colonies in America in clandestine ways, evading the Royal Navy, and developed thereby a useful and growing commerce. Another reaction was to attempt to develop its own trading system in a facsimile of the English system, with a chartered trading company, a tropical colony and an aim to open trade into the supposedly great untapped market of Spanish America.

There had been several Scottish attempts to found colonies, but the necessary population and commercial base within Scotland with which to support and supply such colonies did not exist. Colonies were expensive to set up and required regular supplies of people, food and other goods from the homeland for some time, at least until the colonists found the means to support themselves and had developed an export trade. None of these colonization attempts had succeeded. These matters were also the background to the attempt to develop a chartered trading company.

This was the Darien scheme, which sucked up and wasted a great part of Scotland's financial resources in the 1690s. Investors in the 'Company of Scotland' came from all sections of society. The scheme's manifest impracticalities and stupidities seem to have passed by everyone involved who had any knowledge of the world, including William Patterson, the originator (who characteristically escaped virtually unscathed from the debacle). No English investors would have anything to do with it, certainly not once the English government pointed out the problems. King William refused any assistance, and the determined hostility of Spain for the past two centuries to any other European power attempting to trade with its colonies was completely ignored; Spain was an ally in the contemporary Nine Years' War, but would clearly look askance at any encouragement for the scheme by William's government. Not only that, but all those taking part displayed a complete ignorance of how to settle a colony in the tropics from new, and this was a recipe for disaster in itself.

The scheme failed in all aspects, and rather than accepting that they had been misled by the promoters, and gullible, those many Scots who had suffered tended to blame the English. This did not matter much in itself, for common sense would have revived sooner or later and demonstrated that they themselves were at fault, but it did add an element of personal loss for many Scots to the gradually souring Anglo–Scots relationship.

King William had found that the weakening of his royal power in favour of the English Parliament had been replicated in Scotland, where the decision of the Estates that the relationship of people and king was a contractual one, and not one of hereditary right (still less by divine right), had translated during the 1690s into the increasing independence of the Estates, and therefore an increased separation from the policies of the government in London.

The Treaty of Ryswick in 1697, which ended the War of the League of Augsburg, reduced the hostile foreign pressure which had helped to hold the union together since the Glorious Revolution. It came just as the Darien scheme was getting underway, but even then was causing difficulties. The freeing of the Royal Navy from its wartime activities also now drew attention once more to English hostility towards Scottish trade with English North America. To paranoid Scots, and there were probably plenty of them by the late 1690s, this could all be interpreted as a deliberate English policy designed to weaken, even destroy, Scotland, though it is more likely that any damage to Scotland was merely a side-effect of the increased customs rates and duties in England which were levied in order to increase government revenues and so pay for the war. The one flexible source of such revenue was customs duties, which the Royal Navy was now enforcing.

Scottish public opinion, if such a concept can be entertained at this time, seemed in this whole period after the Glorious Revolution to be displaying a strong tendency towards collective hysteria. The war had no doubt contributed to this, and the English restrictions which impinged on Scottish commerce. But one main contribution was surely the collective anxiety about the issue of the union, which in the years after the Revolution seemed to be failing. Scotland, it must be repeated, was a poor country, with only a small population and few resources, and was marginal in all senses. It was not, and never could be, as wealthy and productive as either England or Ireland, which were at lower latitudes and had fewer mountainous areas. It seemed that it had given up its monarchy – a source of wealth for at least some of the people – and had gained only discriminatory treatment by the English. The Revolution had, above all, been an English affair; the decision on the royal succession had been an English decision. Scotland had found that it had no input into such matters. The failure of the Darien affair appeared to confirm Scotland's marginality, its sense of being dragged along in the wake of the English, who paid it no heed. The Darien scheme made a poor country even poorer, as well as leaving it the butt of contempt.

By the time the disaster of the Darien scheme was becoming clear, the government of William of Orange was already disliked in many parts of Scotland. He had little interest in Scottish affairs. He would have liked to maintain the episcopal organization inherited from Charles and James, but the Scottish bishops he encountered were supporters of James, and so he let the plan of eliminating Episcopalians, bishops and priests, go ahead without interference. But his government was assigned its share of the blame, whether it was merited or not, for the complexities and difficulties which followed, including the massacre of some MacDonalds in Glencoe in 1692.

Dislike of government – foreign, warlike, neglectful – increased in the later 1690s as famine spread. A sequence of cold years reduced agricultural production and resulted in a series of poor harvests, with resultant starvation and increased deaths. Here again, the basic problem was the undeveloped economy of the country, which left no margin of wealth or resources to meet such calamities, together with the poor agricultural quality of much of the land, which was overwhelmingly minimally productive rough grazing. While government could hardly be blamed for the weather, it was inevitable that those in need would consider that the government should be doing something to relieve the distress. But all Europe was suffering, and until 1697 the armies and navies involved in the war absorbed all, if any, surpluses. Even when peace was signed, in that year, it took time for supplies to become available and transport to be organized. England, of course, was much more productive and wealthier, and did not suffer to anything like the same degree as Scotland, but even so had hardly any surplus to export.

The alienation of many Scots from the Revolution government based in London, therefore, had many causes, but it was perhaps the religious element which proved to be decisive in the longer term. No doubt blame for the Darien scheme's failure could be cast on the London government, but this was a matter of the Scots' attitude of collective denial, and they did really understand that it was their own gullibility which was the base cause. Similarly, they might blame the government for not relieving the famine, but when harvests recovered this would be less of a problem and would be forgotten. But the religious decisions being made throughout Scotland were a constant nagging issue which had much deeper political effects.

The decision of the Estates to go ahead with the establishment of a national Presbyterian Church had theoretically required the ejection of ministers who, for whatever reasons, did not agree with or accept that decision. This had also happened in England, but on a much smaller scale, and involved only those clergy – 'non-jurors' – who could not accept the succession of William and Mary and the exclusion of James VII; it was not thus an issue of wider scope which involved the whole organization of the Church. In Scotland, several things came together to exert pressure on non-juror ministers: antipathy to Presbyterianism, support for Episcopalianism, the requirement to take the oath of allegiance to King William and Queen Mary, and therefore to deny the right of James VII to be king, and the opinions of the heritor or heritors, the lords who had the right of presentment of ministers to the parish or parishes in their territory. The Presbyterian system in theory handed that power to the elders of the local parish; in practice, the old system continued, and attempting to deny the heritors their original powers alienated many of them from Presbyterianism. As a result, considerable numbers of Episcopalians remained in their parish manses, to the general contentment of the heritors and usually of the parishioners as well. The national Presbytery, which sent out supervisors to ensure the insertion of acceptable ministers in recalcitrant parishes, in many cases found it quite impossible to remove the incumbents, particularly those at a distance from Edinburgh. They could be denied access to the church by armed mobs, and even if they did remove the recalcitrant ministers, there was probably no acceptable candidate available to fill the vacancy, either because the men who were presented were rejected by the parish, sometimes by force, or there simply was no man available even to be presented.

Politically, this meant that the opinions of the Episcopalian ministers and their heritors remained very strong and tended to reinforce each other. Ejected ministers were often given refuge by men of the aristocracy, and each reinforced the anti-Presbyterian opinions of the other. This religious opinion usually coincided with the belief that King James was still the rightful king. The vengefulness of the Presbyterians, a result in part of their dogmatic beliefs, but also of the memory of their own earlier persecution at Episcopalian hands, compelled an equivalent dogmatism in reply. The apprehension of enmity, local support and persecution shifted many men of some authority in Scotland – ministers and lords – towards Jacobitism.

Scotland by 1700, therefore, was populated by many who were still loyal to King James, especially since he was now at a distance. The government of King William was unpopular, and the apprehension existed among many Scots that England was acting in ways which were deliberately inimical towards Scotland. (It is more likely that the English parliamentarians were so absorbed in their own affairs that Scotland never entered their considerations – but such indifference was perhaps even more annoying than any deliberate slights.) In the war just ended, the Scots had found themselves at war as a result of a revolution in England. This could more or less be accepted, since the enemy aimed to overthrow the Glorious Revolution settlement, James was obviously a Catholic and the king was now required to be a Protestant. But the disenchantment with the Revolution government had begun to shift opinion back towards support for the Jacobites.

To a degree this also reflected the condition of England, where the death of King William in a riding accident in 1702 could be quietly celebrated by his political enemies. On the other hand, the Revolution settlement itself seemed to solve the issue of the balance between Parliament and king. There may be pro-Jacobite sentiments, but it would be highly unlikely that a Stuart restoration would be permitted to include the restoration of James's absolutism. James himself died in 1701, leaving a child as his successor.

The Union Crisis

The crucial events which brought the crisis of the union to its culmination came in 1701–04, beginning with the realization of the disaster of the Darien scheme, and going on with the series of royal deaths, including James and William in 1701 and 1702. The collapse of the Darien business came in 1700, though its failure had been well anticipated, and the aftermath continued for some time. Whatever blame was cast at William and the English government, the fact remained that Scotland had come out of years of famine and starvation into a period when vast sums of money were seen to have been wasted on a worthless scheme. The demoralization had its effect on the issue of the union, and eventually the English understood this, and of course took advantage.

In 1700, the death of King Charles II of Spain opened up a major international crisis which brought on the War of Spanish Succession from 1702, though already in 1701 France and Austria, the sponsors of the two claimants to the Spanish throne, were fighting each other in Italy. In 1701 also, while the international crisis was still developing, James VII and II died in his palace in St Germain. His son, James Francis, was 13 years old at the time, and this might have been thought to cause the French king to pause for a time. Instead he had the boy recognized as King James VIII and III by a public proclamation as soon as the death of the elder James was verified, fully in accordance with his belief in absolutism and divine right, of course. This provided a powerful boost to William's policy, above all in England, where Louis XIV's blatant interference in England's internal affairs was much resented.

William III had already seen that the new war would eventually expand, and set about constructing a durable alliance to combat France, and Louis XIV's deeds and overt hostility helped him in that. William had just about succeeded when he died. His successor as monarch was his sister-in-law, the second daughter of James VII and II, Queen Anne; his political successor was John Churchill, Duke of Marlborough.

The succession of Anne was part of another controversial English decision. The Westminster Parliament had enacted a new Act of Royal Succession the year before, laying out a line of succession which was designed to exclude James and his family. Neither William nor Anne had living children and so it was necessary to decide on the succession after Anne. Her own succession was not really controversial, and could be accepted. The English insistence on a Protestant to succeed led to Sophia, Electress of Hanover, as the next in line. She had adult sons, so this would guarantee the Protestant succession for the foreseeable future. She was also, if Catholics be excluded, the next in line by descent, the great-granddaughter of James I.

To Scottish Protestants, this solution to the problem was more or less reasonable and acceptable. If James VII was to be excluded, then so must his son, who was known to have been brought up as a Catholic. What was not acceptable in Scotland was that the English Act should be passed without any consultation with the Scots, and that Scotland was nevertheless included in the plan. William, however he was disliked, was their king too, and Anne would be their queen, but to exclude the Scots completely from any consultation over the succession was not something they could accept, and to do all this in such a high-handed way was distinctly insulting.

Louis XIV, who had been generous in giving James and his family shelter and sustenance, had gone much further than he needed to do when the elder James died by proclaiming his son as James VIII and III. This was one of the main items which drove the English Parliament (and William) to declare war on France in 1702. But, again, this declaration of war was done without consulting the Scots. By an illegal manipulation of the Scottish government system, the Scottish Privy Council deliberately and illegally avoided calling a meeting of the Estates, which should have been done within twenty days of a royal death. It should then have been Parliament's decision on peace or war, but it was fully appreciated that Scots' annoyance at the time was such that there was a strong possibility that war would not actually be declared, or at best that there would be prolonged arguments about it. The Council itself finally declared war.

By this time the question of a more complete union had been raised, not just as a possibility, but by King William himself. His refusal for much of his reign to bother much with Scottish issues had finally given way to an acceptance that a full union of England and Scotland would be preferable to the constant complaints and disagreements he had faced. For a variety of reasons, including the difficulties he faced with the English Parliament, William at last came out in favour of the union, though he did so only in his last message to Parliament, and died before he could do any more than make the suggestion. The underlying assumption was that bringing in Scottish members would help contain the opposition being mounted by a group of English members.

In Scotland, the issue of union was now taken up, but in such a way as to demonstrate to the English that Scottish resentment at English behaviour was boiling over. The Scottish Parliament which met until 1702 had been the recalled Convention of 1689, never yet replaced, but now, in 1703 and a new reign, a new Parliament was elected, and was soon shown to be fully enraged at English behaviour. Several Acts were passed which were aimed directly at the English practice of ignoring Scottish opinion, wishes and sentiments.

The Act anent Peace and War took from the sovereign (and thus also from the Privy Council) the right to declare war on behalf of Scotland, so in future Scotland might not be dragged into an 'English war'. Only a positive decision to declare war would bring Scotland in. There was thus to be no further example of the country being hustled into war without discussion, as had happened the previous year. One of the more serious effects of this had been to expose Scottish shipping to attacks by French privateers, in part because the (English) Royal Navy refused to protect those ships; Scotland did not have a navy of its own, though plenty of the merchant ships were armed. Perhaps partially in response to that particular threat, but also hoping to raise revenue, the Wine Act permitted the import of wine even from countries at war with Scotland. Lords and barons were not to pay the customs duties, as was the usual practice, but since these men formed the major market for wine in Scotland, half the effect of the Act, which was actually intended to raise revenue, was nullified.

It was, however, the Act for the Security of the Kingdom which was the real blow at English behaviour. It dealt with the two most obnoxious English actions. First, it stated that only the Scottish Parliament had the power to name the queen's successor. That would only be the same as the person who would succeed in England so long as the English agreed to free trade between the two kingdoms and with the English colonies. Also, the next king must be Protestant, and of the ancient royal family of Scotland. This last was the real threat. Such wording could be stretched to include the Hanoverians, who were descended from James I, but it could also mean James VIII and III, the young son of James VII and II, if he would become Protestant; other candidates could probably be found by searching the Stuart family tree. (There were reminiscences here of the crisis of succession in the 1290s.) Further, English guarantees concerning the Scottish religious settlement were required; there was to be no more imposition of Episcopalians on the Scottish Church system, such as had happened several times in the last century, and was still favoured by both King William and Queen Anne.

These Scottish Acts laid down the Scots' conditions for a deeper union. It is obvious that the Scottish Parliament's aim was not actually renewed independence, and they certainly did not wish to have to proffer the Scots crown to James VIII, except *in extremis* – the memory of the experience of accepting Charles II in 1650 had not faded. Both King William and the Scots had come to the same conclusion: that the only way forward was to replace the Union of Crowns with a more effective economic union. By putting forward certain conditions, the Scots were in fact offering to bargain. They were suggesting that the union should consist of a common sovereign, a single trading area enclosing at least England, Scotland and the overseas colonies (but Ireland was not mentioned), and should leave separate and distinct the establishments of religion. These were minimal conditions, but clearly other areas were available for discussion. Yet the option of renewed independence also remained, and the continued existence of the Scots Parliament would mean that such would continue to remain after the union was agreed. Meetings between commissioners from both countries were inconclusive, but in the process the Scots did suggest that the union should be one of the two Parliaments, which would achieve their economic union without a lot of detailed negotiations. By entering the English Parliament (which is what would necessarily happen), the Scots would simultaneously enter the English economic area. No decisions were taken, however, and hostile manifestos continued to be produced.

However, the weaker party's attempts to threaten or blackmail the stronger party carried risks, and the Scots were soon facing a powerful reply. The Scots Parliament had used the Wine Act as a rather weak and self-interested weapon against the government in 1703, and tried again in 1704 with the Wool Act, which prohibited the import of wool (a major English product), but allowed its export, for Scotland was a significant exporter of woollen goods. These were in fact only minor blows, which irritated the English without harming them. The English reply was much more comprehensive, and yet precisely targeted.

The Scots' suggestion of forming a full and parliamentary union was taken up, and the implied negotiations were similarly accepted. But the English Parliament – that is, the government – replied to the Scots threats by adding to this acceptance the threat that if no agreement could be reached, all the Scots who were resident in England would be classified as aliens, with the likelihood that they would be expelled. In another measure it was threatened that Scottish exports of coal, linen and cattle to England would be prohibited. The Scots threats were parried in this way, and the magnitude and potential effect of the English threats greatly surpassed them.

It was clear that the English government was prepared to consider a full 'incorporating' union to replace the Union of Crowns, as had been suggested by the Scots commissioners. The English economic threat was precisely directed at the Scottish nobility, who would be particularly exposed if the aliens legislation went into effect, since many of them had used the wealth they had collected in their Scottish estates to purchase English estates, or had intermarried with English noble families. They risked expulsion, and probably the confiscation of those English estates. Further, the three trades listed as liable to be blocked were exactly those in which the Scots baronage were involved; export of these goods was a major source of currency, for coin in Scotland was not plentiful, and much local trade was still conducted by exchanging goods for goods, without cash involvement. The question of the union of the two kingdoms was thus being addressed in particular to the Scottish nobility, who had particularly profited from the Union of Crowns. They were especially influential in their own localities, and strongly influential both in the Scots Parliament itself and in choosing other members, who were often their tenants, neighbours or clients.

Union

The English ploy worked perfectly. The Treaty of Union – an international treaty between two sovereign states – included concessions favouring the Scots nobility in their trading interests, their control of local courts in their localities (the 'regalities') and in recompense for the failure of the Darien scheme to the extent of £230,000, to be awarded to those who had invested – and the major investors were those very same Scots nobles. (One might see the treatment of the Scottish aristocracy in all this is a case of carrot-and-stick, with the stick wielded first.) Probable sources of opposition were also neutralized – the autonomy of the burghs was guaranteed, the independence of the Presbyterian Church was assured and it would be able to continue persecuting Episcopalians and Catholics; Scots law was to be the rule north of the border. The Scots Parliament was therefore squared, though for form's sake it voted on every article of the negotiated treaty. The treaty was a document actually produced by the London government, but it could hardly be said that the Scots had no input – they had themselves suggested the basic terms, the union of parliaments, free trade and the independence of the Churches and of the law of the two countries. The English acceptance of these terms, incidentally, showed clearly that the government in London was fully aware of Scots prejudices and requirements, as well as the location of political power in Scotland in the aristocracy; it was the aristocracy whose preoccupations were being soothed.

There was, of course, opposition to the union. In England, the Tories, out of office, claimed that the treaty endangered the Church of England, but were blocked when the Archbishop of Canterbury denied this and refused to call a meeting of the Church's Convocation at which Tory criticisms would have been voiced. The treaty went through both Houses of the English Parliament in seven weeks. In Scotland, the issue was much more difficult as it was seen in terms of the extinction of the Scottish Parliament, and even the destruction of Scotland, rather than the wider opportunities which were opening up. The Jacobites were in two minds over opposing the treaty. Those who opposed could not do so for Jacobite reasons, since this would open them to the charge of treason; other Jacobites agreed to the union on the assumption that once it was passed it would provoke widespread dismay and opposition, to their benefit. If their man did become king, the old divisions which had caused so much trouble for earlier Stuarts would also reappear, notably the problem of the Presbyterian Church, whose position was now protected by the treaty. There was a good deal of popular opposition, though how far the possible consequences were really understood by anyone outside parliamentary circles is totally unknown. It is unlikely that the prospect of the extinction of the Scots Parliament produced much popular dismay; it was hardly the most beloved of Scottish institutions.

This was perhaps the most surprising part of the whole treaty process. In exchange for the Scots Parliament voting itself out of existence, forty-five Scottish members would be added to the English – now British – Parliament, and sixteen Scottish peers would be elected – by their own peers – to the British House of Lords. To the English, this was the crucial element, since it had been the activities of the Scots Parliament which had brought about this internal British crisis, and getting rid of it would presumably help towards political peace in the islands. By enfolding Scotland into the English Parliament, where Scots would amount to less than ten per cent of the members – a generous allocation in view of the small Scottish population and wealth – the Scots would be unable in most cases to exert very much influence. Just in case the first election of these new members went 'wrong', they were to be selected by the outgoing Scots Parliament, which was itself elected – or chosen – in 1703, and which would by then have voted for the treaty. It is noticeable that this effectively extinguished the obnoxious provisions of the recent Scottish Acts of Security and Peace and War with regard to the succession and the choice of war or peace.

In England, a number of politicians were surprised that the Scots had not bargained for better terms, but it is difficult to see what improvements could have been asked for. The major issues had always been trade and religion, and in both of these the Scots had gained what they had aimed for – free trade with England and the English empire, and a firm establishment for the Presbyterian Church. The disappearance of the Scottish Parliament may have been a blow, but it was always implied in the discussions that this would happen.

The Tories in England argued that the union should be a federative association, in which the separate Parliaments would continue to exist, but that there were two Parliaments was exactly the problem. Instead, what had resulted was an incorporating union, but one which was only one step onwards from the Union of the Crowns. A true incorporating union was what had happened with England and Wales, where Wales was fully part of England from 1542: Church, law, Crown and all. Instead, the Scottish-English union consisted only of the Union of Crowns and now of Parliaments, leaving the rest separate. The Tories in England were wrong; the Scots had come out of the negotiations with everything they wanted, and what had resulted was actually a version of a federation.

The new union was, therefore, a very limited measure. If two states were united, as England and Wales had been, the least one might expect is some harmony of law, religion and legislative measures. The union of Scotland and England existed only in this last element. The result was that in many important ways, Scotland remained quasi-independent. The Scottish Presbyterian Church accepted the union by agreeing to be left alone to go on purging Episcopalians, a matter of concern to the Church of England. Scottish laws were left entrenched in theory, though in fact many aspects of the legal system were overridden by later legislation from Westminster, when new laws were passed which applied to the whole of the United Kingdom, as they inevitably must. Above all, the Scottish nobility was collectively conciliated, and cooperated in the union in order to secure their own interests. It is not so much, as later opponents of the union charged, that they were bribed, as that they were not economically damaged, as had been threatened by the English proposed measures, and they were, like the Church and the lawyers, to be left alone in their local power. The Scots politicians had achieved what they had aimed for: access to the English market and English colonies, and, incidentally, protection for their ships from the Royal Navy.

Bibliography

Brown, Keith M., *Kingdom or Province? Scotland in the Regal Union, 1603–1715* (London: 1992).

Dand, Charles Henry, *The Mighty Affair: How Scotland lost her Parliament* (Edinburgh: 1972).

Devine, T.M., *Independence or Union, Scotland's Past and Scotland's Present* (London: 2016).

Devine, T.M., *Scotland's Empire, 1600–1815* (London: 2003).

MacInnes, Allan I., *Union and Empire, the Making of the United Kingdom in 1707* (Cambridge: 2007).

McKenzie, John M. and Devine, T.M., *Scotland and the British Empire* (Oxford History of the British Empire, Companion Series) (Oxford: 2011).

Prebble, John, *The Darien Disaster* (London: 1968).

Riley, T.W.J., *The Union of England and Scotland* (Manchester: 1978).

Smyth, Jim, *The Making of the United Kingdom, 1660–1800* (Harlow, Essex: 2001).

Watt, Douglas, *The Price of Scotland, Darien, Union and the Wealth of Nations* (Edinburgh: 2007).

Chapter 10

The Union Challenged

From 1707, the (newly) United Kingdom consisted of the union of three countries – England, Wales and Scotland – while Ireland was attached as a conquered subject state. The two unifications of countries which had taken place had of course different origins and processes. That of Wales with England began as a conquest, which was then for two-and-a-half centuries a conquered province, and was united finally by a legislative accomplishment. That of England-plus-Wales with Scotland was a negotiated agreement confirmed by legislation and by the enactments of the two countries' Parliaments. It was then followed by nearly half a century of wars, disputes and rebellions in which foreign interferences, and Scottish dismay and opposition, challenged the existence of the union, at least that of England and Scotland. There are therefore clear parallels between both unions. (It may be noted that Ireland as a conquered country was, in the seventeenth and eighteenth centuries, in much the same position as Wales between 1288 and 1542, including the military occupation, its irregular rebellions and the intrusion of English and Scottish 'settlers'.)

The populations of none of the three united countries had been consulted in the formation of the unions, though the English and Scots Parliaments had been involved. In the case of Wales, the essential decisions had been English, in particular by two English kings: Edward I, the original conqueror, and Henry VIII, the final unifier. In the case of Scotland, the Treaty of Union had been the result of deals made between the small ruling groups in each kingdom – in effect, oligarchies – in a process marginally more consultative than that of Wales. It is hardly surprising, given these methods, either forced or secretive, that both unions faced serious and major challenges. In order for a union to move on from the original agreement or conquest to acceptance by the populations, a challenge to this union had to be met and defeated; only then would the majority accept the new conditions.

The challenge to the original conquest in Wales had culminated in the rebellion of Owain Glyndwr, who controlled much of Wales between 1400 and 1410. He failed to remove the authority of the English king or of the Marcher lords (some of whom supported him), but the extent of his authority at its height implies that the unification of Wales had been accepted by the Welsh. The imposition of the Council of Wales and the Marches from 1471 did something to bring the Marcher lords under royal control, and finally the Act of Union abolished them. This brought about the full unification of Wales as well as its union with England; that is, Welsh unification was a by-product of the unification of England with Wales, for the process had required that Wales itself become unified first. Paradoxically, the rebellion of Owain both confirmed the work of Edward I and anticipated that of Henry VIII. The Council of the Marches was retained, becoming an instrument of Charles I's systematic evasion of Parliament in the 1630s; it lingered on until final abolition in 1691.

The process of unifying England with Scotland was even more troubled than that with Wales, but it had a number of similarities. The Union of the Crowns of 1603 was revealed as unworkable and had been disliked in both countries from the start, involving as it did an English conquest of Scotland and several Scottish military expeditions deep into England. Much of this violence would not have occurred if they had not been joined in such a loose union. After 1688, it was a union which looked ever less likely to endure. The Union of the Parliaments came when it was clear that separation would be a disaster for both countries.

The effective political authorities in both countries were thus merged. There was no Scottish equivalent of the Council of Wales and the Marches, which prepared the way for the union with Wales, but the activity of the two Parliaments in their disputes and negotiations between the Glorious Revolution and the union had similarities. It was necessary that the two government systems be harmonized; in both cases this meant the slow imposition of English systems on the smaller countries. Given the greater size, wealth and population of England, this should have been seen as inevitable by both Welsh and Scots, but the process certainly fuelled resentment. In both cases this process involved the imposition of new laws, new taxes and new administrations, often by transferring the well-tried and effective English systems wholesale to the other countries.

The symptoms of disunity in Wales and Scotland only slowly disappeared. The most obvious point of disunion was language: in Wales, English and Welsh; in Scotland, English, Scots, Gaelic and Norse. At the time of Henry VIII's union, English had made only a small penetration into Wales, but by the mid-eighteenth century it had spread well over the border into the former Marcher lands (which in many cases will have been bilingual for many decades by then). South Wales was also in part bilingual, especially in Dyfed, where English and Flemish settlers had been established centuries before. Nevertheless, Welsh proved able to maintain itself successfully, though bilingualism was required for some aspects of everyday life.

The division was more complex in Scotland, and English/Scots had been making powerful inroads to a much greater extent. It had begun, of course, as the normal language of south-east Scotland, including Edinburgh and the Lothians. By the time of the union the two main languages, English and Gaelic, had largely come to occupy distinct geographical regions – English in the Lowlands, including the north-east, and Gaelic in the Highlands and a diminishing part of Galloway. The Norse language, which had dominated in the Northern Isles, was rapidly fading before English.

This language division in Scotland had more consequences, since by the time Gaelic was restricted to the Highlands and Islands, it also reflected a social division between the clan societies of the Highlands – largely based on pastoral farming – and the arable-farming and urban-dwelling Lowlanders, and this of course became a serious matter in the reaction of the Scots to the union.

Scotland had other divisions as well, in particular religious, and here there is a contrast with the Welsh religious condition. In Wales, the population became divided between several varieties of Christianity: Anglican, Presbyterian, Baptist and Quaker, together with a not insignificant population of Catholics. But all of these were spread more or less evenly throughout the country. Later they were joined by Methodists and Wesleyans, but no one congregation predominated in any particular area after about 1700. If anything there was a social division, emphasized by separate religious allegiances for the landowners tended to be Anglican, indeed English, in part because this was necessary for their participation in local and national government, and their social inferiors were of any one of a variety of dissenters. This was a deliberate division between two social layers, reflecting their language and national differences. Since the majority of both classes had been Anglican in the seventeenth century, the proliferation of Dissenter sects made the withdrawal of most of the Welsh from that Church a mark of their disenchantment with the gentry, and eventually opposition to gentry influence and power.

In Scotland, on the other hand, Presbyterians tended to dominate in the central and southern Lowlands, with the more extreme version of Presbyterianism predominating in the south west, where the Cameronians had mounted futile rebellions in the reign of Charles II, but had also been used to defeat Dundee's army at Dunkeld in 1689. Episcopalians were strong in the north-east. The Highlands included several Catholic clans, but others were Episcopalian and some Presbyterian. This geographical division reinforced the language division already noted, but less so a social division; the aristocracy largely shared the same religion with their tenants – even enforced their choice of religion on them.

Scottish Discontent

Languages, religions and lifestyles tended to reinforce each other, making the lack of social unity in Scotland particularly obvious. Furthermore, the failure of all governments (from the Romans onwards) to establish their authority in the Highlands, particularly in the face of the continuing legal existence of the independent regalities (where the lords enforced and administered their own law), was a further reinforcement of these divisions. So when the issue of the union with England came up and the Scots discovered that their Parliament had abolished itself, the various parts of the country reacted in rather different ways.

It seems clear that many of the Scots disliked the union, but it was also apparent that they could not organize themselves to oppose it because of their social, religious and geographical divisions. They fairly soon discovered that the new Union Parliament, dominated as it was by English politicians and Members of Parliament – an inevitable consequence of the disparity of wealth and population between the three constituent countries – was quite prepared to legislate for the whole country, England and Scotland and Wales, as one. Complaints were made that this breached the terms of the Treaty of Union. This is a matter which resonates even now, with historians pointing out that subsequent taxes or administrative measures were supposed to have been 'against the terms of the treaty'. But such a treaty reflected the situation as it existed at the time of the conclusion of the treaty. No treaty could ever predict what changes and new laws would be necessary in the future, nor could it be so prescriptive as to prevent the newly united Parliament from carrying out measures which it considered necessary to apply to the whole of the united country. Surely any worldly wise politician expected Parliament to legislate for the whole of the United Kingdom, and such measures would include enforcing customs duties and imposing taxes, as well as defending the whole country. For Scotland this would include opening the English and colonial markets to Scottish merchants, which was one of the main aims of the Scots all along.

The Jacobite Reaction, 1708

The resentment which emerged as the fact of the union was appreciated provided a social and political atmosphere which was guaranteed to attract the intrigues and plots of the Jacobites, and seemed to them a useful vehicle to use for their own purposes. Since the union had taken place during the great war with France and Spain (the War of the Spanish Succession, 1702–13), there was an apparent incentive for the French, who were sheltering the pretender James Francis (James VIII, the 'Old Pretender'), to attempt to exploit the situation.

James pushed for an expedition to be organized to Scotland in order to take advantage of the disturbed condition of the country in the wake of the union. One force was developed and gathered at Dunkirk, but the French were reluctant to become too involved in the British Isles while Marlborough and his Dutch-German-British army was hammering at the fortresses on the northern frontier of France – the sanguinary Battle of Malplaquet was fought in the same year as James' expedition. So when James sailed in a small fleet of ships with some soldiers for Scotland it was with a less than enthusiastic French commander, Admiral Forbin, and a less than enthusiastic French government behind him. Forbin had attempted to explain to Louis XIV the difficulties the expedition faced, but had been rebuffed. There is no doubt that the king understood perfectly well the difficulties, but he refused to allocate more resources. The expedition was thus reliant on a strong response in Scotland. The intention was to land in Fife, but when the French fleet approached there was no sign of any welcoming force.

There had been considerable preparations in Scotland for James' arrival, and there was much rejoicing in Edinburgh when it was learnt that the 'king' was in the Firth of Forth, but coordination was completely absent. The arrival of a Royal Navy fleet under Admiral Byng drove the French vessels northwards, and one of their ships was captured. James begged to be put ashore, even without French soldiers, but Admiral Forbin would not take the risk: the person of the Pretender was too precious to French policy to be endangered. The British fleet seemed threatening, though Byng's force was not actually in sight. Eventually, despite James' anguished pleas, the French sailed off. The British government was satisfied. They feared as much as anything the presence of the Stuart Pretender on British soil, particularly in Scotland, but they also had no wish to capture him, since whatever they then did to him or with him – perpetual imprisonment or execution – would be incendiary. Byng's ships 'chased' the French across the North Sea for a time, but carefully late. In effect, the British and French co-operated in preventing James from taking any action; for the French he was too useful as a threat to hold over Britain; to the British he was too dangerous a commodity to be allowed to land or, if captured, to either hold or execute.

The whole expedition was badly organized, poorly supplied and timorously commanded – in short, it was a fiasco, and rebellions cannot afford to look ridiculous. In the back of French government minds, however, was the further thought that such an expedition might not actually be necessary. They were well informed about the vicious, cut-throat state of political opinion in Britain. The widespread Scots annoyance at being dragged into the union was one aspect, but in England it was also understood that the Whig government was deeply unpopular, as was its war, and that at any time the Tory opposition might come to power on a programme of making peace; the Tories were reportedly very sympathetic towards the Jacobite cause. The Tories toasted the death of William III, argued against the European war, had opposed the union and were generally sympathetic to the accession of James VIII – but they were also Anglican to a man and to their core, and it was this which was their starting point. Unless James could guarantee the Church of England, its privileges and its position, the Tories' keenness for him would slump. James made it clear he was a loyal Catholic and would not change; to him, unlike the French Henry IV, London was not worth abandoning the Mass. This left him bereft of support from the Tories.

The 'Fifteen'

James learned lessons from the failure in 1708, and when a new opportunity arose he did his best to seize it. The Tory government which finally gained power in 1710 pursued its anti-war policy to the extent of making a secret separate peace with France, thus deserting its country's allies; the peace was officially concluded in 1713, but the British forces had effectively withdrawn from the war two years before. The death of Queen Anne in 1714 brought into effect the Royal Succession Act of 1701, by which the Pretender was specifically excluded by reason of his Catholicism, and the crown was to go to the Electress Sophia of Hanover. She had died in June that year, two months before Anne; her successor was therefore Sophia's son, the Elector George. This, to many in England, and probably to most in Scotland, was deeply unpopular and was a signal for a rising against the Westminster government and its schemes.

All calculations, then and later, show that the majority of Scots favoured the succession of James VIII. Calculations of English opinion are much less sanguine, but there is no doubt that James had, shall we say, considerable political support in parts of England. In London, however, the Hanoverian supporters, mainly Whigs, in concert with the Elector George, but also with some of the Tories, succeeded in proclaiming George I in all due legality and ceremony. They then appointed a majority of Whigs to the Privy Council, which was the crucial government organ at the time. Parliament had been dissolved at the queen's death, no elections had yet taken place, there was no monarch present and the Privy Council was therefore the legal governmental authority. (Note the resemblance to the similar role of the Scottish Privy Council in 1689.) A list of the names of suitable men to be added to the Privy Council had been produced by King George, and two extra men, the Dukes of Argyll and Somerset, already members, turned up at the meeting which had been convened by the Tories, and came to dominate it, expelling some Jacobites and installing the new king's nominees. It was in essence a *coup d'état*, but in contrast to what their opponents would now have to do, it was one conducted, like the royal proclamation, with all due legality.

If the Jacobites were to attempt to put their man on the throne now, it could only be by means of a rebellion against the legally constituted government. The whole procedure in London was in accordance with the stated wish of Parliament and the legal forms were followed. Any seizure of power by the Tories would have been just as much a *coup d'état* as that conducted by the Whigs, but it would have also violated the legal requirements of the situation. This also blocked many of the Tories, who might have joined an uprising in England. They might claim that James was the rightful king, but they based this assertion on legal principles; the proclamation and the Privy Council *coup* were clearly legal, so the Tories were trapped into indecision.

Tentative moves supporting James in England were begun, but were easily suppressed, and the two principal political leaders, Bolingbroke and the Duke of Ormonde, fled to France, where they could not be effective. In the English north-east, a set of Catholic nobles and gentry organized a badly developed rising. They headed into Lancashire, where it was known that there was a considerable Catholic population, but precisely because it was overwhelmingly Catholic it failed, facing widespread indifference and hostility from non-Catholics, and was suppressed without too much difficulty in a clumsy battle at Preston. In France, James VIII made it clear in a public comment that even for the crown of Britain he would not renounce his Catholic faith. The French government by this time, having succeeded in making a reasonably favourable peace with Britain, was hostile to any Jacobite adventure; if it did conspicuously support James, it might find itself at war again. Such Tory support as there was in England therefore faded rapidly in the face of James' obduracy and the absence of their likely political leaders.

In other areas the Jacobites were more decisive and had more success. A meeting at Braemar of Highland lords agreed to raise an army, and put it under the command of the Earl of Mar, who had been Secretary of Scotland in the previous Tory government. Once the force gathered, detachments moved into the Scottish north-east and gained control at Aberdeen and Perth. But Mar's new army was not large, and the Highland chiefs had not produced all the forces he expected. The Duke of Argyll, who had been one of Marlborough's senior commanders in Flanders, had brought together such government forces as he could collect and took control of the vital strategic point of Stirling, with its castle and bridge, thus confining the Jacobite forces to north of the Forth. His force was, however, outnumbered at least two to one by Mar's army.

Mar was beset by indecision and a lack of money and weaponry. He knew that supplies had been dispatched from France along with James, carried in a group of French privateers, and possibly he hoped that their arrival would increase his resources and perhaps relieve him of his responsibility. But in the end he was compelled to face Argyll's smaller force in battle at Sheriffmuir. Despite greater numbers, the Jacobite army failed to win. Further, the battle was fought on the same day as the fight at Preston, also a Jacobite defeat. After the Sheriffmuir battle, the enemy armies separated, but Mar took his force back northwards, while Argyll retained control of Stirling. In the north, Inverness fell to a scratch group of anti-Jacobite lords and tenants. Widespread gloom signalled the Jacobite failure.

In England, the new Whig government, in control of the Privy Council, and with the new king having arrived, had at once set about purging Tories from the ranks of sheriffs, Lords Lieutenant and justices of the peace. These were the crucial personnel in organizing and supervising elections, and the purge was followed by a general election in December 1714 and January 1715. The result was a large swing from Tory to Whig, though this was not only due to pressure from the new Whig authorities. The Whig assertions in the campaign that the Protestant establishment and Protestant royal succession were endangered by a Tory victory were well understood and accepted. After the result there was nothing left for the Tories but acceptance or rebellion.

In Scotland, the issue was not so much religion as the Stuart succession, the crown of Scotland, the union and independence. The widespread popular dislike of the union could be translated into support for the Stuart dynasty, but the various groups in the country who could be called Jacobites failed to coalesce into an organized movement, riven as they were by mutual dislikes and hostilities. An attempt to seize Edinburgh Castle failed through general carelessness – the plotters stayed too long at their drink – and this left all the south of Scotland out of the Jacobites' reach. Even the arrival of James in a French privateer, having eluded his French minders, did not help the rebellion once its general failure was clear. He and Mar left Scotland again within a fortnight of James' arrival. There followed, as in England, a purge of Jacobite supporters, but in this case the fact of an actual rebellion made the purge necessarily bloodier. In England, tainted politicians were impeached and imprisoned for a short time; in Scotland, there were a number of executions.

Defeat did not destroy Jacobite feeling, nor did it persuade those Scots who opposed the union to change their minds. The defeat of the risings did, however, compel them to accept that the union existed and would continue. The Whig grip in power was firm enough to deter any new adventures, including when a hapless Spanish force – the few survivors of a storm at sea – landed at Glen Shiel in 1719, only to be gathered in with contemptuous ease. The longer the union endured, of course, the more acceptable it became. A new generation of Scots grew up within the union, and learned to exploit it, though still influenced in their national feeling by the tales of their parents.

The union had certainly caused a substantial derangement of Scotland's economy, and this was one of the basic causes of the Jacobite surge and of enmity towards the union. One of the immediate triggers of the 1715 rebellion had been the imposition of a Malt Tax, which threatened to reduce the profits of the brewing industry – and increase the price of beer – and this had been one of Scotland's largest industries. At Kelso, on the proclamation of James, the announcement was answered by the crowd shouting, 'No Union! No Malt tax! No Salt tax!', which was scarcely a resounding cheer for the Jacobites. (The treaty had only required that the Malt Tax not be levied during the war.)

The extension of the English customs service to Scotland threatened the livelihood of considerable numbers of smugglers (seamen and fishermen when not smuggling), who were frequently supported in their ventures by the town councillors and mayors. Thefts of confiscated smuggled goods from customs warehouses were not infrequent, especially where the warehouse was guarded by negligent, complacent or participating locals. Since it was frequently claimed that these and other changes and charges had been prohibited by the Treaty of Union – especially so claimed by those who had not read the treaty – the rage-quotient was then increased.

The defeat of the rebellion was a sharp reminder of the power of the union government, and failure dumped plenty of cold water on the potential rebels. After all, smuggling was a widespread problem in Britain, from Kent to Orkney and Shetland. Glasgow's merchant-shipowners had been illegally – from the English point of view – trading with the American colonies for decades. Now they could trade legally, but were rather more likely to have to pay the customs duties they had been evading.

Legal access to the English empire in the Caribbean and North America was one of the benefits to Scots merchants which arrived with the union, and was a factor generally ignored by the complainers. It was, of course, unlike a new tax or the arrival of customs officers, something which would only produce benefits beyond the merchants themselves after some time. The trades in tobacco, sugar, indigo, cotton, rice and other American and Oriental products were becoming heavily concentrated in Glasgow, fuelling the development of that city, but only minimally spreading wealth and employment more widely. The Royal Navy no longer had the task of enforcing the Navigation Acts against the Scots, and could now use its ships to support and protect them. One of the principal Scottish exports to the empire was people: supervisors to Jamaica and the West Indian slave plantations, merchants and clerks to India, soldiers to everywhere and civilian emigrants to America. The British Army and the Royal Navy had also become open to Scots recruits. It all took time to be realized, of course, and Scots in the Army and the Navy would hardly be able to spread wealth within the country, being miserably paid, if at all. For example, it was only in 1742 that the first specifically Scottish regiment in the British Army was constituted, out of several local militia companies. They were formed into the Black Watch (which mutinied unsuccessfully when the men discovered that they were destined for India).

The resentment displayed by the Scots at their union with England was mirrored in England by a similar dislike of being yoked to Scotland. It was assumed, rightly, that the Scots were particularly keen on securing access to English wealth, and there were memories of the unpleasant behaviour of Scots armies in England in the seventeenth century. On the other hand, this English resentment towards the union was much less virulent than that of the Scots towards England in the union. The union could be seen as a useful insurance against trouble from the north when at war with France, though the successive Jacobite rebellions were a nuisance.

The 1715 rebellion prompted the London government to undertake some attempts to ensure that any future rebellions might be more easily contained. Above all, there were efforts to install military power into the Highlands. There already existed Fort William at the south-west end of the Great Glen. (The Spaniards landing at Glen Shiel were heading directly for Fort William, whose garrison was quite sufficient to stop them.) To this was added Fort Augustus at the mid-point of the glen, and with a garrison at Inverness these could be said to control the whole line of that route. Other garrisons were at Glenelg, facing towards Skye, and at Kingussie in Strathspey, but these were small, and consisted mainly of troops recruited in the Highlands, which were therefore not necessarily reliable. General Wade set about constructing roads to open up military routes from the south, but these also made it easy for Highland armies to reach the south. These efforts did nothing to establish British government control in the islands – the Spaniards in 1719 gathered first at Stornoway – though they perhaps lulled politicians in London into believing they did so.

Prince Charlie's Adventure

One reason, of course, for the slowness of the Scots to accept the union, its changes and its opportunities, was the continuing Jacobite sentiment. Those who hankered for a Stuart restoration also hoped for a revocation of the union. The expulsion of the Stuarts from France and their new residence in Rome tended to emphasize their continuing Catholicism, and this would further the decline in the loyalty of their supporters in Britain; Presbyterians, in particular, now protected by the legal establishment of their Church of Scotland, had become strongly anti-Jacobite. But support did continue, though it was very largely confined to Scotland, and to Catholics and Episcopalians – and some Highlanders. The final Jacobite throw, the 1745 rebellion, was just as much directed against the union as its predecessors, but it suffered, as in 1689, 1708, 1715 and 1719, from inept leadership and a narrow base of support, and by this time the union was more widely accepted. The 1745 rising was for once led by a prince of the deposed royal family in person, Prince Charles Edward, but he was a political, religious and military lightweight. It seemed all too typical of him that it was only after the failure of the rebellion that he switched his religious allegiance from Catholicism to Anglicanism (in 1750, on a clandestine visit to England). It was, of course, ten years too late, at least, and anyway an Anglican would be hardly reassuring to Presbyterians, with their memories of Charles I and Charles II, nor to the Catholics whom he had deserted.

The 1745 rebellion again came during a foreign war, and once again was beset by poor leadership, divided counsels and indifferent French support, even hostility in Paris. There had been a serious and substantial French plan to invade England in 1744, which failed because of a storm in the Channel and the interposition of the Royal Navy, so invading Scotland after the failure of that invasion plan was hardly sensible timing. The lack of direct French interest in Jacobite success, once again, was shown by their refusal to permit an invasion of Scotland to coincide with the intended invasion of Kent, which aimed to capture London and dictate peace terms there. But the fact that the British were at war in 1745 did mean that their armed forces were mainly being used overseas, and that those inside the country were few and scattered in garrisons and bases. This allowed the rebel army to march virtually unopposed as far as Derby, winning minor fights at places like Prestonpans and Inverness. By the time Prince Charles' army reached Derby, however, its control of those parts of Scotland it had seized was already disintegrating.

There were also large areas the rebels never reached, and their one substantial and politically important conquest, Edinburgh, slid back under their opponents' control as soon as their army left. Much of the territory north of Inverness was never under rebel control, while Argyll and the south-west remained particularly hostile. The rebellion's military victories were won against untrained and inexperienced forces which were often outnumbered, and could be overwhelmed by the unleashed 'Highland charge'. When they finally came up against a real army – trained, armed and disciplined, if under the unimaginative command of the Duke of Cumberland, although an imaginative command was not needed – the Highlanders who composed much of the Jacobite army were easily and comprehensively defeated. The Highland charge was good for only one attempt, and once stopped it was finished. In a long fight, victory automatically went to the professional army. This defeat had been its likely fate, of course, from the start, and was certain once the British government had gathered a large enough army in Britain to cope with it.

The punishment which followed was harsh, but then this had been a rebellion designed to overthrow the whole political system of the United Kingdom, in a time of war against the traditional enemy, and it was the fourth such attempt. A sample of the likely political replacement if the rebellion had succeeded was Prince Charles' airy abolition of the union of England and Scotland 'by decree' while in Edinburgh Castle. There was no reference to consultations, no question of any Act of Parliament and no consideration of what should replace it. If that was a sample of Stuart intentions and methods, their government would have been careless and erratic in the extreme, and would probably have been only short-lived. It is no wonder that the English, even the Catholics, almost totally failed to join him, or that the Scots were by a great majority either hostile or indifferent to him. When he appointed Jacobite governors for Scottish towns, many of them were refused entry; most of the Scottish nobility held aloof, often hedging their bets, sending one son to the government forces and another to the Jacobite, and the longer the rebellion lasted the less support it had. It was a comprehensive and dismal failure, and deservedly so.

This result largely solved the problem of the union and that of the still partial unification of Scotland. For the first time since the English Republic (and only the second time ever), a substantial, modern and efficient army penetrated into the Highlands, and at the same time the government – English, Scottish or British – had a strong incentive to keep the army there and to use it to physically conquer the Highland region. This is what was done, after the defeat of the essentially Highland army at Culloden. Scottish complainers tend to dwell with rather too much relish on the horrors of this process, but it is no more than could have been expected – and, of course, explaining and exaggerating the horrors is a way of deflecting attention from the pointlessness and failure of the rebellion. Nothing else could have been expected. The British Army would not simply withdraw, leaving the Highlands uncontrolled and ready to mount another futile rebellion in another thirty years.

The changes which were enforced were, first of all, a fairly brutal exploitation of victory, in which any Highlander who had weapons was regarded as a rebel or a potential rebel, and treated as such. Casualties were considerable, but numbers are impossible to discover – hence the exaggerations by those determined to complain. Perhaps more important was the confiscation of the estates of those who had rebelled, followed by the abolition of the regalities (in English legalese these became 'heritable jurisdictions'); compensation was offered, usually claimed to excess, and eventually settled at about a quarter of that which had been claimed – and so at about the actual valuation. But the result was that the government came to own substantial territories, and to control the administration of justice, which is only what should be expected of a modern government.

More roads were built, and since these were organized by turnpike trusts they were rather less focused on military needs and more upon the needs of the civilian population. Measures were taken to promote new agricultural practices, though without much noticeable effect. Following the recruitment of the Black Watch, several more Scottish regiments were raised, which simultaneously provided the British government with a quantity of good soldiers, which they used overseas, notably in Canada and India, and which removed a reservoir of military-grade personnel from the Highlands; any further rebellion thus became considerably less likely. One may note that, given the hostility of much of the Highlands to the Jacobites, a similar conquest would have happened had the Jacobites won, if directed at different 'Hanoverian' clans.

This was the conquest of the Highlands, and the effective unification, at last, of Scotland. Until then, no government, Scottish or British, had had anything but brief periods of power in the Highlands. The change was assisted by the spread of schools, where English became the spoken language, so that the Highlands became a bilingual area just as, at much the same time, did Wales. It also accomplished the unification, so far as it ever took place, of England and Scotland. This was obviously a limited (or partial) union. The original treaty left the religious and legal systems separate; their political systems were also, in many ways separate despite the union of the Parliaments – the electoral system in Scotland with the equivalent of an English rotten borough. But at least the government located in London now had something approaching proper jurisdiction over the whole country.

The legal systems began to mesh in some areas as legislation from the Union Parliament imposed new laws on all the joint countries, though in many fundamental and basic areas they remained separate. Similarly, the two political systems, at first separate, were compelled to become similar as various political reforms were eventually passed which applied to all the countries. For over a century after the treaty, however, the Scottish electoral system was tightly restricted in the numbers of people involved. That is to say, the aristocracy who had secured the union continued to control Scottish political affairs afterwards for the next century and more. It was, of course, corrupt, even more so than the English electoral system.

Conclusion

During the half-century after the Treaty of Union, therefore, the union faced several challenges, some of which have been given the name of Jacobite rebellions. In fact, there was more to it than attempts by hapless Stuart Pretenders to secure the throne once more for their family. The more the Stuarts made their attempts, the less likely it was that they would ever succeed. The romantic sight of 'Bonnie Prince Charlie' in Edinburgh Castle was never enough to persuade hard-headed politicians that they should overthrow the whole political system, which worked well enough for them. No part of Britain would accept a Catholic as king for any length of time. The real result of these rebellions was that measures were finally taken to extend the control of the Lowlands throughout the Highlands. This had been attempted for centuries by Scottish governments but they had never had the power or the resources to succeed; it took the combined efforts of the manpower and resources of the Scottish Lowlands and England to succeed. By 1770, therefore, Scotland had been properly united as a single country, and the whole island of Britain had been united as a single government. The parallel with the process in Wales is clear, though in the case of Scotland the union was of course limited, and this had its effect later.

Bibliography

See also the books by Devine, Lenman and Smith listed in the previous chapter.

Baynes, John, *The Jacobite Rising of 1715* (London: 1970).

Clyde, Robert, *From Rebel to Hero, the Image of the Highlander 1745–1830* (East Linton: 1995).

Douglas, Hugh, *Jacobite Spy Wars, Moles, Rogues and Treachery* (Stroud: 1999).

Forsyth, David (ed.), *Bonnie Prince Charlie and the Jacobites* (Edinburgh: 2017).

Gibson, John S., *Ships of the '45* (London: 1945).

Habraham, Chris and Grove, Doreen, *Fortress Scotland and the Jacobites* (London: 1995).

Harvie, Christopher, *Scotland and Nationalism, Scottish Society and Politics 1707–1977* (London: 1977).

Lenman, Bruce, *Jacobite Clans of the Great Glen, 1650–1784* (London: 1984).

McLynn, Frank, *The Jacobite Army in England, 1745, the Final Campaign* (Edinburgh: 1998).
Prebble, John, *Mutiny, Highland Regiments in Revolt 1743–1804* (Harmondsworth: 1975).
Sinclair-Stevenson, Christopher, *Inglorious Rebellion, the Jacobite Risings of 1708, 1715 and 1719* (London: 1971).

Chapter 11

The Union of Britain and Ireland

T he Treaty of Union of England and Scotland of 1707 followed fairly quickly after the definitive English conquest of Ireland, which was completed by the capture and Treaty of Limerick in October 1691. This conquest resulted from the success of James II in recovering control of the island in 1689 after his flight from London to France. His earlier transformation of the Irish army into a Catholic force meant he arrived to find virtually the whole country already under his power, but he could not complete the occupation, and was soon subjected to a sustained attack by forces sent over or commanded by his supplanter, William III. After defeat at the Battle of the Boyne, James fled once more to France, and the Protestant army relentlessly conquered the whole of Ireland. The war ended at Limerick, the final Catholic holding, with a Catholic surrender, followed by yet another flight of Catholic leaders to the continent.

Many of the men who went to France, where James II lived, joined the French Army. They were followed over the next century by several hundred thousands of their fellow Catholics, and every Catholic country in Europe, from Portugal to Russia, acquired its contingent of refugee Irish, often in the army. Women, recent research has shown, were as numerous in this migration as men. There were, however, still enough military-minded or desperate Irishmen in Ireland to provide many thousands of recruits for the British Army later in the eighteenth century.

The Unification of Ireland

The political result of the victory of the Protestant armies was the return of the Irish Parliament to Protestant control, which was followed by the imposition of a number of deliberately discriminatory acts, collectively called the penal laws. These were directed at eliminating the ability of Catholics to organize themselves, and even, for some, at the possible eventual elimination of Catholicism itself in Ireland. A law preventing the dispatch of children for education abroad restricted them to Protestant schools in

Ireland, or none. Catholics were to be disarmed, and they were excluded from political life, from the franchise and from practicing law. How effective these terms were is difficult to gauge, and later Catholic rebels had little difficulty, for example, in acquiring arms of some sort or in organizing themselves, but by enacting these laws the potential for preventive action by a Protestant government was much strengthened.

This conquest was the decisive unification of Ireland. The partial unification began with Henry VIII's surrender-and-re-grant policy, which brought most of the lords, Old English and Irish, within the political system emanating from Dublin. Over the next century-and-a-half that partial unification was battered by repeated crises – 'rebellions' to the English – each of which resulted in a renewed English conquest and in an extension of English power, above all the Nine Years' War of Elizabeth, the defeat of the Kilkenny Confederacy and the Commonwealth military occupation in the 1650s, and the Jacobite War of 1689–91. Earlier victories had ended with the area reserved for Catholic ownership of the land restricted to decreasingly smaller territories; after 1691 there was no such reservation, and the Acts passed in the years after the English victory clamped a firm English and Protestant grip on all Ireland, which was now fully united. As with Wales, the unification of the country had been accomplished by foreign conquest, and that conquest joined the country to its conqueror.

A New Union of Crowns

The measures of Protestant control originated in the Irish Parliament, and they reflected the fears of the Protestant minority in the country. It was, of course, a less than representative assembly, for, apart from excluding Catholics, who were nine-tenths of the population, it was as subject to aristocratic and landlord influence as was the British Parliament – so it was unrepresentative even of the Protestant population. In this it was much the same as the British Parliament, which was similarly unrepresentative and subject to a powerful aristocratic influence and control. The royal administration was headed by a Lord Lieutenant, in effect a viceroy, and he had to rub along with the Parliament, which became newly assertive after the Protestant victory. When the Lords Lieutenant finally understood that the Protestants were anxious most of all about their own security, it became possible for the two authorities to co-operate. However, the Parliament's powers were limited because of Poynings' Law, a measure dating from the late fifteenth century which in effect subordinated the Irish administration and Parliament to the English Parliament by insisting that any measures originating in Ireland required the approval of the English/British government and Parliament before they went into effect.

Clearly this was a situation which made Ireland part of the British political system, though it was attached in a different way than Scotland before 1707. The situation was also likely to be a further cause of continuous dispute. Periodically, the Irish Parliament attempted to escape from this oversight by agitating for the repeal of Poynings' Law. The question had already arisen by 1698, when a pamphlet asserted that the English Parliament had no right to make laws for Ireland, but this was swiftly answered by an English parliamentary declaration of its right to do so and by the passage of an act declaring that the export of wool to any place but England was unlawful. This did two things. First, it smothered the nascent woollen industry in Ireland, and it now became clear that any Irish enterprise which competed with an equivalent industry in England would receive the same treatment. Second, it demonstrated quite clearly that the English Parliament was determined to maintain its oversight and vetoing power. Ireland was not only to be an island where a minority of Protestants ruled over a great mass of Catholics, but also a poverty-stricken country subordinate to England. Not surprisingly, the issue of the independence of the Irish Parliament arose periodically throughout the eighteenth century.

Ireland was therefore in the approximate position within the British constitutional system of Scotland during the Union of the Crowns from 1603–1707, with its own Parliament and its own political system – in effect it was another union of crowns situation. The difference was that the government in London had a much stronger grip on Irish affairs, because of its ability to reject Irish measures and the British origin of the Lords Lieutenant, though politicians with Irish estates and titles were frequently given the post. There was unlikely to be any equivalent of the near declaration of independence which the Scots used to force the English to pay attention before the Treaty of Union, without a basic preliminary change in the political relationship. The reason, of course, was that it was necessary for the Irish Protestant 'Ascendancy' to be able to call on British military support when necessary – and in fact the main part of the British Army in the British Isles was always stationed in Ireland. This was the crucial element which lay behind all politics: Ireland did not have its own army; the troops in Ireland were always under British control and command.

There were thus plenty of fault lines in Irish affairs to produce continuing problems. There was conflict between the British and Irish

Parliaments, between Protestants and Catholics, and between the more violent Protestants and the usually more tolerant British Lords Lieutenant. Of course, the fewer rights the Irish Catholics had, the more likely they were to use violence to gain, at the least, some revenge. The repression of the Catholics was actually somewhat limited: no serious attempt was made to prevent them worshipping in their own way, and Catholic priests were therefore not driven out, though the bishops were, if they were caught. The result, of course, was that the Catholics became ever more firmly fixed in their faith, but by no means reconciled to their situation.

By the economic measures of the English Parliament, the island was drained of enterprise and wealth. By the penal laws, any ambitious Irishman was prevented from making any progress except by leaving the country. For those who stayed, breaking the English Protestant laws was the only way to any sort of enterprise, and at the same time it was their patriotic, even religious, duty. The economic restrictions and the lack of economic opportunities reduced most of the Irish to peasant subsistence. The Irish population doubled in the seventeenth century, and again in the eighteenth, and this happened without any concomitant increase in the resources to feed that increased population. The sort of agricultural improvements which were taking place in England in the eighteenth century were not repeated in Ireland, so the lot of most was hunger, periodic starvation and famine. Greater profits were available from raising cattle and sheep than arable farming, with the result that the growing of grain was much reduced. The peasantry came to rely on potatoes, a good food, no doubt, but it should have been obvious that reliance on a single food was both unhealthy and potentially dangerous.

There were exceptions to the general depressiveness. In Ulster, the descendants of the Protestant settlers from England and Scotland formed a fairly solid block. As tenants, they had gained a degree of security not available elsewhere by the application of 'Ulster custom', which was not a legal system but was generally accepted by landlords and tenants; this was in part due to their Protestant faith, which they shared with their landlords. The region did manage to sustain a linen industry, despite impeding tariffs originating from London. The city of Dublin flourished as the government centre, with its clerks and lawyers and their ability to spend. Both Cork and Dublin were busy ports, with Wexford and Waterford also doing well from shipping and trade, in particular in the export of cattle. Brewing was stifled by restricting the export of hops from Britain, encouraging illicit liquor production. It was, in effect, impossible to develop any industry without the British Parliament blocking it, and the Irish Parliament was unable to retaliate because of Poynings' Law. Emigration continued, though the direction of migration was now mainly towards America, with Europe second; migration to Britain was, not surprisingly, less popular. But the overall rate of emigration was also increasing.

Rural conditions in Ireland worsened in the eighteenth century, in large part due to the increasing population, while the Protestant oppression did not help. By the 1750s, rural distress had begun to produce rural 'outrages', with various groups – 'Whiteboys', 'Oakboys', 'Hearts of Steel' and 'Peep-O'-Day boys' – who committed property destruction, often by breaking down fences erected to confine cattle on lands where landlords had taken to cattle-raising in place of tenant-farming and tillage. They also menaced those they did not like, and were not above using violence – rural terrorists, in fact. These outbreaks tended to be fairly brief and episodic, but their example and methods were remembered and could be repeated. Trouble could be triggered by such events as a steep rise in rents demanded, as by Lord Donegal in Antrim in 1770, which set off the campaign of 'Hearts of Steel', which lasted two or three years, and died away because many of those involved emigrated to America. The fact that such violent reactions occurred and spread beyond the immediate cause and area so easily should have been a warning, but government and landlord reactions tended to a violent suppression without attending to the causes. They also tended to be local, and the issue was Ireland-wide. Further, the only recourse would have been through the Irish Parliament, which was in effect a collaboration of landlords, and it was understood that only by a relaxation of the Protestant grip, and of the British trade restrictions, could improvement be secured. The Protestants could not contemplate this; they were trapped by their own punitive measures, just as the Irish peasant population was trapped between an increasing population and their inability to increase production – a classic Malthusian situation.

The latent conflict between the Irish and British Parliaments emerged once more in the late 1760s, resulting in a brief parliamentary victory for the 'Patriot' group in the Irish House of Commons, but which in the end the government faced down. The weapons in this conflict were parliamentary votes and resolutions, but the government victory was due to the Lord Lieutenant's ability to prorogue Parliament and then to pick off opponents by dismissing them from lucrative offices, and to gather supporters by rewarding others with pensions and appointment to those forfeited offices. But this conflict was a precursor to a more substantial change. That particular dispute was over by 1772, but only three years later the American colonies broke into rebellion over the very same issue that had agitated the Irish – British parliamentary control over local affairs – and the Irish patriots took due note.

Under normal circumstances, as the minor crisis of 1767–72 had shown, the British government had little real difficulty in seeing off such challenges as might be mounted by the Irish Parliament. Ever since England became a united kingdom in the tenth century, it had disposed of much greater power than any other state in the British Isles, or even any combination of such states. This meant that it was only when the English or British government was distracted or preoccupied with a major crisis elsewhere that one of the minor states could seriously hope to succeed in its anti-English, or later its anti-British, government aims. This had been the case in the thirteenth century, when the Welsh princes from Gwynedd were able to exploit internal English problems during the reigns of John and Henry III. It was similarly so in the campaigns of Edward I and II against Scotland, when it became increasingly difficult for the English power to be exerted because of financial problems, and threats of war from France; and Owain Glyndwr's rebellion came when England was distracted by the successful, but challenged, usurpation of Henry IV. The Irish Confederacy succeeded in the 1640s for a time when England was distracted by the Civil War; in 1703–06, the Scots Parliament could exert disproportionate pressure in part because the government at Westminster was deeply involved in war with France and Spain. So it was in the years after 1775, when the British government was preoccupied first with the American rebellion and then with wars against France, Spain and Holland simultaneously, facing the virtually united enmity of all Europe.

The Irish Parliament and its parties quickly saw the parallel between their complaints and those of the rebel colonists: the power of the British Parliament was exerted unilaterally and without consultation to impose its authority on both. The American cause therefore brought a good deal of sympathy and support from the Protestant Irish, who had access to the Parliament, but the Catholics tended to dislike it, partly because they detested republicanism itself, but also hoping that support for the British government might bring some relief from their disabilities – whatever the Protestants wanted, the Catholics opposed. Instead, it was the Irish Protestant Parliament which was relieved of some of the economic prohibitions, though this was in aid primarily of the war effort, not a political concession.

It was the possibility of foreign invasion which finally brought into existence the organization which was sufficient to compel the British government to make serious concessions. The process appears to have begun at Belfast, where a raid by the American privateer John Paul Jones seized a king's ship in the lough, bringing to local attention their lack of defences and the inability of the government to provide any. They resorted to developing their own Volunteer force, and were copied and emulated by other communities throughout Ireland; with the various units it soon counted a hundred thousand members. They were armed and uniformed, and disciplined to some extent; they were also larger in number by a factor of ten than the regular British forces in Ireland. In 1779, the combined French and Spanish fleet reached the English Channel in great force, and the British fleet was not strong enough to fight them. The possibility of an invasion of Ireland was real, and it is only surprising that these enemies did not make the attempt. Volunteering became even more popular, and it could be argued that it was this force which deterred any attacks.

This marked the crucial change in Irish-British affairs. Until the rise of the Volunteers, the Protestant establishment in Ireland had relied, successfully, on British armed support to deal with the occasional risings and potential invasions. With the British forces fighting in America, in besieged Gibraltar and at sea, there was no force available to defend Ireland, except its own Volunteers. Their existence changed the balance of military power between the two islands, and this became the basis for the political changes which soon emerged.

The pressure on the British government of Lord North was too great for it to resist, enmeshed as it was in wars in Europe and America (and the Indian Ocean). It gave way stage by stage to Irish demands. First was the abolition of many of the economic restrictions so that Irish merchants could trade as freely as British, and contribute to government revenue by their customs duties – though they were still subject to the Navigation Laws. The government resorted to the old methods of handing out places and pensions, and felt it could thereby construct a parliamentary majority, but the opposition had – thanks in part to the existence of the Volunteers, but also to a determined popular campaign – developed a strength which could override the government's machinations. The British government, sensing this, gave up another restriction, by freeing Dissenters from the Test Act provisions, which affected the Ulster Protestants equally. It was still not enough. The opposition had understood – partly because Lord North in making the economic concessions had emphasized it – that all these measures were still at the mercy, or lack of it, of the British government and Parliament, so that the restrictions and penalties could be reimposed virtually overnight – Poynings' Law still ruled in the background – and probably would be when the wartime emergency ended. To make them secure it was necessary to ensure that, as Henry Grattan's parliamentary resolution in April 1780 put it, Ireland's parliament 'are the only power competent to enact laws to bind Ireland'.

The government failed to respond to this demand, and in fact gathered enough support to defeat it in Irish House of Commons. But the demands did not go away, and the Volunteers were always hovering in the background, a latent threat. The Volunteers indeed now began to push harder, holding a convention at Dungannon in February 1782 to emphasize those demands, their strength and their representative nature, which was far closer to the distribution of population than was the Parliament. Even if both Parliament and the Volunteers were predominantly Protestant, a considerable number of members of the Volunteers were Catholics. Another resolution demanding independence of British government control was defeated in the Irish House of Commons, though there was no visible outside campaign aiming to maintain the British connection. But then (1782) the government of Lord North collapsed, to be replaced in London by a Whig administration much more sympathetic to the Irish cause. For the third time, the Irish Commons discussed – or rather orated about – the demand for independence, and this time on a strong hint from the new Viceroy, the Duke of Portland, it was passed unanimously. But neither the arguments of the patriot orators, nor the existence of the Volunteers, had been decisive; the reality of British power in this issue was paradoxically demonstrated by the change of government in London – and it was that change in London which brought the alteration in the situation, not a resolution of the Irish House of Commons.

The Irish Parliament passed a series of Acts to put this resolution into effect: above all the operation of Poynings' Law was so altered that it was effectively neutered. The result was that the connection between Britain and Ireland became very tenuous indeed. The Parliament was made independent of British control, as was the judicial system. The king retained his veto power over Irish Acts, just as he did over British Acts, and the Lord Lieutenant was still appointed by, and was ultimately responsible to, the British ministers in London.

The new position from 1782 had many similarities to that of Scotland with reference to England after the Glorious Revolution of 1688. In institutional terms Ireland was, as Scotland had been between 1688 and 1707, almost independent of England. It was now connected to it by the persons of the king and the Lord Lieutenant, but not much else. However, the British ministers still had considerable powers in Ireland, just as they had also had under William III and Queen Anne in Scotland, and in both cases the reduction of pressure by the British on Irish affairs allowed antagonistic parties to develop in Ireland. The Irish situation soon degenerated into arguments and disputes. The issue of the reform of representation in the Irish Parliament came onto the agenda, not surprisingly when its power had been revealed so openly. This in turn opened up the question of the rights of the Catholics. In both of these issues the Volunteers exerted influence from outside the Parliament – thus the latent threat the Volunteers had posed to British power was now also exerted on the Irish political system. But the power which the Volunteers wielded could only be effective if it was not used. When the Volunteers passed their reform programme on to the House of Commons, where it was presented by the politician Henry Flood dressed in his Volunteer uniform, this was interpreted by the MPs as a threat. The Volunteer programme was rejected, and the House replied with a resolution resenting such 'encroachments' on its competence, and further resolved that parliamentary reform was not needed.

The failure to reform parliamentary representation had two more results: first, the influence of the Volunteers waned when that influence was challenged and rejected, and their numbers declined; second, Parliament remained open to manipulation by the executive part of government, and by the British government, for the real powers of the landed Protestant interest had not been severely affected. Indeed, once the political instability in London which began in 1782 had subsided with the establishment of William Pitt the Younger as Prime Minister from 1784, the strength of the Irish viceroyalty quietly revived, while the susceptibility of Parliament to manipulation by the executive had not changed. The effect of the Volunteers' movement, however, had been to highlight the unrepresentative nature of the House of Commons, and without parliamentary reform, the Irish Parliament would continue to be vulnerable to outside pressure.

The Volunteers began to revive from 1789 under the influence of the events and the ideology of the French Revolution. This also had its effect on the penal laws, which were relaxed stage by stage in the early 1790s as a way of cementing the national unity of Britain and Ireland in the face of a likely new French war. This meant that the unification of the two countries returned to the political agenda, for such national unity was still obstructed by the divergences between the two countries. Once again, the relaxation of these laws, which of course went too slowly to satisfy those urging them onwards, also exposed the continuing problem of the restricted parliamentary franchise and its effect on the influence of the landlords in lending assistance to the executive's strong influence over the Members. Further, the concessions being implemented were half-hearted, and only stimulated demands for all restrictions to be removed.

It was clear in the political manoeuvres which took place in the early 1790s that far from being an independent estate of the realm, the Irish Parliament remained largely under the control of the Lords Lieutenant, and these men were operating as agents of the British government which appointed them. Thus the 'independence' of the Irish Parliament, which it had thought had been attained, had quickly been in effect cancelled by its Members' own methods of work and election. Had the Parliament been able to reform its representative system this would not have happened, but the landlords' interest aligned with that of the British government, and they were fearful of losing their lands and positions if the reforms continued.

In Ulster, a war of rival rural gangs, the Protestant Peep-O'-Day Boys versus the Catholic Defenders, had been developing. In the process, the Peep-O'-Day Boys developed into the Orange Society (and then into the Orange Order), and embarked on a campaign of Catholic persecution in southern Ulster. Less addicted to violence was the Society of the United Irishmen, another Ulster-based organization, which had been energized by the democratic noises emanating from France. It aimed at overthrowing the Irish government system, above all by extending and reforming the franchise. It developed great strength through gathering Catholic support – a democratic reform would clearly have some liberating effect on the Catholics' situation – and by striking an alliance with the Defenders, who had suffered badly at the hands of the Peep-O'-Day Boys. The alliance had developed under the stress of the violence in Ulster into a widely based revolutionary movement, and the Defenders' influence shifted its intentions and methods towards the use of force. Preparations had begun for a rising, in part by seizing or stealing the stored weaponry of the Volunteers, and by manufacturing more.

The aims of the United Irishmen were now not simply reform of Parliament, but independence for Ireland and the severing of the British connection. In a way, and taking due note of the Irish context, this was an equivalent situation to that in Scotland during the period of threat and counter-threat in the early 1700s.

The government began preparations to resist. A force of militia was authorized; *habeas corpus* was suspended; an act was passed to suppress authorised oaths, which was one of the instruments binding the revolutionaries together; and a yeomanry force was authorized to supplement the militia. The militia was organized in companies, over 280 of them, the men serving full-time. It was largely Catholic in its rank-and-file, though generally officered by Protestants, and the companies were normally posted away from their home counties. The yeomanry, by contrast, was usually Protestant.

The demands of the war against France which began in 1793 had once again removed most of the regular troops from the island. The government, faced by a probable Irish rebellion, and therefore also threatened by a probable French invasion in support of the rebels, had no choice but to recruit these amateur forces, though once they were permanently embodied their training was properly managed; as a military force they were probably more effective than the Volunteers. This time the command of these forces, unlike that of the Volunteers, remained under full government control – and indeed, one of the purposes of recruiting the militia had been to attract potential Volunteers and so weaken the latter movement. By definition, the Volunteers were unpaid, whereas the militia received pay, and this was the crucial difference in recruiting full-time soldiers and disciplining them.

It was the militia which the government used to break the United Irishmen in Ulster. They were allowed to employ the same sort of methods as the rural terrorists, torturing suspects and enemies, burning houses and having the option of forced conscription to the fleet. But they were operating in a favourable environment, since the United Irishmen had already begun to lose support as it became clear that they were aiming at revolution and had become more than willing to use violence themselves to achieve their aims. A failed invasion by a French army in December 1796 encouraged the United Irishmen, but had also frightened many others, further sapping their support.

The repression by the militia was also applied against the Defenders in other parts of Ireland, particularly in Leinster and Munster. These were of course linked with the United Irishmen, who came to the conclusion that, despite having a quarter of a million armed (yet untrained) men in their organization, they needed French armed help as well, and began negotiations through Theobald Wolfe Tone, one of their inspirers, who had moved to Paris for safety. But the governments in both London and Dublin had an efficient spy system in operation which was both accurate and comprehensive, and was able to detect both the rebels' plans and those of the French. The rising was planned to begin in May 1798, so in March many of the United Irishmen's leaders were arrested and many of their papers were seized. The planned rising was now largely leaderless.

Risings nevertheless broke out in many areas in May, but their coordination failed, and so the government forces – the militia fought much better than the rebels – were able to defeat the risings separately. The most serious problem came in Leinster, where the fighting lasted for a month, but other risings rarely lasted longer than a week. In most cases defeat was followed by the rank-and-file of the rebels simply melting away and going home.

After the revolts were put down – the crucial battle was at Vinegar Hill in County Wexford in June – two French expeditions arrived, by which time the risings were generally over. The first arrived in August, landing at Killala Bay in Connacht, and was defeated after a month of rather aimless campaigning. The second expedition was intercepted in Lough Swilly in Ulster later and mainly captured. The prisoners taken included Wolfe Tone. These forces were republican in inspiration and sympathy, like the United Irishmen, but the Irish Catholics were still anti-republican, as they had been during the American rebellion, and the invaders were refused any support, while the victorious militia units were mainly Catholic in personnel. Both the rebel United Irishmen and the opposing militia relied largely on Catholic manpower.

The rebellions and invasions of 1798 convinced Pitt that it had become necessary to remove the obstacle of the Irish Parliament and proceed to the union of Britain and Ireland. He sent a capable political general, Lord Cornwallis, across as Lord-Lieutenant, and after a time added a usually capable Chief Secretary, Viscount Castlereagh. Their task was to organize the Parliament's extinction. As in the Scottish union a century before, it was necessary that both the British and Irish Parliaments should vote for the union, and the Acts be passed by both. The process took two years.

The early attempts by Cornwallis and Castlereagh failed in the Irish Parliament, but the vote against union was a narrow one, a case of only a handful of votes. Castlereagh then set about using the usual methods of Irish politics to build support. He made offers of lucrative offices, pensions, cash, patents of nobility and so on to those who could be persuaded to change their votes. A number of by-elections were engineered by enlisting the support of patrons of some seats where sitting MPs were opposed to union; the patrons ensured that the new members were in favour of voting themselves out. The Catholic interest was neutralized through the bishops, who were given to understand that Catholic Emancipation would follow the Act of Union. The Orange Order was also neutralized to a degree, but the Presbyterians were generally opposed. A large part of the British Army was

moved to the island, which kept up Irish apprehensions of a new rising and/
or a new French invasion.

Both sides conducted campaigns throughout the country, appealing
to popular sentiment, but the actual audience for this campaigning was
essentially a small group of Protestants. Neither Catholics nor Protestants
outside the political circles and a narrow group of landlords were at all
stirred by the issue; after all, they did not have the vote and were unlikely
to get the vote, whatever the result. Castlereagh had therefore to operate
with a relatively small proportion of the population, just those with the
franchise. It was the landlords, who controlled the voting system and the
franchise, who had to be persuaded. They could be contacted and persuaded
individually. The parallel with the achievement of the Anglo–Scottish union
is once again clear: in both cases the decision was made by a small group
of aristocrats and landlords who stood to gain personally; the general
population was never consulted, informed or gave its consent.

The various campaigns of persuasion by the government side succeeded.
In the several decisive votes on the union question in February and March
1800, in an unusually well-attended Irish Parliament, the government had
majorities of over forty and rising. The Irish House of Lords and the two
Houses of the British Parliament had already voted clearly in favour of
union, and now there could be no doubt. The union came into effect on
1 January 1801.

The methods of persuasion were, to a later view, somewhat unsavoury,
smacking of bribery and even, given the large force of British troops which
was stationed in Ireland – 40,000 men – of intimidation. But the methods
used were the normal methods of Irish Parliamentary politics, and there
seems to be no reason to assume that any other practice could have been
used. Certainly, a popular campaign would not have changed the minds
of any MPs. Opposition came from particular interests in large part, such
as the Dublin lawyers or the landlords, who saw union as threatening
either their incomes, their power or their rents. The landlords were the
most important, since these were the men who either elected – or rather
selected – the MPs, or who served as MPs themselves. Assurances that
the Protestant Ascendancy would continue were given, though part of the
British plan had been to accompany the union with an Act for Catholic
Emancipation – the new term for the relaxation of the penal laws.

The terms of the Act of Union were largely those which had been
produced by the British government; there was little Irish participation.
There was no question of any negotiation such as that which had preceded

the Scottish Act of Union. The terms were partly financial and partly concerned political representation. The electoral interests of the landlords were regarded as a species of property, and well over a million pounds was disbursed to buy out such interests. The Irish representation in the British Parliament was set at 100 MPs (a reduction from 300 in the Irish Parliament), with thirty-two members added to the British House of Lords from amongst the Irish nobility, figures reflecting the wealth and population of Ireland compared with England (just as had the Scottish representation). A reasonable financial settlement was made in which Ireland's contribution was set at two-seventeenths of the total; the two Anglican Churches, of England and Ireland, were united.

In economic areas, however, the union remained limited, with some customs duties varying between the two regimes, and some restrictions on trade still remained, though a condition of free-trade between the two islands was presupposed, and it was intended that harmonization of duties should take place after about twenty years. (This also got over the question which had been raised early on by the Scots, when new taxes were enacted by the Westminster Parliament, that the Act of Union was assumed to have set up a permanent unchanging condition; the potential to change was built in).

There was, however, to be a separate administration for Ireland, a Lord-Lieutenant was still to be in office in Dublin and the former government offices and officials were retained, often in the hands of the same men as before the union. There was to be a separate financial administration. But there was not to be, as it turned out, Catholic Emancipation. The union was thus similar to that concluded with Scotland in being limited to the Parliamentary area, though the precise elements of the limitations were different, the majority religious group in Scotland, the Presbyterians, was established as the Church of Scotland; in Ireland the majority, the Catholics, were still disabled (as also were the dissenting Presbyterians in the North).

The real problem with the union was thus the British government's failure to accompany the political unification with a measure of Catholic Emancipation. Pitt had virtually promised this, through Castlereagh, in persuading the Catholic bishops to accept the union, but when the moment of decision arrived he found that his Cabinet was divided over the issue, and he was therefore unable to present the king with the united advice to accept the measure, which enabled George III to claim that Emancipation violated his coronation oath; faced with a united Cabinet he would have had to give in. This was claimed to be the seed of the Irish problem for the next century, for the union actually reinforced the Protestant ascendancy, even though the Protestants had formed the principal opposition to the union. At the same time the lack of Emancipation alienated the Catholics, who had been in many cases conspicuously in favour of the union.

The union of the two islands, however imperfect it seems, and how unfair the method of achieving it seems from a later viewpoint, nevertheless was accomplished in the same way as the earlier unifications with Wales and Scotland. The failure to enact Catholic Emancipation may not have made that much difference, for it is virtually certain that Catholic opinion would have eventually come to oppose the union under any circumstances. Unification was nonetheless a major political accomplishment. By the time the union with Ireland was arranged, it was a century since the definitive British conquest of Ireland. (The rebellions do not count as 'conquest'.) Negotiations followed by agreement had become the normal process to reach a unification, and it was clearly the only way by which such a political change could be made.

Bibliography

Barnard, Toby, *A New Anatomy of Ireland, the Irish Protestants, 1649–1770* (New Haven: 2003).

Bartlett, Thomas and Jeffrey, Keith (eds), *A Military History of Ireland* (Cambridge: 1996).

Beckett, J.C., *The Making of Modern Ireland, 1603–1923* (London: 1968).

Connolly, S.J., *Divided Kingdom, Ireland 1630–1800* (Oxford: 2008).

Dickson, David, *New Foundations: Ireland 1660–1800* (2nd ed.) (Dublin: 2000).

Elliott, Marianne, *The United Irishmen and France* (London: 1982).

Fitzgerald, Patrick and Lambkin, Brian, *Migration in Irish History, 1607–2007* (London: 2008).

Foster, R.F., *Modern Ireland, 1600–1972* (London: 1988).

Garnham, Neal, *The Militia in Eighteenth Century Ireland: in Defence of the Protestant Interest* (Woodbridge 2012.

Kenny, Kevin (ed.), *Ireland and the British Empire* (Oxford History of the British Empire, Companion Series) (Oxford: 2004).

McDonagh, Oliver, *Ireland: the Union and its Aftermath* (London: 1977).

Pakenham, Thomas, *The Year of Liberty, the Bloody Story of the Great Irish Rebellion of 1798* (London: 1969).

Sparrow, Elizabeth, *Secret Service, British Agents in France 1792–1815* (Woodbridge, Suffolk: 1999).

Chapter 12

A United Kingdom?

The State of the Union

The Act of Union of 1801 produced a new political entity, 'The United Kingdom of Great Britain and Ireland', but to describe the condition of the state in that way is to consciously evade its actual political condition. Only in the most superficial way were the islands of the 'Atlantic Archipelago' united; a delve below the political surface reveals a whole collection of disunities. Further, none of these disunities were addressed in any systematic way once the political unification had taken place, and change only took place accidentally and was concerned solely with details.

A fully unified state should be integrated at all levels, and in all elements, though only a counsel of perfection would see this as attainable. It should have one language, one religion, one set of laws applicable to all citizens, a universal system of education and a political system which extended its authority over the whole country. As suggested, this is never going to be realized by any country larger perhaps than the very smallest, given the irremediable individuality of human beings (and cannot be said to exist in any state now or any in the past), but it is here set forth as a way of judging the state of integration of the new 'United Kingdom'.

It will be seen that the United Kingdom in 1801 failed on all counts. The majority language was certainly English, and this was spoken in every part of all four countries, but in large parts of Ireland the Gaelic Irish language was the only language of a substantial proportion of the population. The same applied to Scotland, with Scottish Gaelic prevalent over much of the Highlands, and to Wales, where Welsh had been rescued by the translation of the Bible into Welsh (on the orders of Queen Elizabeth I) and then by the stubborn determination of the Welsh to retain their particular language, so that the language was still spoken over much of the country, though English linguists were encroaching, as they had for centuries.

But one may go further. The Cornish language had probably died out by 1801, except among a few elderly residents. At the other end of the country, Norse was still spoken in Shetland and probably in Orkney as well, though it had died out by 1900. Refugees from the European continent fleeing religious and political persecution had been arriving since the sixteenth century. They brought in French and Dutch, and while it was normal for such people quickly to learn English, and their descendants were often monolingual, other refugees continued to arrive regularly throughout the eighteenth century, with a still greater inflow after the French Revolution, beginning in 1789. This, of course, has also been a phenomenon of Britain since 1801, particularly in the twentieth century, with the arrival of German- and Russian-speakers, Poles and Hungarians, Arabs, Africans, Indians and Chinese. Those of the second generation, as with the Huguenots and the Flemish refugees long in the past, are usually bilingual, and the third generation will usually speak English with an English, often a local, accent.

In 1801, there were also dialects of English which were virtually different languages. It is said that rural inhabitants in eastern Yorkshire and Lincolnshire spoke a language which Danes could understand, a relic of the Danish invasions of the ninth and tenth centuries. Some of the urban dialects which developed with urbanization in the nineteenth century were impenetrable to outsiders, as thick Brummie, Scouse and Glaswegian accents are still, and a Northern Irish accent is very difficult for others to understand. This is not to mention the continued use of Manx in the Isle of Man and French in the Channel Islands. So the British Isles, in language terms, have not yet become united, and were still less so in 1801.

The cases of religion and law show the use of political compromise at the expense of unification. To unite England and Scotland after a century of conflict, which had been in large part over the issue of religion, it was necessary for the Act of Union in 1707 to accept the two countries' religious separation. The 'established' – that is, the official – Churches of the two countries continued to be separate entities, and cleaved two distinct versions of Christianity. These two – Presbyterian in Scotland, Anglican in England – were then able to continue to persecute the minority religious communities within their own lands, which meant that the Episcopalians (that is, Anglicans) and Dissenters were persecuted in Scotland, and the Presbyterians and Dissenters in England; Catholics were also persecuted in both, as were any other Dissenters. These persecutions had, however, lessened in intensity in the eighteenth century, and had been reduced to a set of legal exclusions, such as the inability of Catholics and Dissenters to sit in Parliament.

Catholics had been persecuted in many ways in Ireland for two centuries, and their onerous legal disabilities were ignored – that is, maintained – by the Act of Union of 1801. In Wales, a steady move away from the Anglican

Church (which had been the choice of most Welsh in the seventeenth century) took large parts of the population into various Dissenting churches during the nineteenth century. The aim was probably to be distinct from the English-speaking gentry who controlled both the land and the Church; this move was an expression of political and social dissent as well as religious, and it left Wales in a religiously different condition from both England and Scotland, with the Welsh feeling increasingly annoyed at being discriminated against in their own country. The four countries, therefore, by 1801 diverged in religion quite noticeably, with each having a majority of the population allocated to one particular and different Christian cult or sect – and this difference had grown somewhat rather than diminished during the century since the Union of the Crowns.

Just as the 1707 Act of Union left the different Churches supreme in England and Scotland, so it left untouched the separate legal systems in those two countries. In both countries the older legal systems were slowly overridden by new laws enacted by the British Parliament. Grumbles came from Scotland claiming that the Act of Union was thus being violated, but once a united Parliament existed, its enactments necessarily applied to the whole of the united country, and did not affect the conduct of the Scottish legal system. In Wales, elements of Welsh law had remained in use for some time after the Anglo-Welsh union in 1542, but English law was gradually enforced by English-speaking magistrates and England-trained lawyers. In Ireland, the legal system which was designed to maintain control in the hands of the Protestant 'Ascendancy' – elements of which would be unacceptable in the main island – was left in place by the union. The four countries saw some convergence by reason of the actions of the united Parliament, but the prevailing legal systems were so deeply embedded in the social conditions of these countries that this moved very slowly and incompletely, even in Wales.

No attempt had been made to unify the provision of education, and in 1801 this was scarcely seen as having any sort of priority. Two universities in England, four in Scotland and one in Ireland, plus the legal colleges, were considered adequate since so few people were expected to reach a university level of education, though criticism of their complacency was mounting. Below the university level, provision was always patchy and local, with little provision for the poor. Scotland claimed to be a literate country, but the old provision at the parish level was being eroded by 1800, and failed in areas of dense industrialization. England's grammar schools, often legacies of the spoils of Henry VIII's dissolution of the monasteries, served the middle classes and were being supplemented by dissenting academies, and often by parish schools, but few of these were really effective as educational institutions.

All these divergences were compounded by the caste-like social structure of the British population. Since the fifteenth century, at least in England, the government system had been under the control of the aristocracy and gentry, and this situation was unaffected by the inhabitants of the throne or by the several Acts of Union. Indeed, these Acts had in effect annexed to the English aristocracy the great landowners of Scotland, who exercised a similar political control, the Welsh gentry, often of English origin or thoroughly Anglicized, and the Protestant Ascendancy in Ireland. This, in a way, was a success for the union in forwarding integration at the governing level, except that these links gradually reinforced the aristocratic control, excluding others. Although the aristocracy, at least in England, was relatively open to accepting rising newcomers, such acceptance was slow and might take two or three generations.

It follows that, despite this lordly supremacy forming a governing caste over the whole union, the political arrangements of the four countries varied. England-plus-Wales, Scotland and Ireland all had their own political systems before the unions, and these were generally taken over whole in the Acts of Union. The provision of members to the House of Commons by Scotland was thus based on the highly restricted electoral system in operation formed in the Act of 1707, which was based on that operating in the years before then, whereby the forty-five MPs sent to the Union Parliament were (in 1831) elected by only about 4,500 voters. In Ireland, the choice of MPs was dominated by the Protestant landowners and the borough oligarchies, as it had been before 1800 – Catholics were not actually denied the vote, but electoral manipulation denied them election. The great predominance of MPs from England (489 from England, 169 from the other countries) meant that English concerns continued to dominate.

Even more anomalously, Ireland, though technically part of the United Kingdom, still had its own governing system under British control, with a Viceroy appointed from London and an Irish Secretary in the British Cabinet; the country was also a garrison island, with army barracks in most towns – in direct contrast with England, where such institutions were extremely rare. Ireland was thus still a separate political entity despite the Act of Union, a condition justified by the difficulty of governing the island and the unwillingness of the Protestant Irish aristocracy to permit any sort of Irish – that is, Catholic – self-government.

It is therefore, given these caveats, difficult to apply the word 'united' to the British islands in 1801. But some progress in integration had taken place between England and Scotland, at the level of the governing aristocracies, and more had occurred, at lower social levels, between England and Wales. It might have been expected that more progress in that direction was possible in all three countries, and that Britain and Ireland might follow, for all were subject to the need to legislate at Westminster for the whole country. But, just as it had taken two-and-a-half centuries to bring the four countries into what must be seen as no more than a preliminary unification by 1801, so the disintegration of that union has taken two centuries so far, and is not fully accomplished yet, being still a change in motion. The United Kingdom in 1801 was, in terms of the classification of unifications detected earlier, in a stage of only 'partial union'.

The Empire Factor

One of the elements which was persuasive amongst the Scots in agreeing to the union of their country with England had been that the unification would allow the Scots equal access into the English empire. They had held a degree of unofficial access ever since the empire existed, but the lifting of the legal bar, symbolized by the effective extension of the Navigation Acts to include Scotland, was a stimulus to Scots who aimed to profit by the English imperial enterprise. This came in several ways.

Scots had been actively recruited into the British Army since before the union of 1707, but it was the French wars which began in the 1740s and continued with only short breaks until 1815 which pushed forward and expanded the recruitment drive. The formation of 42nd Foot (the Black Watch) in 1742 as a regular regiment of the Army was followed after the 1745 rebellion by a deliberate attempt to drain the Highlands of many of the young men of military potential by forming more Scottish regiments. The regiments thus formed were often clan-based, under their chiefs' command, but by sending them overseas these men could no longer cause trouble at home; and most of the soldiers died in imperial service. Regiments sent to India, for example, stayed there sometimes for decades, and were kept up to some sort of strength by drafts sent from Britain; if they were returned, the men were both old and often wasted by disease. Those sent to the West Indies suffered the ravages of yellow fever.

The British Army, between (and even during) the French wars, was largely situated in Ireland, that being the country most likely to be troublesome;

rebellions took place several times during the Revolutionary and Napoleonic wars. Once there, the regiments actively recruited Irishmen into their ranks. When sent overseas on campaign, therefore, many regiments which had been stationed in Ireland included a substantial element of Irish recruits. Once again, one of the underlying reasons for this was to gather in the young men who might take part in any rebellion. When rebellions did take place, the soldiers almost invariably proved to be loyal to their salt. Of course, those young men in Ireland who could not face being ruled by the English could always emigrate; the Irish diaspora in European Catholic countries was numerous and was constantly renewed by new arrivals.

Scottish and Irish recruits into the British Army therefore became one of the mainstays of the imperial system, and became renowned for their successes, even as they died in great numbers for imperial purposes. Merchants, however, fared better, but most of them operated from home in Britain, using agents in the colonies, India and the United States. From the 1790s, it was this last source from which the cotton was increasingly obtained which was to feed the growing appetites of the new factories. Most of it went to Lancashire, of course, but the connection between Glasgow and the American (former) colonies in the tobacco trade easily transferred to trading in cotton. India was a more difficult trading area for interlopers, since they had to avoid the attentions of, and restrictions imposed by, the East India Company, and then had to penetrate the internal mercantile networks which were under the control of Indian merchants. The former proved to be the less difficult task, partly because the Company was as willing to employ Scots as clerks and soldiers as it was anyone else from Europe. The Scots were often helped in the period between 1780 and 1810 by the influence of Henry Dundas and his son, the Earls Melville, who actively promoted the insertion of Scots into the East India Company; and Scots in the Company proved to be quite willing to assist Scottish merchants in India.

Emigration

A major use of the empire for Scots, apart from using up its soldiers and enabling merchants to become wealthy, was providing destinations for migrants. Attempts have been made to calculate the number of Scots who moved to overseas territories, but the total is no more than approximate, and the estimates vary widely. The number must be in the tens of thousands before 1775. The most popular destination was, in that period, the American colonies, but after the War of Independence began in 1775 the movement to Canada increased. By the early nineteenth century, South Africa and Australia had become worthwhile destinations, and from the 1840s New Zealand was available as well.

Emigrants could be attracted to such new lands, or they could be compelled by various forces to go to them. In the aftermath of British internal wars in the 1660s, 1715 and 1745, Scots prisoners who had fought the English and been captured were sent, usually, to the West Indies, and particularly to Barbados. Few ever returned. The numbers involved were relatively few – perhaps 5,000. Other emigrants who were less than voluntary were indentured labourers and 'apprentices', though again these were fairly few over the whole century. Voluntary migration, however, to North America was constant, and in the new century it was actively encouraged by clan chiefs in both the Highlands and Lowlands. These men wished to convert their lands from peasant occupation to the farming of sheep or cattle, into large estates or even into deer forests. For those affected by such actions, the choices were emigrating overseas, starvation on the margins of their former lands or moving to such places as Glasgow, where they might find work in the new factories.

Some overseas destinations were already in a sense prepared to receive Scottish migrants, in that substantial numbers of Scots had moved there during the eighteenth century – New Jersey, North Carolina and to some degree Georgia in the new United States already had a fairly substantial Scottish population, as did the provinces of Canada, which became a favoured destination after 1775. The scale of this movement increased in the nineteenth century, when the main target was the United States, and was helped by famines and blights at home. It has been calculated that between 1825 and the 1930s, 2.3 million Scots moved overseas, together with 600,000 who moved to live in England.

This was what is now called 'economic migration'. How voluntary it all was is impossible to say. Whatever the precise motives were in driving people out of their homes in Scotland, it was also the possibility of a better life, more food, economic opportunities, access to land and the possibility of jobs which were the attractive element involved. To emphasize the point, the unsettled years after 1919 saw a third of a million Scots go overseas in a single decade; twice that number left between 1950 and 1980. All this was in addition to the constant flow of Scots into England ever since 1603. The population of Scotland was thus greatly restricted as a result, and it has been estimated that about half of the expected 'natural increase' was thus siphoned off to these other territories.

In a way this may be thought the salvation of Scotland. If the emigrants had remained in Scotland so that the population grew to six or seven million, instead of the four million which actually lived in Scotland about 1900, their condition would probably have been dire. Employment would have been difficult to get, and wages would be depressed as a result. The industrialization of Scotland could have been expanded, but for a country with few natural resources (other than coal) it seems unlikely that this would have expanded to soak up the extra population.

It is only necessary to consider the population history of Ireland to see the likely outcome of an absence of migration in Scotland. All the considerations noted in the preceding paragraphs apply the more forcefully to Ireland. The refusal, repeatedly, of English governments to admit any serious commercial or industrial development in Ireland in the seventeenth and eighteenth centuries left the island dependent entirely on agriculture – this was in a country where arable agriculture was not easy, and the main element of agriculture was cattle raising. When the Union government finally instituted free trade in manufactured goods between the two islands in 1824, it was to the benefit of existing manufacturers in Britain, and their ability to undersell any Irish-made goods had the same effect as the earlier prohibition.

As a result the capital, enterprise and shipping which were needed to develop commercially or industrially and to provide employment for an increasing population were absent. The population of Ireland doubled in both the seventeenth and eighteenth centuries, rising from about 1.2 million in 1600 to about 4.5 million in 1800. It almost doubled again in the next forty years, rising to over eight million in 1841. By this time Ireland had a population half that of England and Wales, without the economy capable of supporting that number.

It was impossible in an agricultural country to absorb this sort of population increase without an increase in the land under cultivation. There were no alternative sources of employment, and the only recourse was the constant subdivision of the cultivated land or emigration. By the 1830s, when a new Poor Law was being considered, it was clear that the country was on the brink of disaster already. Destitution was widespread and the rural population had become largely reliant on the potato crop. The potato is a fine food, but in the ground it is liable to fail. There had been several failures of the crop in the first half of the nineteenth century, and in the

Scottish Highlands in 1836 an outright famine occurred when the crop failed. It cannot be said that warnings had not emerged that reliance on the one crop was extremely dangerous.

The potato failure in the 1840s happened because of the activity of a new potato disease, a fungus, which persisted in the ground in the next years. As was usual in a famine, one year's hunger can often be survived by a population, but failure in the second year and later turned the famine into a disaster. There were no resources available for the relief of distress – the rest of Europe was also going through a famine period, and the blight attacked the potato crop in Scotland and Belgium as well. Death and migration were the results.

The population fell by about two million between 1841 and 1851. Half of this reduction was due to deaths and the other half to large-scale emigration. But the real result of the crisis was that emigration continued after the end of the famine, at a reduced rate compared with the famine years, but at a constantly high rate compared with the 'normal' years. In the eighteenth century, as the population doubled from two million to over four million, emigration took about 350,000 Irish abroad, mainly to the Americas. In the nineteenth century, emigration took over 7.5 million Irish overseas, the great majority (5.8 million) to North America. The population fell from over eight million in 1841 to 4.5 million in 1901, when it was the same size as 100 years before.

The British Empire, despite its apparent size, was not capable of absorbing such numbers any more than was Ireland. The migration destinations within the empire had only a limited absorption capacity – Australia is largely hot desert, Canada mainly cold desert, South Africa fully occupied and New Zealand small. Some 1.4 million of the emigrants went to Britain, and 350,000 did go to Australia and New Zealand, but it was only the United States which could take in and accept the huge numbers of people who were leaving Ireland. This heavy concentration on moving to North America, however, changed in the twentieth century. The second greatest flow of Irish abroad in the nineteenth century was, ironically, to Britain, and this continued and increased in the twentieth century.

There was thus a clear contrast between the migrant experiences of Scots and Irish. Wales was different again. Welsh migration was on a much smaller scale than that from either of the other countries – or than that from England, which was almost entirely of migrants searching for an improved life. About 100,000 Welsh-born were listed in the United States' census of 1890, and the flow of people to other destinations was similarly comparatively small. Instead, the Welsh tended to move within Wales or into England. The development of industry in South Wales attracted the Welsh from the rural regions. This had not been an option available in Ireland, though the growth of industry in the Central Valley of Scotland had something of the same effect for Scots from the agricultural areas. But it is noticeable that the Welsh who did emigrate tended to be skilled men – miners, metalworkers, quarrymen – whereas those leaving from Scotland and Ireland were generally peasants. (Cornish emigration was also largely of skilled miners from the failing tin mines.) There was, however, the same gradual movement from Wales into England for the purposes of acquiring employment, and this was a constant movement from both Scotland and Ireland from 1500 onwards.

This is a further element in a movement of people, which has already been noted in passing. One of the main destinations for emigrants from all the Celtic lands was always England. This was a movement which was largely independent of famines as in Ireland, or clearances in Scotland, for the attraction was always the availability of work in industrializing England. Scots had also been moving south in considerable numbers even before 1600; Irish migrants similarly moved to the new industrial areas, but mainly in the nineteenth century. This was one of the major elements in the history of the union of the countries, as the people who took part in this internal migration integrated relatively easily with the native English population, thus reinforcing the wider sentiment in favour of the political union.

At the same time, however, it is also clear that those who remained in the 'home' countries perceived the union as something less than welcome. These were often people who had enhanced patriotic beliefs, who resented the notion of leaving their homeland and were often more politically aware and active than the refugees could afford to be. (This was also something felt by many of those who moved away – the Welsh colonists in Patagonia retained their Welsh language; cemeteries in the new lands are full of gravestones on which is recorded the birthplaces, sometimes in emotional terms, of the dead, but they could no longer seriously affect events 'back home'.) The movement of Irish people within the United Kingdom similarly went to areas where work was available – the Glasgow area, Lancashire, South Wales – thereby reinforcing, or perhaps introducing, the Catholic Church in these areas, somewhat to the consternation of the native Churches. The net result was therefore, as always, paradoxical: a greater integration in England, which remained the magnet for all the other countries of the union, but a hardening of an anti-union sentiment in Scotland, Ireland and Wales.

Reforms

The exigencies of the Napoleonic Wars had swept away numerous government sinecures, and had revealed the wealth available for a government if it could institute an acceptable tax regime. Even before the wars, the Pitt government reduced customs duties and thereby largely eliminated evasion and smuggling, meanwhile increasing taxation revenues. The return of peace brought much of the old taxation regime back, including trade protection, the Corn Laws and regressive taxes, benefitting the aristocracy and the landowners; this compounded the difficulties which always follow the ending of a long war. But this period had also revealed the possibilities of popular mobilization, and the half-century after the Battle of Waterloo was filled with popular movements. The pressures to move away from – or break – the restrictive system which had been reimposed increased. Characteristically, this was manifested differently in the several countries of the union.

The Tory governments from 1815 eventually resorted to a series of reforms designed to remedy particular grievances and so reduce discontent, legalizing trade unions, reducing trade tariffs as a move towards free trade and reforming the legal system. The result, which was not intended, was to highlight several issues which had not been on the original agenda. In Scotland this was the general political situation in which a minute electorate could be all too easily manipulated by an able political tactician. This had produced the 'Dundas Despotism' during the Napoleonic Wars period, in which Henry Dundas had so organized politics in Scotland as to maintain a personal political control by manipulating elections and providing kickbacks and sinecures to the bribable and his supporters. This had not been a very efficient system, though it had helped to maintain government control of the House of Commons by lining up Scottish MPs in its support. It has been called 'totalitarian' as a more insulting term than mere 'despotism'. It was hardly brutal enough for such a description, but it certainly relied in part on distorting the law and was widely detested. It crumbled after Dundas lost office, but the fact that one man could so control the whole electoral and political system in one of the countries of Britain was alarming.

Ireland might well fall into the same condition, for its electoral system was equally vulnerable to manipulation. The Irish Act of Union had not damaged the dominance of the landlords over the Irish electoral process, and Catholics, though in theory entitled to vote, were unable to elect their co-religionists because no Catholic could take his seat in the House of Commons. In Ireland, therefore, the main issue was Catholic Emancipation; it was felt this was promised at the time of the union, but then refused. Emancipation went rather further in its demands than political rights, but these were soon seen as the essential element before any further changes could be achieved. The first stage was to ensure that Catholics could elect one of their own and see him in the House of Commons, and therefore these men would exert pressure for further relaxations of the Irish penal laws.

The problem of representation was, for the other countries, the main issue. By focusing at last on the need to reform the representation of the House of Commons, it was generally supposed that further reforms could and would inevitably follow – which assumption was also the source of the opposition to reforms. None of the 'Celtic' countries could insist on such reform, for they were not strong or numerous enough in the House of Commons to do so. In England, however, matters had changed decisively since the 1780s, when the issue had first been raised. Industrialization had shifted the concentration of wealth, and the movement and growth of the population had revealed a series of risible inequities in the electoral process which could no longer be defended. The Welsh system, curiously, did not exhibit any of the corrupt factors visible elsewhere, though it was clearly dominated in many areas by an Anglophone aristocracy.

The campaign to alter the electoral system centred inevitably on persuading English MPs to agree to the changes, in part because separate Acts were required for Scotland and Ireland, whose existing systems had been set out in their Acts of Union. Once an English reform had been achieved the others would follow. Despite these separate bills, the whole House of Commons voted on all three, and similarly in the Lords – a characteristically confusing detail. The reform was a major constitutional crisis, perhaps the most decisive such conflict ever, not excluding the Civil War and the Glorious Revolution of 1688, and it was only passed when the House of Lords was compelled to accept the changes or face the prospect of a permanent Whig-Liberal majority being imposed on it – and a spreading tide of disorder showed the Lords the possibility of violent change being imposed.

The overall result of the changes was to increase the electorate in England by 50 per cent from 435,000 to 653,000 men, in Scotland by fourteen times (from 4,500 to 65,000) and by double in Ireland (49,000 to 90,000). There was a small shift of seats from England to the other countries, but this was not enough to seriously affect the balance of geography. One of the main results was to make it more difficult for candidates to manipulate the vote to bribe the electorate, but neither of these practices actually ceased.

Despite the changes, there was still a great variation in the sizes of electorates between the smallest English constituency (about 200 voters) and the largest (about 18,000 voters), and the distribution of population was not reflected in the seats in the House – Ireland's population was half that of England, but it had only a quarter of the seats of England (105 to 472), which included Wales; Scotland had only a third of Ireland's population and a sixth of England's, but its seats amounted to only an eighth of England's and half of Ireland's. It may be concluded that any attempt at an equitable redistribution was not the object of the exercise. Yet the inequitable elements of the former system had been the basis for the demands for change; further changes were certainly going to be demanded. The essential result, therefore, was that the old system had been made subject to change, and this could be repeated.

The real trigger for the reform had been elections in Ireland where Catholic voters had been mobilized by the Catholic Association and had been marched to the polls under clergy command, where they cast their votes for candidates in favour of Catholic Emancipation. This had succeeded in the county elections in Waterford and Louth in 1826, and in a by-election in County Clare two years later, and if it could be done there it was possible to do it in most Irish counties. This had led, after the usual delays, discussions and arguments, to the passing of Catholic Emancipation in 1829, a measure which was accompanied by an alteration in the qualification of voters in Irish county seats so as to exclude most Catholics. This was therefore the first breach in the electoral and political system. The agitation for the Reform Acts came next, in part inspired by the successes of the emancipators in Ireland.

Sure enough, a whole series of reforms to other institutions followed – changes to the electoral registration system, to the system of local government, the Poor Law and regulation of factory conditions, among others. Many of these changes were dealt with country by country, so there was a Municipal Corporations Act for England, but a Burgh Act for Scotland and an Irish Municipal Reform Act. Once again, by providing similar measures for each country, Parliament was at the same time emphasizing that they were all part of the United Kingdom, and also all different. It would hardly be said that this marked any real progress in expanding the scope of the union of the four countries.

Bibliography

Adams, Ian and Somerville, Meredith, *Cargoes of Despair and Hope, Scottish Emigration to North America 1603–1803* (Edinburgh: 1993).

Beckett, J.C. Bekett, *The Making of Modern Ireland, 1603–1923* (London: 1966).

Brock, Michael, *The Great Reform Act* (London: 1973).

Checkland, Olive and Sidney, *Industry and Ethos, Scotland 1832–1914*, 2nd ed. (Edinburgh: 1989).

Colley, Linda, *Britons, Forging the Nation, 1707–1837* (New Haven, RI: 1992).

Cromwell, Valerie, *Revolution or Evolution, British Government in the Nineteenth Century* (London: 1977).

Devine, T.M., *Exploring the Scottish Past, Themes in the History of Scottish Society* (East Linton, East Lothian: 1995).

Devine, T.M., *Independence or Union, Scotland's Past and Scotland's Present* (London: 2016).

Devine, T.M., *Scotland's Empire, 1600–1815* (London: 2003).

Devine, T.M., *To the Ends of the Earth, Scotland's Global Diaspora, 1750–2010* (London: 2011).

Fitzgerald, Patrick and Lambkin, Brian, *Migration in Irish History, 1607–2007* (Basingstoke, Hampshire: 2008).

Foster, R.F., *Modern Ireland, 1600–1972* (London: 1988).

Fry, Michael, *The Dundas Despotism* (Edinburgh: 1992).

Fry, Michael, *The Scottish Empire* (East Linton and Edinburgh: 2001).

Harvie, Christopher, *Scotland and Nationalism, Scottish Society and Politics, 1707–1977* (London: 1977).

Jenkins, Geraint H., *The Foundations of Modern Wales, 1642–1780* (Oxford: 1993).

Karras, Alan L., *Sojourners in the Sun, Scottish Migrants in Jamaica and the Chesapeake 1740–1800* (Ithaca NY: 1992).

Kenny, Kevin (ed.), *Ireland and the British Empire, Oxford History of the British Empire Companion Series* (Oxford: 2004).

MacDonagh, Oliver, *Ireland: the Union and its Aftermath* (London: 1977).

MacKenzie, John M. and Devine, T.M. (eds), *Scotland and the British Empire, Oxford History of the British Empire Companion Series* (Oxford: 2011).

Morgan, Kenneth O., *Revolution to Devolution, Reflections on Welsh Democracy* (Cardiff: 2014).

Pearce, Edward, *Reform! The Fight for the 1832 Reform Act* (London: 2003).

Pentland, Gordon, *Radicalism, Reform and National Identity in Scotland, 1820–1833* (Woodbridge, Suffolk: 2008).

Phillipson, N.T. and Mitchison, Rosalind, *Scotland in the Age of Improvement*, 2nd ed. (Edinburgh: 1996).

Porter, Andrew (ed.), *The Nineteenth Century, Oxford History of the British Empire* (Oxford: 1999).

Porter, A.N., *Atlas of British Overseas Expansion* (London: 1991).

Webb, R.K., *Modern England from the Eighteenth Century to the Present* (London: 1969).

Part III

SEPARATIONS

The achievement of the full political union of the four countries of the British Isles in 1801 was the prelude to the beginning of that union's disintegration. This has not yet been wholly accomplished by those who find the union inconvenient, but they have made some progress, and this is the overall subject of this section. It is, however, also necessary to indicate the uses to which the union has been put by its citizens; that was partly the subject matter of the last chapter, which overlaps in some degree the matter of this chapter.

It may be noted that the process of disintegration has so far taken a century, since the Sinn Fein election of 1918. It seems quite suitable that it has been slow; after all, the process of unification took 1,400 years to accomplish.

Part III

SEPARATIONS

Chapter 13

Nationalisms

Ireland

Just as an Irish initiative began the agitation which brought about the Reform Act of 1832, so it was the continuing problem of the relationship of Britain and Ireland which finally began the process of breaking up the United Kingdom. The basic aim of most Catholic Irish throughout the nineteenth century, as it had been since the Elizabethan conquest, was to remove themselves from British control. The accomplishment of the union itself was followed by a minor rising ('Emmet's') as early as 1803, though this was not really a direct reply to the unification. Almost as soon as the Reform Act was passed, Daniel O'Connell began organizing sympathetic Irish MPs into a distinct party whose aim was to repeal the Act of Union. The question was repeatedly brought forward by Irish politicians, while British governments repeatedly ignored this fundamental bent of Irish politics.

O'Connell and his party set their sights on repeal, but they got nowhere in the face of opposition from the rest of the House of Commons, not to mention the House of Lords. Apart from that hopeless task, he found that a side effect of his agitation was to destabilize Ireland, where many Irish were less concerned with the hopelessness of repeal and more immediately interested in dealing with some local issues. An early issue (and one which resounded in Wales as well) was that of the payment of tithes, collected from landowners (who recovered the cost, and more, from their tenants) and was paid to the Anglican Church of Ireland, despite the fact that in some areas there were no members of the Anglican Church. The Catholic population was thus being taxed to support the Anglican Church. (In Wales, it was Dissenters who were similarly being taxed.) The agitation, including a general refusal to pay the tithes, led to a partial reduction in the possessions and expenses of the Anglican Church, including the suppression of ten dioceses. The cost was widespread rural unrest and a revival of the agrarian secret societies, several hundred murders, assaults and incidents of arson. The government replied with a Coercion Act, which in effect suspended the operation of the legal system in favour of martial law.

This began a pattern of action and reaction, agitation and coercion, which was to be repeated constantly throughout the nineteenth century. The immediate aim of the Irish varied with time, but the underlying demand was always to get away from the British connection. To go through the details is not necessary, since they have been discussed endlessly in other accounts. Briefly, a new agitation for repeal came in the 1840s, but was overtaken by the great famine of 1845–49 and the subsequent mass emigration. This reduced the pressure on the British government for repeal, though they received plenty of blame for not reacting adequately to the disaster. It did, however, set up a situation in which the shortage of labour on the land brought disputes over rent levels and security of tenure (as had happened after the Black Death in England in the fourteenth century).

An Irish Reform Act of 1850 greatly increased the Irish county electorate and reduced that in the boroughs; the landowners and borough oligarchs found their power decreased. This enhanced the support at elections for demands for further reform. In 1852, forty of the Irish MPs were elected on a tenant-right platform, a demand that the more tenant-friendly Ulster Custom be extended to the rest of Ireland. This became the next demand, though the movement soon collapsed. The coherence of Irish politicians in fact regularly failed. It was obvious that only with a charismatic leader, capable of controlling his followers in Parliament and leading them more distantly in Ireland, and holding them to a clear programme, would the Irish make progress in the demands they were making. O'Connell had been such a leader; those of the 1850s and 1860s were more mundane, and the next would not appear for two more decades.

The threat of foreign intervention in Ireland had long been one of the main justifications in British minds for controlling the island. Spain in 1601 and France in 1688, 1796, 1798 and at other times had intervened militarily, though they had been defeated in all cases. One of the motors for such interventions had been the existence overseas of large communities of Irish exiles, often recruited into foreign armies and more than willing to be used against Britain. The great emigration from Ireland which came from 1845 onwards until the end of the nineteenth century placed even larger exiled communities in the United States, but also in British colonies. Not surprisingly, the Irish in the USA – a country fundamentally hostile to Britain throughout the nineteenth century – organized to support their beleaguered fellow Irish at home. This was a new intervention frontier which was important for the next century-and-a-half.

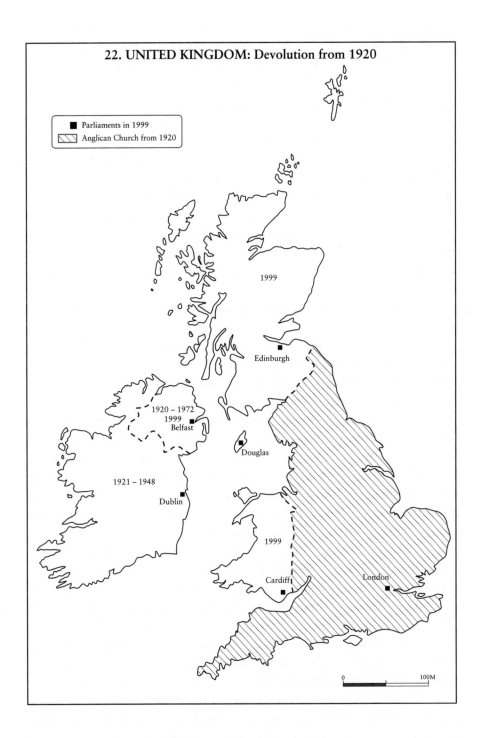

22. UNITED KINGDOM: Devolution from 1920

Parliaments in 1999
Anglican Church from 1920

1999

Edinburgh

1920 – 1972
1999
Belfast

Douglas

1921 – 1948

Dublin

1999

Cardiff

London

0   100M

The Irish in America organzsed as a result of their connections back to Ireland. The Fenian Brotherhood began in 1859 in the USA, but they were soon overwhelmed by the Civil War – in which many Irish served in the Union Army, gaining military skills. In Dublin, James Stephens founded the Irish Republican Brotherhood, and it was as a branch of this that the Fenians originated. The IRB was another secret organization, perhaps rather better organized than earlier ones, and it continued in existence much longer than those; its aims were essentially repeal of the Act of Union and Irish independence. It was composed of men with sometimes differing aims, varying from land reform all the way to repeal. The original aim of secrecy never worked, because it required publicity to thrive and continue, and in fact one of the Fenian successes lay in exploiting events to gain publicity and sympathy. The IRB did, however, set up committees which were quite capable of secretly arranging events without sanction from the wider membership.

The Fenians had a violent tinge. An attempted attack on Canada in 1866 failed, defeated by the Canadians with ease, but it also turned out that the United States was unwilling to contemplate a war with Britain, at least at that point. 'Fenian outrages' in Britain, with bomb attempts to release prisoners in Manchester and Clerkenwell, gave the organization a bad name, at least in Britain, but certainly drew attention to its aims.

In the year after these bomb attacks, 1868, W.E. Gladstone became Prime Minister. Gladstone had identified several areas of Irish life which he felt required reform, though these did not include repeal. He disestablished the Anglican Church of Ireland, thus at last solving that problem. He set about reforming the landownership situation, and set up a scheme by which government money would be made available to settle tenants on their own plots of land, the money to be repaid over a long period.

This was all very well, but, as he must have known, these reforms were no more than palliatives. Indeed, he had claimed when appointed as Prime Minister that his 'mission' was 'to pacify Ireland'. This could certainly be done by redressing some obvious grievances, but it would not solve the Irish problem, though it was the approach all British governments had adopted. By solving specific issues it was believed that Irish discontent could be redressed, and Ireland would thereby be brought into a condition where it approximated to England or Scotland. The Catholic Church in Ireland, for example, could become a national Church, on the pattern of the Church of England in England or the Presbyterian Church in Scotland. As each problem was identified – emancipation, tithes, religious disabilities, land reform – each was dealt with in isolation. It was thought, thereby, that by reforming these elements in Ireland, the country would be, as Gladstone put it, 'pacified'.

It was, in essence, an attempt to cement Ireland into the union of the four countries, eventually on similar lines to those of Scotland. The trouble was, it was all too grudging and too late. Repeal had been in effect a demand for separation, and was an Irish aim as early as the passage of the Act of Union; it had been so ever since, underlying every individual grievance. The two sides were operating from different basic aims – the British to integrate, the Irish to separate – and this did not change.

In 1872, the lawyer Isaac Butt founded the Irish Home Rule movement, which evolved into the Home Rule League in time to field candidates in the 1874 general election, and to see sixty of them elected. The issue of land reform continued to agitate opinion in Ireland, but Home Rule now became the main campaign aim. The movement found its characteristic spokesman in Charles Stewart Parnell, who was able to lead his party in the election of 1885 to a position in the House of Commons where it held the balance of power between the main parties; a newspaper report quickly emerged that Gladstone had been 'converted' to Home Rule. His Liberal Party therefore gained the support of the Irish party and Gladstone became Prime Minister once again.

There followed ten years of political manoeuvres, murders and scurrilous campaigns designed to undermine Parnell and Home Rule. Attempting to push through a Home Rule Bill, Gladstone found that he was not supported by all the members of his own party. A substantial faction, led by Joseph Chamberlain, broke away as Liberal Unionists and allied themselves with the Conservatives. Gladstone went into opposition once more.

The Conservative government of Lord Salisbury which followed, with Arthur Balfour as Irish Secretary, set about dealing with Irish grievances – all except Home Rule, of course – in particular by a serious concentration on the problem of land and rents. This was a political reaction to Gladstone's acceptance of a Home Rule policy for the Liberals, which had pushed the Conservatives (and the Liberal Unionists) into emphasizing their attachment to the union. It had also raised the ire of the Ulster Protestants, who stressed their opposition to the prospect of a Catholic-dominated Irish government regime.

The attempts to destroy Parnell were unsuccessful, but his position in the Irish Party was fatally undermined when he filed for divorce. As a Protestant in a party mainly of Catholics, he had always had a precarious position; the notion of divorce (and a wider revelation of the existence of his mistress, the wife of one of his colleagues) was disastrous to him. He was successful in being re-elected as leader in 1890, but in December of that year, in a six-day debate over his position, the party split into Parnellites and anti-Parnellites. He died the next year.

This decisively weakened the Home Rule Party. The issue had also divided Gladstone's Liberal Party, with the result that it went into opposition for almost the whole time between 1885 and 1905. Meanwhile, the Protestant majority in Ulster was energized at the prospect of being subject to a Catholic government in Dublin, and was roused by, among others, Lord Randolph Churchill, who, in fiery speeches, campaigned in opposition. Gladstone returned to power briefly in 1892–94 with a majority in the House of Commons in favour of Home Rule, but the House of Lords was adamantly opposed. Yet the issue of Home Rule continued, though with the death of Parnell and the split in the Irish Party, the heat went out of the issue.

Until 1880, Ireland had been one of many issues which concerned British governments; as with all of them, it fluctuated in prominence. From 1880, however, it assumed a dominating position, as the issue which defined every party. This was Gladstone's achievement by adopting Home Rule as a policy for his party. For the next thirty and more years, Ireland and its government was the issue around which all policy and all policies revolved. It also had its effect in the other constituents of the union. The term which became invoked for the assertion of the identities of the 'Celtic' countries was 'nationalism'.

Scotland

A split of a different sort had largely paralyzed Scottish politics after the passing of the Reform Act in 1832. A growing dispute within the Church of Scotland finally brought the two sides to separate in 1843, in the 'Disruption'. The 'official' Church of Scotland, established by the Act of Union, continued, but was clearly diminished in both numbers and authority; its dissident rival was the Free Church. For decades there followed disputes over the loyalty of congregations and the ownership of churches and lands, together with further splits, unions and reunions among the various groups. This had its effect on the union, since the Church of Scotland established by the Act of Union of 1707 was now divided, as was the Scottish population. Nevertheless, the political union proved, largely because of English indifference, to be able to accommodate the 'Wee Frees' and leave the matter to the Scots.

It was this English indifference which was particularly galling for many Scots, who had an inflated idea of themselves and their importance in the economy and the empire. Yet at the same time many Scots did not wish to see any English 'interference' in their affairs. The small numbers of Scottish members in the House of Commons made it difficult for them to exert any strength, and their MPs had a strong tendency to cleave to the Liberal Party, which further muted their voice. On several occasions Parliament found that the autonomous Scots legal system stood in the way of kingdom-wide legislation. It was not clear, for example, that the Bank of England could legally operate in Scotland – it did not even try, once the difficulty was identified. A campaign to retain the note-issuing facility by Scottish banks was undertaken, helping to deter an English encroachment. Reform Acts were separately passed for both countries. It became the practice to pass specifically Scottish measures in other areas, which in fact might mean that an Act was passed for England, but the parallel Scottish measure was then delayed. This might have awkward, even dangerous, consequences. A Public Health Act in 1848 applied to England alone, but no similar Scottish measure appeared until 1867, even though the need for reform was as urgent in Glasgow as it was in Liverpool and London. A Sanitary Act in 1865 could not be applied to Scotland because of legal complications. On the other hand, an Education Act of 1872, passed at much the same time as a similar Act for England-plus-Wales, was a much more effective instrument for bringing children into schools than the English Act, and established a system much less subject to disruption and interference. Scotland was distinct again.

Scotland and England-plus-Wales were always separate states, just as Ireland was separate. But the Scots were not agitated over the union, as the Irish were. They had, of course, their own government system, their own Church (even if it was split), their own legal system and so on, to which now were added separate measures, such as health policy. Despite a certain awkwardness and occasional annoyances, Scotland and England rubbed along generally in a satisfactory way, largely by ignoring their differences.

But conditions were changing. The Highland area went through a traumatic series of problems, with the clearances caused by landlords and clan chiefs, famines and blights in the 1830s and 1840s, and eventually a 'crofters' war' in the 1880s. This inflicted serious damage on the Gaelic language and culture, to which disdain and some hostility from English speakers (English and Scots) was added. In the Lowlands, something of the same changes were also taking place, though not on the same scale as in the Highlands. Meanwhile in the Central Valley, the industrialization which came with the cotton mills, shipbuilding and coal mining inflated the cities in size and brought in migrants from the Highlands and Ireland. Wealth was created, but poverty was widespread.

Scotland had long defined itself in contrast to England, and the growth of the great cities brought in a new aspect of that contrast. The Glasgow area in particular attracted to itself many displaced Highlanders, but also many displaced Irish, particularly after famines, and these new arrivals set up conflicts. The agitation in Ireland, which grew to a demand for Home Rule, had its effect in Scotland as well, where several, usually brief, societies came into existence to emphasize Scottish distinctiveness. One demand by many Scots MPs in 1869 was for a separate Secretary of State for Scotland, but this had been refused by Gladstone; it was later instituted by Salisbury's Conservative government in 1886, though he was only a Secretary for Scotland, not a Secretary of State. By this time a variety of departments and appointed boards, dealing with such subjects as fisheries, the Poor Law, public health, prisons, education and agriculture, had been set up by a variety of specific Acts and at various times in the preceding generation. The Scottish Office now took all these within its department, but the Secretary did not have a great deal of control over their activities, though he had to answer questions concerning them in the House of Commons. Nevertheless, the existence of a Secretary for Scotland did bring rather more concentrated attention to Scottish matters, and began a process of parliamentary accountability to the boards which had been absent before. This distinction included the institution of the 'Goschen Formula', whereby government spending in Scotland was to be in proportion to its population; in Parliament, a Scottish Grand Committee existed from 1894, to consider specifically Scottish matters.

It was all very piecemeal, and tended to be palliative rather than a properly sustained policy. It did, however, continually emphasize Scotland's difference. The example of Ireland stimulated the formation of a Scottish Home Rule Association, yet this was only one more manifestation of Scottish self-esteem and had little or no effect. That is to say, the palliatives in Westminster had succeeded. Scottish political energies tended to go elsewhere than towards a demand for Home Rule, notably into trade unionism and socialism.

Wales

The case of Wales had been generally subsumed in English affairs since the Tudor Acts of Union, but by the 1880s this had begun to change.

The basis of this change was twofold: first, there was a great increase in the population generally, together with a new concentration of that population in the South Wales industrial area; and second, there was a decline in the population in the rural areas of North and mid Wales brought about by the general agricultural depression of the 1880s, together with some local failures of mining and quarrying enterprises. The political and social effect was to radicalize the population in both parts of Wales, though in slightly different directions. This was displayed in the elections between 1868 and 1885 with the defeats of several landowner candidates. From 1885 on, the Anglican-landowner Conservatives consistently failed in Welsh elections, though the anti-Conservative vote went to the Liberals in the rural areas, and eventually to Labour in the south, where trade unions developed strongly. From 1885 onwards, it was clear that Wales was always going to be voting differently from England.

The Irish Home Rule agitation had its effect in Wales, as it did in Scotland. Cymru Fydd ('Young Wales') had been founded in 1866 as a Welsh cultural movement, but became nationalist in the 1880s; its advocacy was, however, not for Home Rule in Wales but for equality with England, thus insisting on a certain distinctiveness in Wales. In this situation the movement was easily defeated, or deflected, by legislation which dealt with Welsh affairs specifically. The Sunday Closing Act of 1881, a response to the temperance movement which was strong amongst the Nonconformists in Wales, applied only in Wales; the County Councils Act of 1889 brought democratic elections to local government, and the Liberals won control of all but one of the Welsh counties in the subsequent elections. But an attempt to create a version of the Scottish Office and thereby bring under one government office the several authorities and boards in Wales for the Poor Law, public works, health and so on failed. The plan was for its members to be chosen by the county councils, but no agreement could be reached on the representation of the councils in the body, since Glamorgan would predominate. Such a Welsh Office would have been a step towards equality with England, but was not seen to be a serious requirement for Wales.

Yet there was in all these specifically Welsh measures a distinct development of the consciousness of being Welsh, manifested in a further series of specifically Welsh measures – for example, in education, the founding of the University of Wales – to add to those boards and departments which continued mostly autonomously, though without any overriding authority other than the Home Office in London. There were distinctive Welsh causes, like Sunday closing, which were rooted in the Nonconformism of the majority of the population. The disestablishment of the Anglican Church in Wales became a notable cause, taken up, like Irish Home Rule, by the Liberal governments, and like the latter it became entangled in the domination of the House of Lords by the Conservatives, one of whose priorities was the defence of the Anglican Church. The first disestablishment bill vanished with the fall of the Liberal government in 1895 and a second was overtaken by the constitutional crisis of 1910; but the Parliament Act of 1911 finally allowed the measure to pass in 1914, though by this time few people were seriously exercised over the problem.

Ireland Again

The arrival of a Liberal government in 1905 and its huge victory in the election of 1906 revived the issue of Irish Home Rule (as well as that of Welsh disestablishment). Yet the Liberal majority in the House of Commons was so great that the Home Rule Party had no scope for pressing the government into acquiescence with its demands. Nor did the government make any attempt to push forward Home Rule, since the Conservative majority in the House of Lords would, as it had in 1894, inevitably block the legislation. This it did with several other Liberal measures, culminating in the refusal to pass the Budget in 1909. The following general elections – two in 1910 – returned Liberals and Conservatives to the House of Commons in approximately equal numbers. The Liberal government continued with Labour and Irish support, so once again the Irish party held the balance. The first business which followed, therefore, was the Parliament Act, which imposed restrictions on the ability of the Lords to thwart the Commons. The next point of business was a Home Rule Bill.

In the meantime, the Ulster Protestants had voiced their strong objections and were energized both by their leader Sir Edward Carson and by the leader of the Conservatives, Andrew Bonar Law, who in effect offered unconditional support for whatever the Unionists did to thwart Home Rule – a green light for their military organization. The Commons repeatedly passed the government's bill, and the Lords repeatedly rejected it, until in 1914 the provisions of the Parliament Act were invoked, and, having passed the Commons for the third time, the Bill was made law. The Unionists in Ulster still resisted, in effect threatening civil war, while a group of Army officers in Ireland indicated that they would refuse to fight against the Ulstermen. Both the Ulster Volunteers and their counterparts in the rest of Ireland, the Irish Volunteers, collected arms and drilled in military formations.

The intransigence of the Ulster Unionists was not quite complete. The obvious solution to the threat they posed was to exclude Ulster, or part of it, from the operation of the Home Rule Act, and this became the Ulster Protestants' aim. This the Irish refused to accept. A long conference at Buckingham Palace in July 1914 failed to reach agreement, but when the Home Rule Act was to be implemented it included an amendment, not actually passed by Parliament, which would later allow for the 'exclusion' of an unwilling area, county by county.

The discussions had continued while the international diplomatic crisis that led to the Great War trundled along less obviously and less publicly. When the war began and spread in the first days of August, all sides in the Irish dispute were relieved of the need to make any decisions about Ireland. The threat of an armed Ulster rising ceased, the British officers' disloyalties were redirected to fighting Germans, and the chief of the Irish party, John Redmond, offered the Irish Volunteers as soldiers for the British forces. The Home Rule Act was at once suspended from operation.

Redmond found that his backing for the war effort led to his support in Ireland dwindling. Whereas the Ulster Volunteers enlisted in large numbers, virtually *en masse*, into the Army – and suffered the casualties to be expected – the Irish Volunteers were much less enthusiastic, and suffered an immediate split when a relatively small militant group refused to participate in the war. Redmond had included the phrase 'wherever needed' in his offer of the Irish Volunteers, which meant that they, like the Ulstermen, went to France and the trenches. It was this phrase which brought the split in the organization. Those who objected to it assumed the name 'Irish Volunteers' to indicate that they were willing to serve but only in Ireland; those who enlisted became the 'National Volunteers' and became the soldiers in France. At home, the organization became demoralized as more and more of them disappeared into the British Army and its cemeteries. The Ulster Volunteers participated enthusiastically in the war in order to earn credit with the British government, but this was something the Irish Volunteers – 'Irish' or 'National' – were unlikely to get under any circumstances.

As the fighting continued, the cost was seen to rise steadily. Voluntary recruitment in Ireland was notably less enthusiastic than in the rest of the United Kingdom, though this should have come as no surprise, and support for the anti-war groups increased. Two other organizations, the now rather venerable IRB and its associate Sinn Fein, which had been founded in the last years of peace, linked up with the dissidents. Contact was made with Germany and arms were solicited, though they were successfully intercepted by the Royal Navy at sea. The incident confirmed British fears that a separated or independent Ireland was a likely ally of an enemy in war.

A sub-committee of the IRB planned a rising. The shortage of arms and the lack of obvious support were difficulties, but the rising went ahead at Easter 1916. It was predictable failure, if it was really intended to drive the British out of Ireland. It was suppressed within a week, having hardly extended out of Dublin. When the German involvement became clear, the leaders could be regarded as traitors – an armed rebellion in wartime was clearly treason – and they were executed. This was exactly what those involved in the rising had expected and aimed for, to be a blood sacrifice on the altar of Irish freedom which would inspire emulators. The executions were a mistake, since it was exactly what the dead men had planned for, but at least they did not become living imprisoned martyrs. It is often claimed that this killing swung opinion in Ireland heavily in favour of Sinn Fein and its political allies, but opinions had been shifting in the island for a year and more already, ever since the Home Rule Act had been passed and then suspended, seen as another case of British bad faith.

As much to blame for the change was the apparently never-ending war. Irishmen who espoused the cause of free Ireland could not see any reason why they should be involved in a 'British war'. Sinn Fein had been against Irish participation in the war from the start, and now, with increasing casualties, its judgment seemed to be justified. The exact reasons for the increase in Irish opinion in support of early independence, or at least the implementation of Home Rule, are clearly many. The outcome became clear in the results of by-elections in 1917. The activists had to demonstrate that support existed, and this had to be by means of an election; assertion and ambition would hardly suffice. This had always been the Achilles heel of the militant tendency in Ireland, so that often when some action was attempted, it turned out that their support scarcely existed outside their own small group; it was necessary to demonstrate wide support, not assume it. Now the opinion shift meant that Sinn Fein candidates were victorious in four by-elections during 1917. The candidates made it clear during their election campaigns that they would refuse to take their seats at Westminster, and by the end of the year, with a new wider support, Sinn Fein's political aim had become an independent Irish republic. Sinn Fein's success signalled the terminal decline of the pre-war Irish Home Rule party; it also signalled the certainty that Ulster would not be included in whatever provisions were finally made to implement Home Rule.

These electoral tactics were decisive, and in the general election of 1918, seventy-three out of the 105 Irish seats went to Sinn Fein – twenty-five of them unopposed – and another six went to the surviving Redmondites. Only three of these were elected in Ulster, where most victories went to Conservatives. It was a clear declaration of the wishes of the electorate, both in northern Ireland and in the rest of the island, and should have been enough to decide the issue. But the shift of Sinn Fein's programme to independence and a republic was a move too far for the British government, once more a step behind Irish opinion. The government was still fixated on Home Rule. As a result of the election, this was now essentially the Conservative Party in power in coalition with a relatively small group of Liberals. Fighting ensued, of a particularly unpleasant sort, a mixture of civil war and insurrection, conducted by guerrillas and combated by police, soldiers and official irregulars.

The elected Sinn Fein members of 1918 implemented their promise not to serve at Westminster and organized themselves into the Dail Eireann, the Parliament of the intended republic. Over the next several months, as violence increased, this body set up a government system, modelled on that which they intended to replace. The Dail was eventually declared illegal at the end of 1919, but too late again; by then it had established its presence and authority in Irish minds.

The tactics of the Irish Republican Army were to provoke a British violent response, and thereby appeal to outraged Irish opinion. Their method was to assassinate policemen, on or off duty. Necessarily, the British responded, using their own forces, including the especially recruited Black and Tans and Auxiliaries, who were technically police reinforcements but had a strong tendency to act independently, even riotously. Intimidation and reprisals by both sides spread. The actual numbers fighting on each side were not large – the active members of the IRA have been suggested to have been no more than about 5,000 at any one time – and in early 1921 the British government was considering plans to flood Ireland with a quarter of a million soldiers, which would probably have crushed the insurgents, though at what cost does not bear thinking about. Beyond these numbers and the military operations by both sides, there was also widespread disorder in the island. As the fighting and murders continued, there came a steady hardening of opinion in Ireland in favour of Sinn Fein's programme, while elsewhere in Britain opinion was becoming sickened at the violence.

This was, however, not a war which Sinn Fein could win. It and the IRA could only create mayhem and murder. The real decisions must come from London: the British government and its assessment of opinion in Britain.

During the first half of 1921, the British forces made substantial progress in containing the IRA, including several successful captures of arms, which was likely to cripple the IRA's fighting ability. Some sort of British victory might well have resulted later in the year if the massive reinforcements being considered had been imposed, though again, as with Sinn Fein's defiance and determination, how long this would have been considered a victory is questionable. A new Irish Act, the Government of Ireland Act, set up two Parliaments, one in Dublin for twenty-six counties in the south, the other in Belfast for the six counties of the north which had Protestant majority populations. The Belfast Parliament was set up, but that for Dublin was not; the Irish would argue they already had one, and the IRA and Sinn Fein used the subsequent elections to choose a new Dail, where Sinn Fein won again.

The British Prime Minister, Lloyd George, provided a conciliatory speech for King George V to deliver at the opening of the Belfast Parliament in June 1921. The speech had a substantial effect in Britain, where anti-Irish sentiment was strong, but where support for the fighting was becoming less adamant. Lloyd George then offered talks to the IRA, this time without the usual preconditions of an insistence on certain constitutional issues or the surrender of arms, and this was accepted by Dail president Eamon De Valera. There followed, as would have been expected, an intricate and difficult series of discussions, though they began by agreeing to a truce in Ireland in July.

The treaty was negotiated in a conference in London, and was agreed in December 1921 and ratified by the Dail in January 1922. This was the moment when, in actuality, Ireland (less the six counties of Northern Ireland) became independent. The Republic had to go through a civil war between those who saw the treaty as inadequate and others who were prepared to accept it. During 1922–23, the violence therefore continued, but in a new election for the Dail in June 1922 an overwhelming number of new members elected were in favour of the treaty. Technically, the south, Eire, now the Irish Free State, was of dominion status within the British Empire (like Canada or Australia), but this was never taken seriously in Ireland.

The Ulster Parliament soon adopted measures to control, even persecute, the Catholic minority within its boundaries, which was about a third of the whole (420,000 Catholics to 840,000 Protestants). The armed police were recruited exclusively from Protestants, and their auxiliary force, the 'B' Specials, similarly. Segregation was enforced in housing and education, and funding for both favoured Protestants. This Protestant government thus implemented the very regime they had claimed to fear would be imposed on them in an Ireland-wide Home Rule state.

The links between the Free State and the British Empire were steadily eroded by Irish measures over the fifteen years after 1923. The final connection went in 1938, when the British residual right to occupy several ports in Ireland in wartime was surrendered, and Eire announced its intention in 1939 to remain neutral in Hitler's war. Once again, the fear in Britain was that this meant that the German enemy might gain access to Ireland in war.

The issue for the Irish, therefore, was the ability to rule themselves; the issue for the British was that, in a world full of weaponry and international enmities, Irish neutrality might mean Irish hostility. Ireland actually escaped the war, and neither Germany nor Britain invaded it, though both powers were less than scrupulous about neutral 'rights' – the British violated the neutrality of Norway, Iceland, Vichy France, Persia and other countries openly, and other states clandestinely.

The removal of most of Ireland from the United Kingdom broke the spell of the unity which had been so painfully constructed over such a long time. The Irish cultivated a longstanding resentment at the way they had been governed, not surprisingly, and the manifest reluctance of nineteenth-century British governments to consider seriously Irish complaints until forced to do so only rubbed salt in those wounds. Every concession to Ireland took a generation to be gained, and the list of grievances was therefore never ending. The eventual independence of Ireland came about in large part because of British refusal to face the issue until it was far too late.

In 1920 or thereabouts, as Ireland slid away from his kingdom, King George V is said to have remarked that they should have listened to Mr Gladstone back in the 1880s, when he first espoused Home Rule. But the royal hindsight had it wrong: Ireland would have still gone independent, and probably not quietly. The British would not have let it go at all easily.

Nationalism in Scotland

The experience of detaching Eire from the United Kingdom was searing for all involved, and it is instructive that no later nationalist party in Britain has adopted the same tactics – with the significant exception of the later Sinn Fein in Northern Ireland, who regarded the Ulster regime as illegitimate. The issue of devolving government powers to local legislatures had been in the air since Home Rule for Ireland became a serious political issue,

282 The United Kingdom

and Scotland and Wales had been the obvious political units for such devolution. But demand was minimal, especially by contrast with Ireland, and little more than discussion ensued. The Welsh failure to agree to a grand overseer of government functions in Wales was in fact also a rejection of the idea of Welsh Home Rule. In Scotland, the Scottish Home Rule Association existed from 1886, but made no mark. It helped draft a bill in 1927–28 which was based on providing a similar status for Scotland as the Irish Free State had achieved in Ireland, but it was so extreme that one might assume that it was produced in order to be rejected, and sure enough it was dismissed by the House of Commons overwhelmingly. There is no sign that this dismayed more Scots than the leaders of the Association itself.

The combination and sequence of issues which had driven the Irish problem – religion, land, language, hunger, national resentment and dislike for British rule – was unique to Ireland, and was generally absent from Scotland, which had its own Church, legal system, a particular national pride, no serious land problem (despite the crofters) and very largely governed itself. So the only issue in the 1920s was that of the governing authority, which was less than urgent. This began to change in the 1930s, when the Conservative-dominated government reacted to the Depression of those years with little imagination, but this again was not a Scottish issue but one affecting many areas of the United Kingdom. From 1922 onwards, Scottish voters consistently (except in 1931) voted against the Conservatives, and from 1945 the Labour Party had a consistent majority of Scottish seats; such was also the situation in Wales. This situation could well fuel discontent when a Conservative government was in power.

The Scottish Home Rule Association was only one of several nationalist groupings which emerged in the 1920s. They all failed to make any impact in the only way which counted – in elections. In 1934, several groups came together – the Home Rule Association, the National Party of Scotland, the Scottish Independent Labour Party and the Scottish Self-Government Party – to form the Scottish National Party. Its antecedents were mainly in the ILP and the NPS, which had the most political experience, and its main organizers came from both; it was thus of a leftish bent in its policy, but it thereby competed with the Labour Party and the communists, though neither of these adopted a nationalist platform, regarding such ideas as inadequate to their purposes. The SNP also competed with the Liberals, who had a substantial presence in Scotland and successfully elected several MPs at each election. The SNP thus competed in a crowded field, and made little progress. Despite helpful by-election results (though no victories), it had therefore made little political impact by the time the Second World War began.

The SNP did moderately well to survive, in adverse conditions. It faced a major difficulty in the British electoral system and in the unwillingness of the major parties other than the Liberals, grievously divided, to contemplate any sort of devolution of political power. The Conservatives had evolved into an explicitly Unionist party under the impact of the Irish problem. The Labour Party was concerned to gain power in order to carry through its own social and economic programme, in which nationalism was irrelevant or an obstacle, and in which there was no scope for reducing the power of the central British government. The Liberals had been the only party interested in local devolution, but had gone into steep decline, fuelled by repeated splits, since 1916.

Nationalism in Wales

There was a similar basic difficulty for the Welsh nationalist party, Plaid Cymru, which was formed in 1925 out of two earlier groups. Like the SNP, Plaid's aim was at the least Home Rule for Wales, but it also had the problem of determining why this was required. One of its founding organizations had been the Welsh Movement, which was mainly concerned over the well-being of the Welsh language, but the majority of the Welsh population by now lived in English-speaking areas in industrial South Wales, and the voters there had been captured by the social programme put forward by the Labour Party, voting solidly Labour since 1922. The early aims of Plaid Cymru were therefore devoted to advocating the Welsh language, which was not a particularly popular cause in the English-speaking areas, so little political progress was made on those terms.

Conclusion

The differing results of the nationalist organizations in the four countries of the United Kingdom since the Irish Act of Union in 1801 were the outgrowth of the previous histories of the several countries. England was complacent, with no obviously significant nationalist movement, and was largely content with its general political control of the kingdom of as a whole. It is not possible to write any sort of description of an English national movement.

Ireland was the very opposite. From the time of the Act of Union – indeed ever since the English conquest in the reign of Elizabeth I – the main Irish political aim had been to gain, or regain, its independence and freedom from

British control. This was clouded at times by the temporary emergence of particular issues – emancipation, repeal, the famine, land and rent reform, and others – but underlying all these was the basic issue, often largely ignored or dismissed by the British, of separation and independence. This distinctive historical background did not exist in either Wales or Scotland. To be sure, Wales had been conquered by the English kings, and when Plaid Cymru held its first conference, it chose symbolically to meet at the site of Owen Glyndwr's Welsh Parliament at Machynllech. But the process of integration with England had been gradual, and the Anglicization of Wales had been very slow and was long incomplete – the landlords who became the target for vilification from the 1860s were in fact usually of Welsh descent and often spoke Welsh. Scotland had not been conquered, except briefly by Oliver Cromwell's New Model Army; it had voluntarily joined in the union with England, and so had retained its distinctive institutions under the umbrella of the Act of Union. For neither of these countries was there any real support for the idea of independence throughout the twentieth century.

So the condition of the four countries, which had long been individually distinct, continued to be so through the twentieth century. The threats from enemies during that century were sufficiently disagreeable and constant to restrain the Scots and the Welsh from any extravagant demands for political autonomy. For the British, the interference by foreign powers in the affairs of Ireland in particular, which had occurred frequently between 1600 and 1800, was a sufficient reason for holding onto the island, in the governments' minds at least, who could argue with some conviction that an independent Ireland could well be the basis for a threat to the whole. The interference of Germany both before and during the Great War only reinforced that conception, and during the Second World War the anxiety was similar and constant. The threat of attack and subversion between 1910 and 1990 was therefore one of the basic reasons for the failure of Scottish and Welsh nationalists to gain any ground. It was the reduction of that threat with the collapse of the Soviet Union which released the Scots and the Welsh from their acceptance that their existence within the United Kingdom was necessary for their own well-being.

Bibliography

Most of the books listed in the previous chapter are relevant to this. In addition, the following may be consulted:
Blake, Robert, *The Decline of Power, 1915–1964* (London: 1985).

Brown, Stewart J. and Fry, Michael (eds), *Scotland in the Age of the Disruption* (Edinburgh: 1993).

Harvie, Christopher, *No Gods and Precious Few Heroes, Scotland 1914–1980* (London: 1981).

Kinnear, Michael, *The British Voter, an Atlas and Survey since 1885*, 2nd ed. (London: 1981).

Lawlor, Sheila, *Britain and Ireland, 1914–23* (Dublin: 1983).

Lyons, F.S.L., *Charles Stewart Parnell* (London: 1977).

Morgan, Kenneth O., *Consensus and Disunity, the Lloyd George Coalition Government 1918–1922* (Oxford: 1979).

Morgan, Kenneth O., *Rebirth of a Nation, Wales 1880–1980* (Oxford: 1981).

Morgan, Kenneth O., *Revolution to Devolution, Reflections on Welsh Democracy* (Cardiff: 2014).

Stevenson, John, *British Society 1914–45* (Harmondsworth: 1984).

Stewart, A.T.Q., *The Ulster Crisis, Resistance to Home Rule, 1912–14* (London: 1967).

Walsh, Maurice, *Bitter Freedom, Ireland in a Revolutionary World, 1918–1923* (London: 2015).

Chapter 14

Referendums

The Emergence of the Nationalists

In 1945, for the first time, a candidate of the SNP, Dr Robert McIntyre, was elected to Parliament. This was at a by-election at Motherwell in April; Parliament was dissolved in June and the seat was lost in the general election which followed. McIntyre was elected not so much because of his politics, still less in support of his ideas of Scottish independence, but as a gesture of the annoyance that the electorate felt at the delay in calling the general election, and perhaps weariness at the end of a hard and debilitating war. He was one of a number of similar candidates elected during the war by voters voicing their discontent. Voting for the SNP was seen as a protest in an electoral system where the two main parties were so dominant that there was normally little chance of a vote having any effect. The SNP remained at the protest level for five decades.

It took a major effort to gain seats in Parliament for an unknown and inexperienced party, and no SNP candidates succeeded again until Winnie Ewing in the by-election at Hamilton (the constituency next to Motherwell) in 1967. Labour had achieved a majority of 16,000 in the constituency in the general election the year before, but the elected member took a government job after only a year, thereby subjecting the voters to the annoyance of another election, the third in three years. Labour selected an elderly councillor to stand as a reward for long union and political services, assuming that anyone standing for Labour would automatically win. Mrs Ewing, a far more attractive, able and interesting candidate, won handsomely. Like the protest vote at Motherwell in 1945, this vote took a clear and direct aim at the complacency of the established parties, but also at the whole political and constitutional system. In this connection, it is not irrelevant that Hamilton and Motherwell had the highest proportion of Roman Catholic voters of any Scottish constituencies.

Mrs Ewing's victory came at a time when the Labour government of 1964–70 was going through a most difficult patch. Combined with the local party's bland complacency, this is the most obvious explanation for its defeat – and the seat was once again won for Labour in the next general election in 1970 (although Labour lost power). Nevertheless, it was the SNP which was beginning to make the political running in Scotland.

In the preceding decade it had set about establishing itself as a national party, and not just one which appeared occasionally at by-elections with an amateur candidate suddenly popping up out of nowhere, with a disorganized campaign, though usually enthusiastic. Local branches were established and the central party organization was developed. Some policies other than mere nationalism were devised, for it was a standard criticism that such parties had one issue only, and were very vulnerable when asked as to what else they would do if in power.

In 1966 at the general election, the party won 5 per cent of the Scottish vote – but where its candidates stood (in a third of the constituencies) it had registered a vote of over 14 per cent. On a national (Scottish) scale, that would make it the fourth party in size, not far behind the Liberal Party. In four by-elections between 1966 and 1970, its vote ranged between 20 and 46 per cent. On the other hand, in the general election of 1970, when rather more was at stake than local Scottish issues and a chance to protest, its vote was just 11 per cent and it won only one seat. It was still a party of protest; when big things were in question, it was disregarded.

This all highlights that the contest for a Scottish government was an electoral matter. It was not to be a repeat of the disastrous process which was Irish independence. Still more so was this the case in Wales, where enthusiasm for any sort of Home Rule was extremely limited, and non-existent for independence. Wales followed well behind Scotland – though the political process was constantly electoral. The early moves were aimed at gaining a specifically Welsh voice in government, just as the campaign for a Secretary of State for Scotland had been aimed at that very target. The response by the parties at Westminster had been the same. Just as the Scots were at first fobbed off with a minister without much power, so the Welsh were given an unelected 'Council for Wales and Monmouthshire' in 1948. It was supposed to advise the central government on Welsh matters, but since it was unelected and responsible to that government, it had as little effect as the original Scottish minister.

Devolution

In both Wales and Scotland, the issue was discussed and disputed in terms of votes and elections. Plaid Cymru did succeed in 1964 in persuading the new Labour government to create a Secretary of State, having supported Labour in the preceding election. Yet this was essentially an electoral move by Labour, which felt that continuing to deny this minimal concession would fuel the Welsh nationalist vote, which given the electoral mathematics in Wales could only be at Labour's expense. To a degree this worked, and the Plaid Cymru vote remained low, with just two or three constituencies (all Labour) being taken in the next thirty years. The Secretaries of State were not, in the event, seen in either Scotland or Wales as of much use in furthering the local interests; they might sit for Scottish or Welsh constituencies, but they were part of the London government.

The next stage in the demand-and-concession process was devolution, the process of moving powers from central government in London to a locally responsible body, which meant establishing a local Scottish or Welsh Assembly to exercise those powers. It raised all kinds of difficult questions – on finance and taxation, for example, and exactly what powers the assemblies should have – but by 1970 it was in discussion, again from the major parties' viewpoint as a means to defect the nationalist vote to themselves, not the nationalist parties.

Northern Ireland

It was noticeable that the Northern Ireland Assembly was rarely invoked as an example by the mainland nationalist parties. It had fallen on evil days in the 1960s, and hardly provided a helpful pattern for the devolution of power elsewhere. By the 1960s, reform of the system put in place in the 1920s had begun, with results which can only be described as disastrous.

Tentative concessions towards greater equality and improved civil rights for Catholics naturally produced demands that they should be taken further. At the same time, this produced contrary Protestant demands that the process should be stopped. Improved civil rights for Catholics seemed, to the Protestants, to threaten their established supremacy. The situation degenerated to virtual civil war, and since the Northern Ireland government and Parliament were clearly unable to solve the problem, they were suppressed in 1972 and power was 'returned' to the British government in London. This was hardly an inspiring example of the devolution of powers from the centre.

Northern Ireland descended into a new set of 'troubles', which cost the lives of at least 3,000 people over the next twenty years. The partisanship of the police force compelled the intervention of the British Army, which then provided a target for a revived Irish Republican Army. The issue widened, with the Irish government for a time scenting the possibility of the reunification of the island, and the IRA carried out a bombing campaign on the British mainland. The over-simplification of the issue by non-Irish and anti-British outsiders interpreted it as another freedom struggle of a British colony. Anti-British sentiments were revived in the United States, whence funds came through to finance the fighting, former British colonies interfered, self-styled revolutionary dictators supplied funds and arms, and so on. The fighting was thereby prolonged, and the partisan interpretation of events in Northern Ireland continued to bedevil the solution.

Scotland and Wales

These events in Northern Ireland did no service for the cause of devolution on the mainland, but at least the argument there remained political, with little overt violence. It must have been quite clear that it was necessary to keep exerting pressure on successive British governments as they would be persuaded to make successive concessions, often for momentary electoral gains. But just as the case of Northern Ireland was peculiar to itself, so the processes of devolution were different in Wales and Scotland. The Welsh campaign was still centred on Plaid Cymru, originally devoted to the revival and maintenance of the Welsh language. This became its main aim in politics, and its basic political support always lay in those areas where Welsh was still widely spoken – the north and west of the country primarily. The rest of Wales, by now speaking English almost exclusively, was a good deal less interested, and did not appreciate the thought that learning Welsh in the schools would become compulsory.

For Scotland, however, the SNP, if it bothered about language at all, claimed to wish the use of Scots, which is a dialect of northern English. There was also a gesture towards the revival and maintenance of Scottish Gaelic, but this was never a priority. While it could thereby expect support in the Western regions, where Gaelic was still spoken, its only hope of gaining real support lay in the rest of the country, in particular among the heavily Labour-voting regions of the Central Valley, the numerous constituencies between Glasgow and Edinburgh. Votes here could only be secured by appealing to the Labour voters. The victory of Winnie Ewing in 1967 showed the way, since Labour in Scotland remained as complacent as it had been in Hamilton.

Both nationalist parties had a tendency to fade at a general election, when the voters were faced by wider issues. A leftward move of opinion favoured them, while a rightward move reduced their support. So in 1970 the SNP captured one seat (the Western Isles) and Plaid Cymru none, but in the two elections of February and October 1974, with a rise in the Labour vote, the Welsh party gained two seats and then three, and the SNP gained seven and then eleven. By October 1974, for the first time since the election of 1935, there was a considerable number of MPs not of the three main parties, and eventually holding the balance in Parliament. Yet the SNP had still received only 840,000 votes, and Plaid Cymru only 166,000. Any claim either might make that there was a widespread wish for devolution or independence could not be sustained on these figures.

The Labour government of 1974–79 staggered through repeated crises, supported usually by the Liberals and by the nationalist parties. For the nationalists, the alternative was a Conservative government which had toyed with the idea of devolution before being defeated in 1974, but had now become hostile to anything of the sort, while Labour was at least sympathetic. (This was a near repeat of the situation of 1885–86, when the Liberal adoption of Home Rule for Ireland drove the Conservatives into opposing it.) One result had been that the Conservative vote in Scotland, and the seats it won, had steadily reduced in the previous twenty years. The seats won by the SNP in 1974 had been mainly at the expense of the Conservatives. This seemed an opportunity for Labour. If Labour could gain the credit in Scotland for providing devolution, this might translate into votes and undercut the SNP vote. The basic assumption was that the SNP was a one-issue party and that once that issue was resolved its support would dissipate.

The Resort to Referendums

To keep the SNP (and the Welsh and the Liberals) onside, the Labour government in 1976 brought forward a Bill to set up devolved assemblies in both countries. It took time to fight it through the House of Commons, where the government's lack of numbers made things difficult. The unlikelihood of a majority for devolution among MPs dictated a resort to a referendum. This allowed MPs to evade a decision, but opened the way for the one-issue nationalist parties to evade the responsibility of devising a wider programme of government, such as was needed in a general election. To avoid the majority being railroaded by a fanatic minority – a possibility which was clearly apprehended at the time – two conditions were imposed: there must be majority of votes cast in favour, and that majority must be at least 40 per cent of the total electorate. That is, those who did not vote were effectively voting against.

Referendums became favoured by governments and parliaments in order to avoid responsibility for certain measures, but they were not always convincing and not always thought through properly. The Wilson government in 1975 resorted to a referendum to confirm the previous Conservative government decision to join the European Common Market, but this was really a method of dealing with an awkward minority of his own party who were opposed to membership; he knew that, with Conservative support, he would gain approval. Another example was in 1973, when a referendum was set up in Northern Ireland – called the 'border poll' – supposedly to 'decide' whether the province's people wished to continue as British subjects or become part of the Irish Republic. This was guaranteed to bring a pro-British result, since the Protestant population was a majority of the local Northern Ireland population. The poll was boycotted by the Catholic population, who saw it as a phoney exercise and their abstention rendered the exercise essentially meaningless. It did not convince anyone, nor did it stop the continuing violence in the province.

For the Labour Party, the referendums set up by the Scotland and Wales Devolution Act of 1978 were similar in intention and in projected result. It was known that in Wales there was very little support for the idea, and though there was more backing in Scotland, the 40 per cent rule was reckoned to be too great an obstacle to be overcome. The SNP was annoyed at this, but since its argument was that there was a great surge in demand for devolution in Scotland, it could not effectively object. It could also point out that the Labour promise of devolution made in its election manifesto had not been carried out. (Referendums had not been indicated.) The result of the referendum in Scotland was, in the circumstances, somewhat ambiguous.

A majority of those in Scotland who voted did so in favour of devolution, but this was not enough to clear the 40 per cent hurdle. Half of those voting approved, but only 64 per cent of the electorate turned out. Approval was thus only 32 per cent, and even if the 40 per cent rule had not been applied, a majority of only 3 per cent in a straight vote could not be said to have been convincing.

In Parliament, the result destroyed the alliance between Labour, the SNP and the Liberals, and in March the government was defeated in a confidence motion (by one vote). In the subsequent election on 18 May 1979, the Conservatives were returned to power, the SNP was reduced to two MPs and Plaid Cymru to just one. The Welsh devolution referendum, to no one's surprise, had seen a resounding rejection.

Devolution: Scotland

The Conservatives now were wholly committed to opposing devolution, and repealed the Devolution Act. In the vote a majority of Scottish MPs – mainly Labour members – voted for devolution. There was now a growing division between English and Scottish opinion within the Labour Party on the issue. But for the period of the Conservative government – 1979–97 – there was no possibility of another referendum being agreed.

One result of the sequence of events in Scotland was to compel the SNP to choose between devolution and 'separation' – that is, independence. The prospect of a devolved Scottish assembly in Edinburgh was attractive enough to a majority of the party to bring them to support the idea, which in turn meant that they had to deny or evade their former policy of agitating for separation. This had been fuelled by a set of disparate notions, including the claim that independence would be made economically viable by revenues from North Sea oil and gas exploitation, and by tendentious interpretations of long-ago historical events, including the negotiations for the Act of Union, which was portrayed as an English plot. In addition, the Labour government had taken several measures in the late 1970s which seemed to indicate a better understanding of Scottish needs and aspirations, which supported the perceived need for independence.

Thus in the referendum the SNP had been wrong-footed. Support was slanted against them, and Labour support in Scotland was encouraged. Most Scottish MPs after the referendum and the general election, following the defeat of most SNP candidates, still supported devolution, clearly as a means of driving support away from the SNP. The idea had gained momentum, and the long period of Conservative government which followed did nothing to defuse it; indeed some of the government's policies seemed to be encouraging the growth of support for the policy it rejected – and its record was certainly interpreted that way.

For that lengthy time (in political terms, at least) the question of devolution remained in discussion, and became increasingly complicated. The extent of the responsibility which a devolved assembly should have was unclear. The devolution debate centred on Scotland, since the Welsh issue was less urgent, and this meant that any Scottish assembly would clearly expect greater power than a Welsh one. The Northern Irish troubles rumbled on, but there was never any real doubt that some form of devolution would eventually be applied there once more, if only the violence would end and the two sides could be brought to some agreement.

The question of an English assembly also arose periodically. If devolution was applied only to the three smaller countries and not to England, the 'East Lothian question' loomed. This was that Scottish, Welsh and Irish MPs at Westminster would be able to vote on English matters, whereas English MPs would not be able to affect matters which the devolved assemblies considered. Various solutions were suggested, but none was ever adopted. This left it to the Scottish and Welsh members, who could abstain on English issues, thereby demonstrating their separation.

Events outside the United Kingdom had their effect as well. The pumping of North Sea oil had a beneficial effect on the British economy, and above all on the balance of payments, and was eyed with some greed by Scottish Nationalists, who talked about 'Scotland's oil', though this presupposed a change in the internationally agreed sea boundaries, which was highly unlikely. The end of the Cold War in 1989–91 reduced the political and military threat from Russia, and the expansion eastwards of the European Common Market – now the European Union – opened up a wider market. One result was that the political support for the union was reduced for the first time since the union of England and Scotland in 1707, for the viability of an independent Scotland was thus thought to be increased. It was, however, still only a small country, with a population of only four million. This would make it one of the smallest of the European states, but the Nationalist argument was that its economy would be helped by 'Scotland's oil' and by the supposed tradition of Scottish enterprise and commercial sagacity.

The problem was, of course, that none of these assumptions was either correct or reasonable. Scotland had become a largely commercially inert welfare-dependent country, with no useful natural resources –the oil and gas would not last long, even if Scotland's claim was accepted. (One of the SNP's leaders, Alex Salmond, was an economist working on oil in a bank; he surely knew how nonsensical such a claim was, yet he voiced it and promoted it.) It was assumed that if the country became independent it would become a member of the European Union – but this turned out not to be so, at least not for several years while an accession treaty was negotiated. Nationalists repeatedly claimed that Scotland would continue to use the pound, despite unanimous and unambiguous refusals by Westminster politicians. Nor was the assumed English subsidy going to be forthcoming. These issues had to be thought through, but most were blithely assumed to cause no difficulty. Those in favour of devolution proved to be deaf to any reasonable contrary arguments. For Wales, the questions were less urgent and less momentous, since the issue of independence scarcely arose. The decline of both the steel industry and coal mining seemed, as in Scotland, to cut the ground from under any argument that the country could survive without English financial support.

All this meant that the SNP had to go beyond its aim of independence and consider actual plans, intentions and expectations which could be discussed, argued over and perhaps refuted. It was clear from the devolution referendum in 1979 that two major obstacles lay in its path – the need to persuade a clear and decisive majority of the Scottish people that independence was something that they wanted, and the need to overcome the general hostility to the idea at Westminster. But a third problem grew steadily as time passed: the inability of the Nationalists to be rational. The first two of these problems were amenable to discussion and persuasion; the last was not.

The economic and social policies pursued by the Conservative government between 1979 and 1997 provided plentiful targets for opposition attacks. Yet in Scotland and Wales, the nationalist parties were quite unable to capitalize, though the SNP did make a practice of claiming that the Conservative policies were directed specifically against Scotland. Inevitably it was the Labour Party which gathered most opposition support; it was the only party with a chance to form a government. The Conservatives under the right-wing Margaret Thatcher were constitutionally Unionist. The Liberal Party had a long-standing policy of devolution of some sort, and had gained electoral and numerical strength from a schism in the Labour Party ranks. As a result, the nationalist support went to Labour and Liberals. Throughout the Conservative domination, therefore, the nationalist parties made little political headway, securing only two or three seats each in any general election. In the end it was the Labour Party which offered another devolution project.

The antipathy towards the Conservative government translated in the 1997 elections to a wholesale defeat of Conservative candidates in Britain, but particularly so in Wales and Scotland. Not a single Conservative MP was elected from Scotland or Wales. Plaid Cymru and the SNP elected four and six MPs respectively. This, of course, cleared the way for Labour to institute devolution, and rendered the old arguments less relevant. The new Labour government under Tony Blair was strong enough in Parliament to ignore the old awkward arguments, such as the requirement for a majority of the electorate vote and the 'East Lothian question', and push straight ahead without restraint.

Assemblies

The Labour victory in 1997 included a manifesto provision for devolution, to be accepted or rejected in advance by the Scottish and Welsh electorates on straightforward majority votes. This time, therefore, if a simple majority of those voting wished for a devolved assembly, one would be set up by a new Act. This avoided the long debates of 1976–78 and saved parliamentary time, and almost guaranteed that devolution would take place.

The referendums actually produced divergent results. In Scotland, three-quarters of those voting voted for devolution, but the turnout at 60 per cent meant that only 45 per cent of the electorate voted for devolution. However, every part of Scotland did vote in favour, particularly strongly in the Central Valley, a distinct shift of opinion. In Wales, the result was much closer, with half of those voting approving devolution, but on a turnout of only half the electorate – so only a quarter of the Welsh voted for a Welsh assembly, and this was with Labour advocating it, hardly a ringing endorsement of the policy.

The map of the referendum results, however, showed that the approval for devolution had spread beyond the former restricted areas which had elected nationalist MPs. In Wales, approval was strong in the Welsh-speaking areas of the north and west, but it had now spread into the industrial south, a region where the unsettling industrial changes of recent years had been particularly difficult. The apparent approval and advocacy of the Labour government had been helpful here, of course, in solid Labour territory. The English-speaking areas of the former Welsh Marches, on the other hand, were against, including Pembroke; Monmouth (which had been renamed Gwent and summarily transferred to Wales) had been especially hostile to the idea.

In Scotland, a second question was posed, asking if the new assembly should have 'tax-varying powers' – which would mean tax-increasing powers. This raised much less enthusiasm, and two regions of Orkney and Dumfries and Galloway voted against. It is curious also to see that the regions which had earlier regularly elected SNP MPs, particularly the north-east, were only moderately approving.

The Labour government went ahead with devolution bills for both countries. A Parliament and an 'Executive' was set up for each country, though with strictly limited powers. The overriding authority of the Westminster Parliament was reiterated, though it was clear that further areas of authority were transferable once the assemblies had organized themselves. (The Scots argued for a new Parliament building, but since it was paid for by the British government they did not suffer from it going well over budget.)

The assemblies then had to be elected, and the results suggested that there had been little change in the basic political preferences of both electorates. A form of proportional representation had been added to the constituency election system, so that some members were elected directly from a constituency and others were allocated in proportion to the total voting strength of the party countrywide. The aim was to prevent a clean sweep by one party, though the Labour Party assumed that it would have a perpetual majority in both assemblies. It was approved by all the major Westminster parties, each for different reasons. Labour feared losses to the SNP, which was articulating a left-wing policy; the Conservatives feared that the Assembly would have a permanent Labour majority, and saw that the new system would operate to rescue the Party in both countries; the Liberals had long been advocates for some sort of proportional representation. All the main parties were determined that the SNP should not profit too much from their claim to be the leading advocates for devolution and independence.

Meanwhile, progress of a sort had been made in restoring a devolved Assembly in Northern Ireland. The fighting had largely died down, and the assistance of the Irish Republic's Taoiseach and the arbitration of a former United States senator, George Mitchell, together with a reduced Army presence in the province, finally brought forth a settlement, the 'Good Friday Agreement' in 1998. To forestall a return to exclusively Protestant rule, the 'Executive' was to be a coalition of the two largest parties, which in the event were the Democratic Unionist Party and Sinn Fein, extremists and deadly enemies.

All these new assemblies had difficulty in operating. In Northern Ireland, the two main parties found it all too easy to find ways to disagree, and the British government had to suspend the Assembly in 2000, though it was restored in 2002, and then operated with some success for fifteen years. In Scotland, the Assembly elections of 1999 and 2003 resulted in Labour as the largest party, and it governed in coalition with the Liberals; the Conservatives, meanwhile, recovered somewhat. The SNP was the most vocal opposition, inevitably. But the Labour regime was dull and unenterprising, even within the restrictions imposed by the Act.

The Labour Party in Scotland had scarcely changed since the defeat of the party's uninspiring candidate in the Hamilton by-election in 1967. The first First Minister, Donald Dewar, had been well liked and dynamic, but he died after only a year in office. His successors were of the old mould, dull apparatchiks who came out from the depths of the party, men scarcely known outside it. After several years, they could point to no more than minor achievements, so that taking powers over Scottish railways in 2005 (though the railways were privatized and the powers were strictly limited) could be hailed as 'the most significant devolution of new powers' since the Parliament was created.

It was thus hardly a surprise to anyone but the Scottish Labour Party that it suffered a thumping defeat in the Scottish Assembly election of 2007. The SNP was returned as the largest party, with one seat more than Labour, and the smaller parties held the balance. The First Minister, the SNP leader Alex Salmond, therefore headed a minority administration, supported by the Greens. His primary aim was not so much to govern Scotland as to prepare for independence. To that end the 'Scottish Executive' was renamed the 'Scottish Government', but the only transfer of new powers related to planning and nature conservation – the new name was, in effect, a political stunt. The SNP did little in the way of government, making no use, for example, of the tax varying powers, and so failing to address real and immediate issues, though it abolished medical prescription charges and claimed to provide free university education. On the whole it was in danger of sinking into the same hole as Labour. Eventually the SNP began to formulate useful policies which would make it an attractive party for other reasons than its advocacy of independence. A Bill was introduced to hold an independence referendum in 2010, but it failed to pass – not surprisingly since all the other parties were against. The SNP must have known that it would fail, so it was never more than a political gesture to its supporters – it was another stunt so that the SNP could then claim that the will of the people was being thwarted. Even if the Scottish Bill had passed, the government in Westminster would need to approve, and without a majority in the Assembly, the SNP could not argue that it had the backing of the electorate; approval from Westminster was thus highly unlikely.

The SNP's only serious competition remained Labour. The Scottish Labour Party had gone through several leaders since 1999, and fought the

2011 election with yet another dour, unimaginative and uncharismatic leader, not to mention a completely uninteresting and complacent programme. Since the only way to persuade the Westminster government (a Conservative-Liberal coalition from 2010) to agree to an independence referendum was to show a strong demand from the Scottish Assembly, the Labour Party's dismal performance in the 2011 Scottish election (following on from its dismal and uninspiring performance in government) was a great contribution to the SNP's strategy; in 2011, the SNP won an overall majority.

The Welsh Assembly had none of these turbulent changes, though in no election did any party gain a majority of seats. The contrast with Scotland lay in the lack of any desire in Wales to go for independence, as well as even more restricted powers for the Assembly, so that politics revolved around rather more mundane and unexciting matters. A referendum in 2011 did approve an increase in the Assembly's powers, and these were included in an Act in 2014. The referendum did show a small increase in approval for devolution, with only Monmouth/Gwent voting against, but the turnout was only a third of the electorate; so the extension of the Assembly's powers was therefore approved by only a fifth of the voters. There were criticisms that the performance of the government of Wales had been less than admirable, and the lack of enthusiasm for the Assembly was clearly at the root of the generally lacklustre performance by the government, not helped by the inability of the largest party, Labour, to secure a majority.

Independence Referendum

The main problem was the issue of independence in Scotland. The clear victory for the SNP in the Assembly elections in 2011 led directly to the independence referendum three years later. Yet there was a disjunction between the SNP's electoral support and the desire for independence. This was a legacy of the SNP's original position as a vehicle for protest, in particular against the policies of the Westminster government under the Conservatives, and against the complacent Labour policy in Scotland. In the 1990s, the Conservatives in Scotland had received a drubbing, suffering largely at the hands of the local Labour Party, in reaction to Conservative dominance at Westminster. It survived only because of the second vote system for the Assembly elections. Now in the next decade it was the turn of the Labour Party in Scotland to suffer, this time at the hands of the SNP. There was a further disjunction, between the votes for the Scottish Assembly and the votes for MPs at Westminster; in the Westminster election of 2010 there were no losses for Labour in Scotland, whereas in the UK overall it lost over ninety seats. Complacency in Scottish Labour continued.

The independence referendum held in 2014 finally broke the mould of Scottish politics, a matter which had clearly been in preparation for twenty years. The campaign was extraordinarily involving, and the eventual turnout at about 85 per cent was higher than in any earlier Scottish election or referendum. The SNP succeeded in tweaking the system to its advantage, by extending the right to vote to 16- and 17-year-olds, by the wording of the referendum question – which was phrased so as to attach the more positive Yes answer to independence – and by Scots living outside the country being excluded, though in other votes they would have had the vote. The campaign was the worst kind of single issue business, full of distortions, exaggerations, lies and half-truths on the Yes side. There were even stories of threatening messages being sent to the media that advertising would be withdrawn if they recommended a No vote – suggesting a totalitarian strain in the SNP. Given the right to choose the date of the referendum, the SNP chose the 700th anniversary of the Battle of Bannockburn, exhibiting a naive faith in the totemic qualities of their distorted version of Scottish history. The No campaign was widely criticized as tedious, unimaginative and dwelling on negatives – but it was at least largely honest.

The Yes campaign's methods were countered by some vicious press coverage, which in most cases had no pretence of impartiality or accuracy. The other main political parties were solidly behind the No campaign. A most effective intervention was by the Chancellor of the Exchequer, George Osborne, that in the event of independence Scotland would be economically on its own, with no support from the remnant-UK. On the other hand, Osborne's manner – southern English, Eton-and-Oxford and Conservative – made him a prime target for Scottish loathing as much as his austerity policies were detested. His warning was one of many which were never heeded, and when mention by the Yes campaigners were dismissed airily.

Labour enlisted in the No campaign as well, but this did not sit well with many of the Labour working class in Scotland, who were beguiled by the prospects of independence and wealth and had been encouraged in the past to support devolution. The Party also appeared to have become a Tory lackey in the campaign, and was tarred with the Conservatives' unpopularity. This was to produce a sea-change in politics in Scotland.

The question of devolution had already largely sunk the Conservatives; the question of independence was about to do the same to Labour.

The last few days of the campaign saw an extraordinary sequence of events. First came an opinion poll which suggested that – for the first time in the campaign – there was a majority for independence; this seemed reasonably convincing, since it came on top of a steady advance in the polls for the Yes campaign. The London Parties reacted by offering, two days before the vote, a series of further devolution measures which would be, as the former Labour leader Gordon Brown termed it, 'a modern form of home rule'. Conservative Prime Minister David Cameron and Labour leader Ed Miliband paid visits to Scotland, effectively for the first time in the campaign, provoking chuckles and jokes from SNP leader Alex Salmond, but then the latter had no real answer to this late No campaign, and in political terms, this late offer was a sensible move, and was in line with one of the alternatives Salmond himself had claimed to want – it was termed 'devo-max'. (If the London politicians had intervened earlier they would have been accused of being Englishmen interfering in Scotland's private business.) One result of the threat that the Yes campaign might succeed was to persuade the No voters to turn out at the vote. The consistently negative earlier polls had led to the widespread assumption that No would win without difficulty. This new poll energized them.

One reaction to the long No dominance in the polls was that the Yes campaign forsook the practicalities of achieving independence and began to adopt a mystical, utopian view that all would be well in Scotland if only it was independent – problems would disappear, social equality would arrive, peace would break out, and so on. The process was to be a leap of faith. As such, it would be bound to end in tears.

A particularly good example of the Yes campaign's ludicrous tactics was a claim that independence was necessary to save the National Health Service from cuts imposed by the Conservative London government. But there had been no 'cuts' (except in the minds of self-serving health service union members), and the devolved Scottish government itself already controlled the Scottish health service, so if it was suffering from a lack of resources it was the 'fault' of the government which was claiming to 'save' it. The claim, in other words, was a lie. It was not the only example – the claim for the revenues of 'Scotland's oil' was another. An old complaint centred on the US and Royal Navy nuclear submarine base at Holy Loch off the Clyde. This was to be removed, supposedly in order to prevent the Glasgow area from becoming a target for enemy bombs. But in a nuclear war, every city in Britain would be a target, and Holy Loch as well. The argument for safety was, to any person with the slightest knowledge of affairs, deliberately and consciously misleading, an insult to the voters' intelligence – but many voters were so befuddled that they accepted such arguments without serious consideration. If the Yes campaign had won, Scots' future would have been bleak indeed.

The result of the vote was a clear refusal by the electorate to endorse the idea of independence, though it was a much closer result than had been contemplated earlier. Only four regions (Dundee, Glasgow, North Lanarkshire and West Dunbartonshire, all areas with an above average population of Roman Catholics, of Irish descent) voted for independence. The overall vote against was 55 per cent out of the eligible voters who turned out; to put it the other way round – under 38 per cent of the adult population voted in favour of independence. (Since the referendum, this proportion has remained much the same in the opinion polls; it is only a few per cent greater than the vote in the first devolution referendum in 1979.) The turnout at over 84 per cent was high enough so that neither side could convincingly cry foul or suggest that they had been cheated – though the No campaign might have pointed to the Yes campaign's lies, half-truths and distortions, and to its earlier manipulation of the eligibility criteria.

The political effect was that the devolved Assembly gained the new powers promised by the Westminster party leaders two days before the vote. The details were to be published on 30 November – St Andrew's Day – and legislative details to be worked out by 25 January 2015 – Burns' Night; two could play such historical cards. The Act was passed in March 2016, and provided for extensive new powers to be taken up by the Assembly. Needless to say, this did not satisfy the SNP, which muttered every now and then about holding a new independence referendum, though the opinion polls on the question were discouraging. The SNP had to buckle down to some serious governing at last.

The general election in 2015 demonstrated the political earthquake which had taken place. The Labour Party suffered a massive defeat: each of the three main parties returned only one MP in Scotland; the SNP gathered fifty-six Westminster seats; Labour fell from forty-one seats to one, the Liberals from eleven to one. The result, as always with the British voting system, was highly misleading. The SNP's actual support was 'only' 50 per cent of the overall vote, though it won in over 90 per cent of the seats. The next year, in the Scottish Assembly election which followed the increase in powers, the SNP lost its majority, losing six seats, while the Conservatives staged a significant recovery, gaining sixteen, as did both the Greens and the Liberals. The Labour Party meltdown continued, losing thirteen seats. The Scottish electorate had recovered its balance. In the immediate aftermath of the 2014 referendum and the 2015 elections, there were ecstatic, if journalistic, claims of a 'democratic revolution' and that Scottish politics had changed forever. The electorate, however, was as unimpressed at this as it had been of the case for independence.

Bibliography

Many of the books listed in the previous chapter are relevant to this. In addition, the following may be consulted:

Aughey, Arthur (ed.), *Nationalism, Devolution and the Challenge to the United Kingdom State* (London: 2001).

Bogdanor, Vernon, *Devolution in the United Kingdom* (Oxford: 1999).

Butler, David, *British General Elections since 1945* (Oxford: 1989).

Childs, David, *Britain since 1945, a Political History*, 2nd ed. (London: 1986).

Cowley, Philip and Kavanagh, Dennis, *The British General Election of 2015* (London: 2016).

Devine, T.M., *Independence or Union, Scotland's Past and Scotland's Present* (London: 2016).

Evans, John Gilbert, *Devolution in Wales, Claims and Responses, 1937–1979* (Cardiff: 2006).

Geoghegan, Peter, *The People's Referendum, Why Scotland will never be the same again* (Edinburgh: 2015).

Harvie, Christopher, *Fool's Gold, the Story of North Sea Oil* (London: 1994).

Hassan, Gerry and Barrow, Simon (eds), *A Nation Changed? The SNP and Scotland Ten Years on* (Edinburgh: 2017).

Hennessy, Peter and Seldon, Anthony (eds), *Ruling Performance, British Governments from Attlee to Thatcher* (Oxford: 1987).

Hennessy, Peter, *The Kingdom to Come, Thoughts on the Union before and after the Scottish Referendum* (London: 2015).

Irish Times, *Scotland's Moment: The Story of the Referendum* (Dublin: 2014).

Kavanagh, Dennis and Cowley, Philip, *The British General Election of 2010* (London: 2010).

MacWhirter, Iain, *Disunited Kingdom, How Westminster won a Referendum but lost Scotland* (Glasgow: 2014).

MacWhirter, Iain, *Tsunami, Scotland's Democratic Revolution* (Glasgow: 2015).

Marwick, Arthur, *British Society since 1945* (Harmondsworth, Middlesex: 1982).

Morgan, Kenneth O., *Rebirth of a Nation, Wales 1880–1980* (Oxford and Cardiff: 1981).

Sked, Alan and Cook, Chris, *Post-War Britain, a Political History* (London: 1979).

Tonge, Jonathan, Leston-Bandeira, Cristina and Wilks-Heeg, Stuart, *Britain Votes 2017* (Oxford: 2018).

Not Yet a Conclusion

It has been a long story – and it has clearly not yet ended. The course of British unity spreads from the sixth century AD until the present, when that unity has broken at one point and is apparently breaking down elsewhere. One may omit the Roman period, perhaps, though its imposition of unity on the southern part of the main island by a process of conquest was a method which the English also chose to use in uniting their part of the island. The Scots were less belligerent in unifying their part, but it was war which brought unity to Wales and Ireland. In uniting the islands into a United Kingdom, war turned out to be less than useful, and negotiation the best route.

The story of the unification is one of erratic developments and unusual interruptions. It seems quite clear that the Anglo-Saxons would have achieved the unity of England themselves in time, but they were forced into unifying their kingdoms by the brutal intervention of the Danish Great Army. This was clearly a wholly unexpected development. No Viking army had made anything like a serious attempt to conquer any territory permanently until then. In the winter of 878, it looked very much as though they had succeeded. The revival of Saxon power under Alfred after his winter refuge in the Somerset marshes was even more of a surprise than the landing of the Great Army and the revelation of its aims in the first place.

In a sense, of course, the Vikings did win when one considers a much longer term. The conquest of the united England by the Danish kings, and then a second conquest by the Normans, originally a Viking intrusion into France, could be seen as the return of the Great Army. Neither of these conquests could have been anticipated, still less the brutal process by which the loosely united Anglo-Saxon kingdom was battered into a new unity by William the Conqueror.

Once that had been achieved, the rest of the British Isles could be conquered whenever an English king chose to do so, but they were repeatedly distracted from this process by other interests, particularly by their wish to rule large areas of France. William the Conqueror, Henry II and John all made tentative attempts at expeditions into their Celtic neighbours, and all ended up fighting in France. Edward I felt that he had been provoked into conquering Wales, and then took the opportunity of a Scottish crisis to impose his suzerainty, but he also was distracted into warfare in France and left the job to his son and grandson, who failed to finish it.

Yet it was quite clear that a determined English attempt at conquest would probably have succeeded in Scotland. Wales was effectively acquired, while the success of a minor Anglo-Welsh-Norman expedition into Ireland had demonstrated that a complete conquest of that island was certainly possible with determination and the application of sufficient resources. However, in all three cases the work lay incomplete. The Scots succeeded in maintaining their independence, though at the cost of widespread damage in both Northern England and much of Scotland; the Welsh conquest left the Marches untouched; and in Ireland, the intervention of Edward Bruce effectively ended the English conquest, with more destruction and devastation.

Whether all this and the limitations of their activities was appreciated by the English in later years is not clear, but it seems certain that the new methods adopted by Henry VIII were grounded in political sense and experience and understanding of conditions in all these countries. Wales was united by Acts of Parliament; Scotland was enticed by a royal marriage and an attempt at a second. As all too often in English relations with Scotland, things went wrong, helped by French interference. In Ireland, the king's authority was expanded by his more conciliatory surrender-and-re-grant policy and his encouragement of settlement by English colonists. This led to the preliminary Irish unification achieved at the very end of Elizabeth's reign, and in the same year by the inheritances of James I – whose collection of kingdoms owed almost everything to Henry and Elizabeth.

After a thousand years of intermittent conflict, including several attempts by English kings to accomplish what James I achieved by inheritance, these events are as surprising as any. The reputation of Henry VIII for bluff and hearty extravagance, self-indulgence, readiness with the executioner's axe and a ludicrous marriage policy renders his intelligent, careful and productive policies towards England's Celtic neighbours another surprise. Then came the seventeenth century, a period of quite extraordinary upsets, conflicts, temporary results and reversals, ending with a new and tighter unity than James I had achieved. In the process, the traditional method of attempting that unity, military conquests, succeeded and was abandoned.

After the actions and activities of Charles I, Oliver Cromwell, Charles II, James II, two or more revolutions and constant quarrels, the eventual achievement of the Act of Union in 1707 is yet another astonishment.

The kingdoms ruled by King James I to Queen Anne formed a 'composite monarchy' in present-day political studies-speak. For some reason historians are reluctant to use the term 'federalism' in connection with monarchies, but James' composite kingdom was clearly a federal state. The three kingdoms each had their own government, money, laws, Church and so on, and these conditions were continued under the Acts of Union. The Acts of Union with Scotland and Ireland left large contentious areas of government and society in local hands. That there were wars between these autonomous areas in the early years is hardly surprising, given the potential for conflict they exhibited, but other monarchical and republican federations have also had such conflicts. These conflicts did not destroy the federation, which has survived the seventeenth-century wars, the Acts of Union and the rebellions against them, and even to a large extent the excision of southern Ireland from its political body. Not only that, but the idea of a federal state has been exported to a whole series of colonies and former colonies of the British Empire throughout the world, with some success. The idea of a federal state is part of British political thought and action.

Of the several attempts in Europe to construct composite monarchies from the fourteenth century onwards, usually arrived at by royal inheritance, only two – Britain and Spain – have endured into the twenty-first century. Neither are secure. Both have constructed themselves by agreement between the various parts, Britain in a rather better way than Spain. Earlier attempts – the Habsburg Empire, Scandinavia and Poland-Lithuania – based on royal inheritance alone have broken apart or have been destroyed. It was always clearly necessary to underpin the royal headship with clear institutional development. Poland-Lithuania did this, but its parliamentary system was chaotic and the royal succession became a plaything of the powers, so that its neighbours were able to take off slices of land repeatedly until the whole country disappeared. The Spanish union has been subject to massive strains and may well not endure, though much devolution has been deployed to several of the provinces. The strains in Britain have brought the separation of most of Ireland and much autonomy to Scotland, Wales and Northern Ireland. All of these changes came about unexpectedly, just as did those which had created the United Kingdom in the first place.

That is to say, there is absolutely no point in attempting to predict what will happen during the rest of the twenty-first century (and later) to the British union, tempting though such speculation may be. One thing is clear, that the absence of external pressure is one of the major factors in reducing the union's cohesion. Repeatedly, the threat from outside has thrust the several countries into making, maintaining or strengthening their union: the Vikings, France repeatedly – notably under Louis XIV and Napoleon – Germany under Wilhelm II and Hitler, Soviet Russia and now perhaps the European Union, if the removal of Britain from the EU ends in hostility. Such threats are not finished. In particular, the vote in the 2017 referendum to pull out of the European Union has set up new strains bearing on the union. (This referendum was another blatant case of lies and untruths, though in this case these were successful in persuading a majority of voters to leave.) England may have voted to pull out, but neither Scotland nor Northern Ireland wished to do so, and this could well have adverse effects on their willingness to remain part of the British union. It is quite clear from the referendum on independence that over a third of the Scottish population wishes to move into independence; the question has already arisen that Scotland might become a part of the European Union as an independent state. It might take no more than an uncharacteristically swift decision by the EU to detach Scotland.

On the other hand, once Britain has removed itself from the European Union it will face a whole variety of new geopolitical and economic threats – from a reviving and militant Russia, an increasingly isolationist United States (an old if erratic enemy) and quite possibly a disdainful EU. An improvement in democratic accountability in the European Union might also help – the perception, at least in Britain, that the European system of government is overbearing and undemocratic is one of the major causes of Britain leaving the union. That union is going to have to face the issue of its military component fairly soon, and especially without the military support of Britain it is going to look vulnerable and weak, and there are other strains than the British resignation within it. When Europe arms itself, the position of Britain will then itself be vulnerable.

It will be clear from all this that it is out of the question to make any seriously believable predictions about what is going to happen. The history of the achievement of British unity is so littered with unexpected developments and reversals that no one can be expected to produce any worthwhile guess as to the future. What is quite certain is that the story of political unification in Britain, or its reverse, has not yet finished, and that the only safe prediction is that the unexpected will continue to happen. The history of a united Britain is not yet near a conclusion.

Bibliography

See books on devolution listed in the previous chapter, along with the following:

Burgess, Michael, *The British Tradition of Federalism* (Leicester: 1995).

George, Stephen, *An Awkward Partner, Britain in the European Community* (Oxford: 1990).

Hester, Michael, *Internal Colonialism, the Celtic Fringe in British National Development, 1536–1966* (London: 1975).

McKay, David, *Federalism and European Union, a Political Economy Perspective* (Oxford: 1999).

Middlemass, Keith, *Orchestrasting Europe, the Informal Politics of the European Union 1973–1995* (London: 1995).

Siedentop, Larry, *Democracy in Europe* (London: 2000).

A Brexit Afterword

This book has been written while the convoluted political crisis involved in extracting the United Kingdom from the European Union, curiously summarised as 'Brexit', has been going on. Halfway through the production process, when the typescript was delivered to the publisher, it was suggested that an afterword be included, in May 2019, discussing in reflective mood the effect on the unity of the composite kingdom of leaving the union. Alas, for plans. Why wait until May? At this moment (April 2019) it looks as though the problem is set to continue into next year; and then there will be the transition period with multiple areas of dispute. A reflective mood is hardly possible. For those who foam at the mouth at the hideous prospect, as they would say, of being subject any longer to the European Union, this is outrageous, intolerable and not to be borne. For some, however, (whisper it) the later the date of the separation the better.

Substantial effects of this difficult business have been visible even before the Brexit process is completed. The referendum in 2016 suggested that the four constituent parts of the kingdom saw things differently, though it is not quite clear that the essential decisions were being made over membership of the European Union or something else. The preference of Scotland, for example, for remaining within the Union looks very much as though the prospect of the United Kingdom leaving it was another opportunity for secession into independence; that is, Scotland was voting for something other than membership or not of the European Union. In Northern Ireland the question was less a membership of the European Union and more a question of relationship with the independent Irish Republic – and this has, in fact, of course proved to be one of the more intractable problems involved in leaving. Even Wales, where the question of independence is much less acute than elsewhere, has differentiated itself from England on the question. And in England itself there is a clear division between South and North; not, of course, for the first time in the country's history.

The contortions of Parliament in attempting to discover the most acceptable form of the terms for leaving the European Union has put almost unacceptable strains on the traditional political order – 'traditional', meaning the last fifty years or so, of course. This, of course, mirrors the wider divisions within the country/countries on the issue. It may well be that the political party system will fall apart as a result of the venomous disputes which the process has generated; on the other hand, when the question is settled it is quite likely that the divisions will be forgotten. One cannot know, and prediction is pointless.

The unification of the British Isles has been one of the most successful political settlements in European history. Of the several and varied composite monarchies which developed in the continent at various times, only two have survived for centuries and still exist – the United Kingdom and Spain, and Spain's unity is as much under strain as that of the United Kingdom. The division of the United Kingdom would reduce the whole to one rich country (England) and three poor ones, for Northern Ireland, Wales and Scotland are unlikely to prosper on their own. And without them, England would be politically reduced to second-class status within the European state system.

This would be a great shame. Of the European countries, the United Kingdom has been the most creative, culturally, scientifically, technologically, economically and politically, for the last 300 or 400 years; only France can rival it. One of the elements in that creativity has been the internal peace which resulted from the unification of the islands. It is a pity that Ireland broke away, but at least the problem was largely solved by its move into independence. The access to English resources of Scottish, Welsh and Irish talent was clearly one of the major elements in that creativity. Lack of access would reduce it.

It may be pointed out further that by removing itself from the European Union, the United Kingdom is dealing a serious blow to that Union – a matter of some glee to the English nationalists hunting for Brexit. One of the most important elements in European development over the past half-century, while the United Kingdom has been a member, has been the persuasiveness of British political and economic thought and practice in the internal development of that Union. It is frequently remarked that the European Union is modelling itself on unification of the United States – drawing together independent states, a customs union, freedom to travel and absence of internal borders, and leading on to a single currency and a united defence. In fact, of course, all these elements have been part of British history, and the United Kingdom is a better model for European unification than the United States. Removing British influence from the

European Union diminishes the Union perhaps even more than it does the United Kingdom. Absenting itself from the promise of a European union, with its promise of peace and the prospect of expansion, argues a depressing failure of the British political imagination amongst those advocating removal.

Brexit therefore has incalculable effects for the future. It is a serious blow at the concept of European unification and it looks like being a serious blow at the continuation of British unity.

Index

330 The United Kingdom